The Princeton Review

PrincetonReview.com

college

navigator

Find the School to Match Any Interest
from Archery to Zoology

2007 EDITION

BY THE STAFF OF THE PRINCETON REVIEW

Random House, Inc.
New York

The Princeton Review, Inc
2315 Broadway
New York, NY 10024
E-mail: bookeditor@review.com

© 2007 by The Princeton Review, Inc.

All rights reserved. Published in the United States by Random House, Inc., New York, and simultaneously in Canada by Random House of Canada Limited, Toronto.

ISBN 978-0-375-76583-4

Publisher: Robert Franek
Editors: Adam O. Davis and Suzanne J. Podhurst
Production Manager and Designer: Scott Harris
Production Editor: Christine LaRubio
Illustrations: Andrew Baker

Printed in the United States of America.

9 8 7 6 5 4 3 2 1

Acknowledgments

Many thanks to Suzanne Podhurst and Adam Davis, book editors, for their hard work on this project. Thanks to Suzanne for coordinating and organizing these many lists and to Adam for tirelessly heading up the research team. Thank you also to Rob Franek, editorial director, for constant support, and to Ben Zelevansky, data collection director, for pulling together the objective data for many of these lists.

Lisa Marie Rovito wrote lots of the lively prose; Christine LaRubio brilliantly copy edited it all; and Scott Harris designed and illustrated the interior (avec flair).

Thanks to Tom Russell, Nicole Benhabib, and Shaina Malkin at Random House for their continued belief in and support of The Princeton Review, and for the advice they provided as we planned this project.

Adrinda Kelley
Senior Editor
The Princeton Review

Contents

Introduction

In 1817, Ralph Waldo Emerson began attending Harvard at age 14. Once at school, he was appointed President's Freshman, a designation that allowed him to live there free of charge. Just as Emerson did, you will soon discover that college is one of the best places on earth to make the most of yourself. Out from under your parents' roof and free to dictate your own destiny, you can truly soar—especially if you've chosen your ideal-match college.

> Make the most of yourself, for that is all there is of you.
>
> RALPH WALDO EMERSON

About This Book

Students today have more choices in higher education than any previous generation has. Don't fall into the trap of considering the same ten schools as everyone else you know. Now, more than ever, you can find more—of everything: colleges, majors, extracurricular offerings, you name it. Schools have become more diverse, more specialized in their offerings, more nuanced in their requirements. Add to this the climbing costs of college, and the need to make an informed choice becomes even more apparent. The good news is that twenty-first century students are even better equipped than their parents or grandparents were to find the right school. You've probably traveled more and been exposed through various media to global perspectives. You've honed your talents and skills in high school, and you have a relatively clear idea of what you'd like to experience in college. If you do your research, you can find the right school—it may not even be one you've heard of yet—and you can gain admission.

When it comes to choosing a college, it may seem that everyone wants to share a magic formula for finding the right one. While it's never a bad idea to hear them all out—from your friend's older brother, who's a brainy sophomore studying physics at an Ivy League school, to your Aunt Sally, who transferred three times before she found happiness in the music program at a small school in the Midwest—finding your best college match isn't about magic at all. It's about knowing yourself. It's about taking the time to search high and low for a school that seems to be the higher education form of your very person. It all comes down to matchmaking—determining exactly which schools are going to make you happy and help you grow during those four or so years that will forevermore be known as "college."

FUN FACT

After each football victory at the **University of Georgia**, the chapel bell is rung from the end of the game until midnight.

But how? Before you get there, college may seem like a big mysterious place where teachers are now "professors," your bedroom is now a dorm room shared with one or more strangers, and your mom's famous lasagna is now reserved for special visits home. On the upside, those professors are going to treat you like the adult you now are; you'll discover that living in the residence halls can be one of the most memorable (albeit trying) aspects of school; and every night you'll now have a choice of

Did You Know?

More than two million students apply to college each year—and a lot of them get into their top choice schools. Seventy percent of the Cooperative Institudional Research Program's Freshman Survey respondents gained admission to their first-choice schools; an additional 22 percent got into their second-choice schools. Those are promising odds!

entrees—and a choice of friends with whom to share your meals. While you will be at a new school and perhaps in a new town or state, you'll still be *you*. Taking the mystery out of what you can expect at college involves carefully choosing a school that speaks to you as an individual—no matter how much Aunt Sally wants you to fall in love with her oboe-friendly alma mater.

If you're reading this book, then you're probably looking for something beyond what the schools themselves make available to the general public, and you're in for a treat. You'll read about schools that will give you credit to go scuba diving and schools that serve wine at dinner, among other things. You'll get the lowdown on which schools have the most exciting freshman orientations, the most extensive library collections, and the best honors programs. You'll discover that there are schools that don't look at your SAT scores before they let you in, and schools that won't issue you grades once you matriculate. All of this great information is right at your fingertips.

This book aims to give you a fresh perspective on college admissions by providing information that you probably won't come across while browsing colleges' glossy brochures or interactive websites. In reading about what some schools are doing on their campuses, you'll have a better idea of things you might like to ask about when you plan your own college visits. In finding out about schools at which some students are super-into Ultimate Frisbee (or the steel pan or volunteer work), you may discover colleges you've never heard of before, but that are worth a serious look. Maybe you'll find another reason why a school you've been obsessing about is an even better fit for you than you first thought.

On the other hand, a gander at these lists might alert you to the fact that a school you had placed at the top of your list isn't strong in the diversity department, or that you could find a better fencing program elsewhere. Naturally, no school is perfect. Each will come with its own strengths and areas for improvement. Getting smart about the weaknesses in addition to the strengths of a school will give you a more realistic picture of what's behind the name and the reputation. If you've found a flaw in your top-choice school, does that mean you should write that school off? Of course not! Just keep in mind that every little bit of information will aid you in making your final decision. In browsing these lists, you might just stumble upon something you'll be glad to have found out before you get to campus, instead of being surprised once you're already there. No matter what, you'll come across information that will make you even more elated about packing your bags and making your campus debut, wherever that may be.

You'll discover that the perfect school for you will be the one that has the perfect combination of attributes that reflect your interests, preferences, and values. That could be a mid-sized private school in the Midwest with a stellar video game design major, a top-ranked ballroom dance team, and a dining hall that serves free-trade coffee or sushi. Or it

> **FUN FACT**
> One of **Harvard**'s most famous traditions is called Primal Scream. Students who take part in it run laps, naked, around Harvard Yard at the stroke of midnight on the day finals begin each semester.

could be a large public university in the Northeast that has a reputation for producing CIA recruits, and that houses its students in dorms reminiscent of the Château de Versailles.

There will always be juicy tidbits that schools can't tell you (how they stack up next to hundreds of other schools when it comes to rollerblading), won't tell you (the campus is small and ugly with 1970s-style architecture), or never thought of telling you (the seniors have a longstanding tradition of streaking across the quad every full moon at midnight). But these are things you ought to know—so we're telling you about them.

One additional piece of advice: Be bold in your search and confident in what you have to offer. Think less along the lines of, "Where can I get in?" and more in terms of, "Where will I fit in?" These lists will help orient you toward your best-match schools.

Who Should Be Reading This Book, Anyway?

Anyone who is currently or will soon be looking for that perfect-match college will benefit from reading this book, including but not limited to:

1. Those who haven't started the search. If you have yet to begin looking for a college, this book can serve as a point of entry to the daunting process. Lists are approachable, user-friendly, and straightforward. By reading through these chapters, college-seekers will formulate questions to ask, identify new directions to pursue, and discover a sense of possibility about what is—or could be—in store for them.

2. Those who are in the middle of the search. In the midst of researching and weighing the pros and cons of the colleges you're considering, look them up by name in the index at the back of this book. By ascertaining which lists a school appears on, you'll learn a few more tidbits about daily life on campus to ponder. Want to verify something you've heard through the grapevine or round out your picture of a school before or after you visit its campus? Want to narrow down your list? Want to expand it? Curious about where you might pursue your lit mag/juggling/badminton interests? These lists are here for you.

3. Those who are about to commit to a school. Before you make that life-changing decision and begin announcing it far and wide, take a final look through these pages. Read up on the school of your dreams, and give at least a brief glance to those you're about to turn down. Chances are, you'll pick up

some solid fodder that will only confirm your good taste in choosing the
school that you have. It's possible,
however, that you'll come across a
piece of information that sheds new
light on your final list of schools. It's
not too late to reconsider!

Did You Know?

There are more undergraduate
women than men in the United
States. Ditto for grad students.

4. **Those who have already chosen a school.** By perusing these lists,
you can not only catch up on everything you ever wanted to know (but
wouldn't have thought to ask) about your school, but you can also get some
ideas for clubs, sports, and classes to check out once you arrive on campus.
Maybe you'd like to look into becoming a radio DJ, or maybe you'd like to
dust off your skis now so you'll be ready for your winter class commute. If you
want to do a good deed, look up the schools your friends have chosen and
let them in on a thing or two, too.

5. **Let's not forget…busy guidance counselors!** This quick-reference
book is a smart addition to every counselor's guidance library. It offers a fast
way for perennially busy counselors to address students' highly specific,
often random, and always numerous questions.

Why We Wrote This Book

This book offers information you'd be hard-pressed to find anywhere else. The Princeton Review fields questions every day from students, parents, and guidance counselors across the globe. They want to know: Which schools have excellent photography programs? Which schools are strong in track and field? Which will offer the greatest number of choices for studying abroad? Where can I go to prepare for a career in sports medicine? Will there be a rock climbing wall or snowboarding nearby? Read on—we share our answers with you.

What you'll read in this book is decidedly not a compilation of college-specific profiles. After you use the lists in this book to identify your best-match colleges, you'll be well positioned to delve into specifics about those schools-from enlightening student testimonials to essential admissions policies—and we recommend that you utilize the resources in other publications by The Princeton Review and on PrincetonReview.com to continue your research. In compiling

FUN FACT

Lebanon Valley College has one of the best incentive programs out there. It grants a Vickroy Award—a one-half tuition scholarship—to high school seniors who graduate in the top 10 percent of their class. To retain that hefty scholarship, students have to maintain a 2.75 semester GPA during their freshman year and a 3.0 semester GPA all remaining years. This program rewards hard work, and, as the school notes, offers high-achievers the opportunity to receive a "private college education at a state school price."

the lists in the *College Navigator*, we sought to you help you pinpoint your interests and identify colleges for which you may be well-suited and at which you may further cultivate those interests.

After all, schools have distinct personalities. Getting to know a school and determining whether the two of you would get along well in a long-term relationship involve more than simply scanning tuition figures, comparing your SAT scores to those of entering freshmen, and checking to see if you can take marine biology as a first-year. On paper, a school can appear ideal, especially if it has the right location, the right programs, and even the right price. That's why atmosphere comes in. Whether a school plays it liberal or conservative, rowdy or reserved, athletic or musically inclined, you'll want to know all of the factors that will influence your college experience. Ultimately, you want to find a "partner" that appreciates your intricacies and compels you to explore everything it has to offer. These lists invite the art of college matchmaking. (Isn't it romantic?)

Just Lists?

Just lists?! That's what this book might look like if you're just giving it a quick browse. But these lists offer more insight than a first glance might allow, and they provide more information in one place than you can find anywhere else. Besides, who doesn't like lists? There's a reason why David Letterman's Top Ten Lists have been one of his show's highlights for more than a decade.

Lists offer you the power of comparison. If you're a top-ranked high school tennis player with your sights set on competing in an elite Division I college tennis program, the names of schools on the Great Tennis Programs list will speak to you just as loudly as the ones that didn't make that list at all. If you're toying with the idea of majoring either in social work or sign language, you'll be able to investigate your options for both programs. If one of your top-choice schools makes the lists of schools with helpful career services while another appears on the list of least helpful career services, you'll probably want to file that information away for later use. Your career-seeking days may seem a world away now, but a stellar career services office can make your life a lot easier in the not-so-distant future.

These lists also serve as the perfect springboard for further research. They get your mind in motion and keep you wanting to know more. Talk to your parents, guidance counselor, and friends about your findings. Follow up with the schools in which you're interested, and don't be afraid to ask them what—exactly—makes their particular major/athletic program/student services office so outstanding.

Where Did These Lists Come From?

The lists you'll find in this book are the result of the extensive research conducted by the experts at The Princeton Review. They are original to us and are the result of our desire to give you, your family, and your guidance counselor relevant and up-to-date information that isn't available anywhere else. Accuracy, helpfulness, and breadth of knowledge were our goals—and we held ourselves to the highest standards in achieving them. In formulating these lists, we drew from four primary sources of information:

1. Institutionally-provided data. In determining such lists as schools with the largest and smallest student-to-faculty ratios, we used objective figures that came directly from school administrators.

FUN FACT
At **Deep Springs College** in Dyer, Nevada, the student-to-faculty ratio is 3:1.

2. Advice from the experts. We asked experts from The Princeton Review all across the country. College counselors and tutors work with college admissions offices all the time, and our in-house experts proved highly knowledgeable about some of the best—and at times, most obscure—programs available.

3. Input from guidance counselors. We surveyed guidance counselors, college admissions counselors, and mentors from across the country. Some of these individuals work at public schools, others at private schools, and still others are independent counselors. We asked them not only about which schools have particularly outstanding programs in each of many highly specific areas, but also about the schools at which their former students have enjoyed particular success in those realms.

4. Research. We went out and conducted our own independent research. When we wanted to let you know which schools have produced the greatest number of alumni who went on to become U.S. President, for instance, we did some good, old-fashioned research.

FUN FACT

The former U.S. President Franklin Pierce and the author Nathaniel Hawthorne graduated one year apart (in 1824 and 1825, respectively) from **Bowdoin College**.

In most instances (save the altogether straightforward and objective ones), we used a combination of the information from those four sources to produce a given list. It's true that a certain degree of subjectivity is involved in any book that calls out schools as particularly outstanding at what they do. But each one of our lists is backed by solid research and years of trusted counselor experience. Can a school have a terrific theater program and not be featured on our list of stellar theater programs? Of course. You can rest assured, though, that all of the schools on these lists have truly remarkable programs that caught our attention and the attention of those we surveyed.

Within each list, the schools appear in alphabetical order. We didn't rank them because schools that are strong in the same area may have unique strengths. Two schools may have outstanding film programs, for example, and one may be perfect for aspiring cinematographers and the other ideal for future screenwriters. It's up to you to determine the atmosphere that works best for you. We note with confidence though, that out of the roughly 3,500 schools across the United States, the relatively few that appear on each list are truly superlatives in the given category.

While we have gone to great lengths to ensure that the information in this book is accurate and up to date, we also realize that schools change. They may add or drop majors and increase or decrease the size of their faculty and student bodies. They may tighten their admissions requirements, upgrade their science facilities, build new stadiums, or go coeducational. Always cover your bases and check with a school directly to confirm that you have the most up-to-the-minute requirements, policies, procedures, fees, deadlines, and the like. For our own part, we will continue to update this book periodically so that what you read on these pages agrees with what you'll find on your college visits.

> **FUN FACT**
> The classic film *Animal House*, set on the campus of the fictional Faber College, is based on the experiences of co-writer Chris Miller at **Dartmouth College** and was filmed at the **University of Oregon**.

How to Use This Book

This book is divided into chapters by category, and the chapters are further divided into related topics of interest. In amassing the lists for each of these ten chapters, we gathered information from nearly 2,000 colleges and universities. Academics, majors, career prospects, extracurriculars, and life on campus are all included here.

In Chapter 1, we cover general information, from special program offerings to the nuances of academic calendars. You'll also find information about special campus facilities and options for taking a nontraditional path.

Chapter 2 delves into what you can expect from faculty and advisors at various schools, including information about student-to-faculty ratios and the best premed and pre-law advising programs out there.

In Chapter 3, you'll read about differing academic requirements, find out about stellar research opportunities, and learn about the finest study abroad programs available. Spending a summer or a semester in a foreign country is the highlight of many students' college careers. If you have any desire at all to study abroad before you graduate, these schools offer a solid starting point for your college search.

You're ultimately going to college to gain expertise in a particular field, right? In Chapter 4, you'll read about the best programs in virtually every subject you could want to study—and we also provide enrollment information so that you can get a sense of the (size of the) cohort that may await you.

Once you've gained the necessary expertise in your field of study, we expect you'll want to launch a successful career. Chapter 5 covers career prospects so that career-oriented readers can direct their college searches from the outset.

Your biggest admissions questions will be answered (hopefully) in Chapter 6. Want to know which are the toughest schools to get into, the schools that accept the highest percentage of applicants, or the schools with an incoming freshman class that boasts the highest SAT scores? You'll find all of that information here. Because information about the students who graduate from a school may reveal just as much (if not more) as specifics about the students who matriculate into it, this chapter also has alumni-related information. Curious about which schools produced alums who loved their alma mater so much that they remained actively involved in its academic community? Wondering about which schools have produced prominent alums? Flip to this section and find out.

Many students are especially curious about what life will be like once they finally choose a school and arrive on campus. In Chapter 7, we give you the lowdown on dorms, dining hall food, and the student body. You won't just be attending classes and participating in extracurricular activities; you'll also, in all likelihood, be a part of a greater academic and social community. Get a sense of what that experience will be like—before you buy extra-long twin sheets and a shower tote.

Academics won't completely consume you of course, so in Chapter 8, we give you a rundown of schools that have the best extracurricular offerings in each of a series of categories—including activities for the athletically inclined as well as those involving community service, fine arts, performing arts, and a range of other areas of interest.

If you want to narrow down your search to schools with a particular religious affiliation, look no further than Chapter 9, which lists the schools affiliated with each of thirty-seven faiths.

Finally, we'd be remiss in our matchmaking efforts if we weren't to tell you about the fun stuff. College is about many things, and one of them is having fun. In Chapter 10, read about crazy and fun activities that you can do . . .

for credit! Add the words "and get credit for it" to the ends of these sentences, and you'll notice how much more enticing they sound: Ever want to go to a wine tasting? Ever aspire to go whitewater rafting? (You get the idea.) These crazy for-credit exploits are not the only fun information in this chapter. If you're curious about a school's wackiest traditions, read on. Pranksters, jokesters, class clowns, and those who revel in the absurd, the ridiculous, and the unbelievable will find this section particularly appealing.

FUN FACT
Pace University has border collies on campus to keep away geese—and their droppings.

The table of contents and the indexes will help you identify and then stay on track with what appeals to you—and with what doesn't. If one or more schools keep popping up on the lists that catch your eye, take it as a sign. While you're scanning the contents of this book, we urge you not to be too quick in dismissing a chapter or a type of list as insignificant just because it doesn't seem to apply to you at the outset.

Consider this: You probably don't know now all of the things that may come to play a significant role in your life. Say you're less than athletic and have zero intention of ever playing on a college sports team. Does that mean you can't appreciate the art of spectatorship? Of course not. (You also shouldn't rule out the possibility of discovering your as-yet unknown football prowess.) Check out our lists of schools with the largest stadiums, with great basketball programs, or with professionally-drafted players if you think you might ever want to suit up, or if you aspire to look forward to four years of safe-on-the-sidelines school spirit. If you always wanted to write poetry, then peruse the list of schools that boast awe-inspiring literary magazines. Who knows where that could lead you? If you're a stay-up-all-night-in-the-lab type, look into the schools that lay claim to outstanding opportunities to conduct research with your professors. This is all to say—if you've always had an interest in something, now's the time to explore it.

Speaking of exploring, for a book of this bounty and breadth, including more than just an alphabetical index would be nearly impossible (well, not impossible, but it'd certainly force us to include a complimentary back brace), so we've saved you the heavy lifting and let the internet do the work. Just log on to Princetonreview.com/books and check out the multitude of other indexes available to help you in your search for your college match.

> **FUN FACT**
>
> Former U.S. Secretary of State Madeleine Albright, U.S. Senator Hillary Rodham Clinton, filmaker Nora Ephron, and journalists Cokie Roberts and Diane Sawyer are all **Wellesley College** alumnae.

Some Final Words about Finding the Perfect-Match School

It's worth doing the research to find the perfect-match school for you—we promise. If you've started the process, keep chugging along. And if you've been putting it off, make up your mind that today, starting now, the search is on. Here's why:

No one is going to find the right school for you. This is your deal. This process isn't magic. The best way to find the school that's a perfect fit for you is to start researching early, commit yourself to the process, and take responsibility for making a good decision. We won't lie to you: It's a lot of work. While your high school teachers pile on the exams and papers, you'll need to be talking to your guidance counselor, reading up on schools, visiting them, and eventually applying. Think of it as the biggest and best decision you'll have had the chance to make so far—it's your first real-life adult choice to boot. You didn't get to choose your family, or your house, or the color of your eyes. You probably didn't choose your preschool, elementary school, middle school, or high school. This time, the choice is yours. Make the most of it—and give yourself as much time to do so as possible.

Take good notes from Day One of your college search. You'll have your own method of tracking your lists of pros, cons, and comments for each school. Whether you opt for an Excel spreadsheet or a cocktail napkin scribble, do keep track of it all, starting now. As the months of researching colleges fly by, memories that seemed distinct may become hazy if you're not jotting them down. ("Was it Wellesley or Wheaton that had that great anthro class I sat in on? Could it have been Wesleyan?" That sort of thing can happen.)

Shop around and do your homework. In other words, choose well and you'll only have to choose once. During our many years of helping students apply and gain admission to college, we've noticed one trend above all others: Students who have done what it takes to find the right school tend to be happier campers. Once you've researched schools, made your big list of possibilities, and then whittled it down to a manageable handful, you should visit as many of those col-

FUN FACT

The music group Talking Heads formed at the **Rhode Island School of Design** in 1974.

leges as you can. Talk to as many students and faculty as humanly possible while you're there. Squeeze the juice out of your visit—sit in on a class, stay in the dorms, go to the coffee shop, the gym, the stadium, the bookstore. Take the school's tour, but then take your own, one that is tailored to the things you are most interested in. If you're a big hiker, find out how to get to the nearby trails. If you're looking to find part-time work once you're settled in, take a spin by the job boards at Career Services. When you add up the hours that you'll actually spend sitting in a classroom, it's easy to see that your classes, while extremely important, are still just part of the total experience. The rest of your time will be filled with the things you choose to do.

Don't apply to a school you'd never want to attend. It seems obvious, yet this practical bit of advice is often overlooked. Spend your time and your efforts completing stellar applications for the schools you love—or at least the ones you would be happy attending. You'll want to apply to some reach schools, some match schools, and a couple of safeties, as well. In all cases, make sure that you apply only to schools at which you could envision yourself being a happy, well-rounded, engaged student. If you visited school and didn't connect with the campus, the classes, the professors, or the students, then cross it off your list. You're not likely to sprout a magic connection overnight—and there are enough wonderful schools out there to justify a list comprised only of your perfect-match schools.

Trust your instincts: Birds do, bees do—and you should too.

Many college students who love their schools say they knew from the minute they stepped onto campus that it was "the one." If you're lucky, you might experience that same love-at-first-sight-like sensation. Even if you don't, you'll emerge from your college visit with a lasting impression. Make the most of that impression. Ask yourself: Would I love this place for four years, maybe more? Apart from the din of advice you're undoubtedly receiving from every imaginable source, be sure to listen to your own inner voice. Research (beginning right here with the lists in this book) will take you almost all the way there. Your own good judgment should take care of the rest.

Good luck, and happy searching!

chapter 1

General College Knowledge

In the midst of getting to know your potential perfect-match schools, you'll need to figure out whether you and each of the schools you're considering complement one another. You'll want to think about the obvious considerations—location, size, and price tag—and you'll probably want to take into account some less obvious aspects of daily life—including academic calendar, noteworthy facilities, and special programs. But before you get to the program- and activity-specific information that constitutes most of this book, we'll give you solid foundation in what we're calling General College Knowledge. The information you'll find in this chapter applies to college-wide phenomena. For that reason, the topics covered apply virtually to every prospective student.

For example, we give you the inside word on which schools have been around since the Puritans and which are on the rise. We tell you about schools with unusual academic calendars, those best known for getting their students in and out within four years, and those with exceptional learning disabilities services.

This chapter also delves into where you'll find the best college consortia (AKA partnerships among various colleges in the same region that promote the sharing of educational and cultural resources, services, and facilities so that broader sets of opportunities are available to students), the finest combined bachelor's-master's programs, and the best college honors programs.

You'll learn which schools have the best college art galleries, museums, on-campus gardens, and most extensive library collections. Find out about the schools with the largest stadiums, most Mac- or PC-centric computer labs, largest (and smallest) campuses, and more. These lists will clue you in to the value sets of various schools—as exemplified in how they allocate resources.

If you're considering a nontraditional path, check out our lists of distance learning programs, outstanding community colleges, and noteworthy and technical schools. Considering a two-year school as a springboard into a top-tier college? There's a list here for that, too.

part 1

Everything You Ever Wanted To Know About Your Potential Match Colleges

When I Was Your Age . . .

Oldest schools

- Becker College
- Bowdoin College
- Brown University
- Castleton State College
- College of Charleston
- College of William & Mary
- Columbia University
- Dartmouth College
- Dickinson College
- Franklin & Marshall College
- Georgetown University
- Hampden-Sydney College
- Hartwick College
- Harvard University
- Middlebury College
- Moravian College
- Ohio University—Athens
- Princeton University
- Salem College
- St. John's College (MD)

- St. John's College (NM)
- Transylvania University
- Tusculum College
- Union College (NY)
- United States Military Academy
- University of Delaware
- University of Georgia
- University of King's College
- University of Louisville
- University of North Carolina at Chapel Hill

FUN FACT

Harvard University was founded on September 8, 1636 making it the oldest institution of higher education in the United States.

- University of Pennsylvania
- University of Pittsburgh—Pittsburgh Campus
- University of South Carolina—Columbia
- University of Tennessee—Knoxville
- University of Vermont
- Washington & Jefferson College

- Washington and Lee University
- Washington College
- Williams College
- Yale University
- York College of Pennsylvania

New On the Scene
Youngest schools

- Allen College
- Argosy University—Orange County
- Arizona State University—Polytechnic Campus
- Arizona State University—West
- The Art Institute of California—San Diego
- The Art Institute of Los Angeles—Orange County
- The Art Institute of Washington
- The Art Institutes International—Minnesota
- Baker College of Auburn Hills
- Baker College of Owosso
- Beacon College
- California College for Health Sciences
- California State University—San Marcos

- Cambridge Online Learning
- Canadian Mennonite University
- Capella University
- Cascade College
- Christendom College
- Clark Atlanta University
- The College of Saint Thomas More
- Concordia University—Irvine
- East-West University
- Emmanuel Bible College
- Eugene Lang College—The New School for Liberal Arts
- Everglades University
- Florida Gulf Coast University
- Franklin W. Olin College of Engineering
- Globe Institute of Technology
- Henry Cogswell College
- Heritage University
- Immaculata University College of Lifelong Learning
- International Academy of Design & Technology—Tampa
- Jones International University
- Keiser Career College
- Keiser College
- Landmark College
- Lyme Academy of Fine Arts

- Martin Luther College
- Medcenter One College of Nursing
- Metropolitan College of Court Reporting
- Musicians Institute
- New School of Architecture & Design
- New World School of the Arts
- Northwood University—Florida Campus
- Pennsylvania College of Art & Design
- Pennsylvania College of Technology
- Salish-Kootenai College
- Savannah College of Art and Design
- Shawnee State University
- Soka University of America
- St. John's College—Department of Nursing (IL)
- Thomas More College of Liberal Arts
- Université du Québec a Hull
- University of Advancing Technology (UAT)
- University of the District of Columbia
- University of Hawaii—West Oahu
- University of Illinois at Chicago

○ University of New Hampshire at Manchester
○ University of Northern British Columbia
○ University of Phoenix
○ West Suburban College of Nursing
○ Western International University

Students a-Plenty
Schools with the highest enrollments

○ Arizona State University—Tempe
○ Brigham Young University (UT)
○ California State University—Fullerton
○ California State University—Long Beach
○ California State University—Northridge
○ California State University—Sacramento
○ Colorado State University
○ Concordia University (QC)
○ Excelsior College
○ Florida International University
○ Florida State University
○ Indiana University—Bloomington

○ Indiana University—Purdue University Indianapolis
○ Iowa State University
○ Iowa State University of Science and Technology
○ Lock Haven University of Pennsylvania
○ Louisiana State University
○ Michigan State University
○ New York University
○ North Carolina State University
○ The Ohio State University—Columbus
○ Pennsylvania State University—University Park
○ Purdue University—West Lafayette
○ Rutgers, The State University of New Jersey—New Brunswick/Piscataway
○ San Diego State University
○ San Francisco State University
○ San Jose State University
○ Sierra College
○ Temple University
○ Texas A&M University—College Station
○ Texas State University—San Marcos
○ Texas Tech University
○ University of Alberta

- University of Arizona
- The University of British Columbia
- University of California—Berkeley
- University of California—Davis
- University of California—Los Angeles
- University of California—San Diego
- University of Central Florida
- University of Colorado—Boulder
- University of Florida
- University of Georgia
- University of Houston
- University of Illinois at Urbana-Champaign
- University of Kansas
- University of Manitoba
- University of Maryland—College Park
- University of Michigan—Ann Arbor
- University of Minnesota—Twin Cities
- University of Missouri—Columbia
- University of Nevada—Las Vegas
- University of North Texas
- University of Oklahoma
- University of Phoenix
- University of South Florida
- The University of Texas at Austin
- The University of Texas at San Antonio

- University of Toronto
- University of Utah
- University of Washington
- The University of Western Ontario
- University of Wisconsin—Madison
- University of Wisconsin—Milwaukee
- Virginia Polytechnic and State University (Virginia Tech)
- Western Michigan University
- York University

When Knowing Everyone is Everything

Schools with the lowest enrollments

- Alaska Bible College
- American Academy for Dramatic

FUN FACT

Not only was the **University of California—San Diego**'s Geisel Library named in Dr. Seuss's honor, but it also houses a collection of 8,500 pieces of his work.

27

Arts—West

- American College of Dublin
- American Indian College of the Assemblies of God, Inc.
- Antioch Southern California—Los Angeles
- Antioch Southern California—Santa Barbara
- Argosy University—Atlanta
- Argosy University—Chicago
- Argosy University—Orange County
- Arkansas Baptist College
- Arlington Baptist College
- Art Academy of Cincinnati
- Baltimore Hebrew University
- Beacon College
- Blessing-Rieman College of Nursing

FUN FACT

Lexington College only offers degrees in Hospitality Management and "entrusts its doctrinal and spiritual formation to Opus Dei."

- Boise Bible College
- Bryn Athyn College of the New Church
- Clear Creek Baptist Bible College
- The College of Saint Thomas More

- Colorado Mountain College—Timberline Campus
- Columbia College—Hollywood
- Conception Seminary College
- Deep Springs College
- DeVry University—Charlotte
- DeVry University—Milwaukee
- DeVry University—Portland
- Dominican School of Philosophy and Theology
- Emmanuel Bible College
- Eugene Bible College
- Grace Bible College
- Gratz College
- Hebrew College
- Hellenic College
- Heritage Bible College
- Hillsdale Free Will Baptist College
- Holy Apostles College and Seminary
- Jewish Theological Seminary—Albert A. List College
- John F. Kennedy University
- Jones International University
- Laura and Alvin Siegal College of Judaic Studies
- Lexington College
- Lincoln University (CA)
- Lyme Academy of Fine Arts

- ○ Mannes College—The New School for Music
- ○ Medcenter One College of Nursing
- ○ Metropolitan College of Court Reporting
- ○ Monterey Institute of International Studies
- ○ Nebraska Christian College
- ○ New School of Architecture & Design
- ○ Northcentral University
- ○ Oak Hills Christian College
- ○ Oregon College of Art and Craft
- ○ Pacific States University
- ○ Pontifical College Josephinum
- ○ Roanoke Bible College
- ○ Saint Anthony College of Nursing
- ○ Saint Francis Medical Center College of Nursing
- ○ Saint Joseph Seminary College
- ○ Salish-Kootenai College
- ○ San Francisco Conservatory of Music
- ○ St. John's University—School of Risk Management, Insurance, and Actuarial Science
- ○ Shasta Bible College
- ○ Sheldon Jackson College
- ○ Shimer College

- ○ Southern Christian University
- ○ St. Charles Borromeno Seminary
- ○ St. John's College—Department of Nursing (IL)
- ○ Sterling College (VT)
- ○ Thomas More College of Liberal Arts
- ○ Trinity College of Florida
- ○ Trinity Lutheran College
- ○ University of Judaism
- ○ University of West Los Angeles
- ○ Vandercook College of Music
- ○ Wadhams Hall Seminary College
- ○ Webb Institute
- ○ Wesley College (MS)
- ○ West Suburban College of Nursing

Size Matters

Schools with the largest campuses (acreage)

- ○ Alcorn State University
- ○ Andrews University
- ○ Auburn University
- ○ Berry College
- ○ California Polytechnic State University—San Luis Obispo
- ○ College of Saint Benedict/Saint John's University

29

- ○ Deep Springs College
- ○ Duke University
- ○ Fort Hays State University
- ○ Indiana University—Bloomington
- ○ Iowa State University
- ○ Iowa State University of Science and Technology
- ○ Lehigh University
- ○ Liberty University
- ○ Louisiana State University
- ○ Miami University
- ○ Michigan State University
- ○ Mississippi State University
- ○ North Carolina State University
- ○ The Ohio State University—Columbus
- ○ Ohio University—Athens
- ○ Pennsylvania State University—University Park
- ○ Principia College
- ○ Richard Stockton College of New Jersey
- ○ Rutgers, The State University of New Jersey—New Brunswick/Piscataway
- ○ Sewanee—The University of the South
- ○ Southern Illinois University—Edwardsville
- ○ Stanford University
- ○ Stockton College of New Jersey
- ○ Sweet Briar College
- ○ Texas A&M University—College Station
- ○ Texas Tech University
- ○ Tuskegee University
- ○ United States Air Force Academy
- ○ United States Military Academy
- ○ University of Alaska—Fairbanks
- ○ University of Arkansas—Monticello
- ○ University of California—Davis
- ○ University of California—San Diego
- ○ University of California—Santa Cruz
- ○ University of Connecticut
- ○ University of Florida
- ○ University of Idaho
- ○ University of Illinois at Urbana-Champaign
- ○ University of Iowa
- ○ University of Michigan—Ann Arbor
- ○ University of Minnesota—Twin Cities
- ○ University of Mississippi
- ○ University of New Hampshire
- ○ University of Oklahoma

- University of South Florida
- University of Toronto
- University of West Florida
- Virginia Polytechnic and State University (Virginia Tech)
- Washington State University

Good Things Come in Small Packages

Schools with the smallest campuses (acreage)

- Albany College of Pharmacy
- American Academy for Dramatic Arts—West
- The Art Institute of Boston at Lesley University
- The Art Institute of California—San Diego
- The Art Institute of California—San Francisco
- Art Institutes International—Portland
- Atlanta College of Art
- Barnard College
- Berkeley College—New York City
- Berkeley College—Westchester
- Beulah Heights Bible College
- Blessing-Rieman College of Nursing

- Brandon University
- Burlington College
- California College for Health Sciences
- California College of the Arts
- City University
- City University of New York—Borough of Manhattan Community College
- City University of New York—Hunter College
- City University of New York—John Jay College of Criminal Justice
- City University of New York—New York City College of Technology
- Cogswell Polytechnical College

FUN FACT

Barnard College is a member of the Seven Sisters, an organization founded in 1927 to promote higher education for women.

- Columbia College—Chicago
- Cornish College of the Arts
- DeVry University—Crystal City

- DeVry University—Long Island City (NY)
- DeVry University—Philadelphia
- DeVry University—Westminster
- Eastman School of Music—University of Rochester
- Eugene Lang College—The New School for Liberal Arts
- Georgia Baptist College of Nursing
- Harris-Stowe State College
- Henry Cogswell College
- Jewish Theological Seminary—Albert A. List College
- Jones International University
- Kendall College
- Lesley College
- Lyme Academy of Fine Arts
- Maine College of Art
- Manhattan Christian College
- Manhattan School of Music
- Mannes College—The New School for Music
- Marymount Manhattan College
- Massachusetts College of Art
- Massachusetts College of Pharmacy and Health Science
- Metropolitan College of Court Reporting
- Milwaukee Institute of Art and Design
- Minneapolis College of Art and Design
- Monterey Institute of International Studies
- New College of California
- New England Conservatory of Music
- New World School of the Arts
- Nova Scotia College of Art and Design
- Otis College of Art & Design
- Pace University
- Pacific Northwest College of Art
- Parsons—The New School for Design
- Polytechnic University—Brooklyn
- Prescott College
- Saint Francis College (NY)
- Samuel Merritt College
- San Francisco Art Institute
- San Francisco Conservatory of Music
- Shimer College
- Southeastern University
- St. Joseph's College—New York (Brooklyn)
- Suffolk University
- Texas A&M University—Texarkana
- Thomas Edison State College

- ○ University of King's College
- ○ University of West Los Angeles
- ○ Vandercook College of Music
- ○ Westwood Aviation Institute—Houston

Express Lane to College

Schools from which the greatest proportion of students graduate within four years

- ○ Amherst College
- ○ Barnard College
- ○ Bates College
- ○ Beacon College
- ○ Bowdoin College
- ○ Brandeis University
- ○ Brown University
- ○ Bucknell University
- ○ California Institute of Technology
- ○ Carleton College
- ○ Claremont McKenna College
- ○ Colby College
- ○ Colgate University
- ○ College of the Holy Cross
- ○ College of William & Mary

- ○ Columbia University
- ○ Connecticut College
- ○ Cornell University
- ○ Dartmouth College
- ○ Davidson College
- ○ Dickinson College
- ○ Duke University
- ○ Emory University
- ○ Georgetown University
- ○ Grinnell College
- ○ Hamilton College
- ○ Harvard University
- ○ Haverford College
- ○ Heritage Bible College
- ○ Humphreys College
- ○ Johns Hopkins University

FUN FACT

Ever notice how frequently the number 47 comes up on your favorite television shows (*Star Trek* especially)? In 1964, Pomona College Professor of Mathematics Donald Bentley proved that all numbers are equal to 47. He's responsible for much of the 47-related buzz.

- ○ Kenyon College
- ○ Lafayette College
- ○ Lehigh University
- ○ Lyme Academy of Fine Arts
- ○ Manhattan College
- ○ Massachusetts Institute of Technology
- ○ Middlebury College
- ○ Muhlenberg College
- ○ Northland College
- ○ Pomona College
- ○ Pontifical College Josephinum
- ○ Prescott College
- ○ Princeton University
- ○ Saint Francis Medical Center College of Nursing
- ○ Saint Mary's College of Ave Maria University (MI)
- ○ Samuel Merritt College
- ○ Scripps College
- ○ Shasta Bible College
- ○ Smith College
- ○ Stonehill College
- ○ Swarthmore College
- ○ Thomas Aquinas College
- ○ Tufts University
- ○ United States Air Force Academy
- ○ United States Naval Academy

- ○ University of Pennsylvania
- ○ University of Virginia
- ○ Vanderbilt University
- ○ Vassar College
- ○ Voorhees College
- ○ Washington and Lee University
- ○ Wellesley College
- ○ Wesleyan University
- ○ Williams College

Cruising in the Right Lane

Schools from which the greatest proportion of students graduate in more than four years

- ○ Albany College of Pharmacy
- ○ Anderson University
- ○ California Baptist University
- ○ California Polytechnic State University—San Luis Obispo
- ○ California State Polytechnic University—Pomona
- ○ California State University—Chico
- ○ California State University—Fullerton
- ○ California State University—Long Beach
- ○ California State University—San Bernardino

- Central Michigan University
- The Cleveland Institute of Art
- Colorado School of Mines
- Coppin State University
- Dickinson State University
- Dominican University of California
- Drexel University
- D'Youville College
- Georgia Institute of Technology
- Georgia Southwestern State University
- Humboldt State University
- Illinois Institute of Technology
- Iowa State University
- Iowa State University of Science and Technology
- Kansas State University
- Kettering University
- Massachusetts College of Pharmacy and Health Science
- Michigan Technological University
- Miles College
- Montclair State University
- New Jersey Institute of Technology
- North Carolina State University
- North Dakota State University
- Oak Hills Christian College
- The Ohio State University—Columbus
- Pennsylvania State University—University Park
- Philadelphia Biblical University
- Rockford College
- Saint Mary's College of Ave Maria University (MI)
- San Diego State University
- Schreiner University
- Silver Lake College
- Stevens Institute of Technology
- Texas A&M University—College Station
- Texas Lutheran University
- Tougaloo College
- University of Alaska—Anchorage
- University of California—Davis
- University of California—Irvine
- University of Cincinnati
- University College of Cape Breton
- University of Dubuque
- University of Georgia
- University of Guelph
- University of Idaho
- University of Michigan—Dearborn
- University of Missouri—Kansas City
- University of Missouri—Rolla
- University of Nebraska—Lincoln
- University of Oklahoma

- University of the Sciences in Philadelphia
- The University of Texas at Austin
- University of Utah
- University of Wisconsin—Eau Claire
- University of Wisconsin—La Crosse
- University of Wisconsin—Madison
- University of Wisconsin—River Falls
- University of Wisconsin—Stevens Point
- University of Wisconsin—Whitewater

FUN FACT

The John B. Begley Chapel at **Lindsey Wilson College** was designed by E. Fay Jones, an apprentice of Frank Lloyd Wright.

- Washington Bible College
- West Chester University of Pennsylvania
- West Virginia University Institute of Technology
- Western Oregon University
- Western Washington University

A Hole On Campus?

Schools with the lowest retention rates

- Alliant International University
- Arlington Baptist College
- Averett University
- Berkeley College—New York City
- Central State University
- Chowan College
- Columbia College—Hollywood
- Davenport University—Kalamazoo
- Glenville State College
- Grace Bible College
- Heritage University
- Huron University
- Lindsey Wilson College
- Lyme Academy of Fine Arts
- Messenger College
- Metropolitan College of Court Reporting
- Miles Community College
- Missouri Valley College
- Mount Senario College
- National American University (MN)
- National American University (MO)
- National University
- Patten University
- Shasta Bible College

- ○ Sheldon Jackson College
- ○ Southwestern Christian University
- ○ Sul Ross State University
- ○ Talladega College
- ○ United States International University
- ○ University of the District of Columbia
- ○ University of West Alabama
- ○ Wiley College

Higher (and Higher) Learning

Schools from which the most number of students go to grad school within one year

- ○ Alabama A&M University
- ○ Alabama State University
- ○ Alice Lloyd College
- ○ Allegheny College
- ○ American University
- ○ Antioch Southern California—Los Angeles
- ○ The Art Institute of California—San Diego
- ○ Baptist College of Florida
- ○ Bard College
- ○ Beulah Heights Bible College
- ○ Birmingham-Southern College

- ○ Bishop's University
- ○ California Institute of Technology
- ○ California Lutheran University
- ○ Carlos Albizu University
- ○ Carnegie Mellon University
- ○ Centenary College of Louisiana
- ○ City University of New York—LaGuardia Community College
- ○ Cleveland Institute of Music
- ○ Conception Seminary College
- ○ The Cooper Union for the Advancement of Science and Art
- ○ Deep Springs College
- ○ Delaware Valley College
- ○ Dominican School of Philosophy and Theology
- ○ Eastman School of Music—University of Rochester
- ○ Emory University
- ○ Eugene Lang College—The New School for Liberal Arts
- ○ Faulkner University
- ○ Georgetown University
- ○ Hawaii Pacific University
- ○ Hellenic College
- ○ Howard University
- ○ Humphreys College
- ○ Iona College

- ○ Landmark College
- ○ Lane College
- ○ Livingstone College
- ○ Luther Rice Bible College and Seminary
- ○ Maharishi University of Management
- ○ Manhattan School of Music
- ○ Metropolitan College of New York
- ○ Miami University
- ○ Miles Community College
- ○ Minot State University—Bottineau Campus
- ○ Mitchell College
- ○ Monterey Institute of International Studies
- ○ Notre Dame College
- ○ Olivet College
- ○ Oral Roberts University
- ○ Pepperdine University
- ○ Pontifical College Josephinum
- ○ Reed College
- ○ Sacred Heart Major Seminary
- ○ San Francisco Conservatory of Music
- ○ Shasta Bible College
- ○ Shimer College
- ○ Southern California College of Optometry

- ○ Southern Christian University
- ○ St. Charles Borromeno Seminary
- ○ St. John's College (NM)
- ○ St. Mary's University
- ○ State University of New York— The College at Old Westbury
- ○ State University of New York— Cobleskill
- ○ Texas A&M University—Galveston
- ○ Thomas More College of Liberal Arts
- ○ Tougaloo College
- ○ Trinity University
- ○ United States Military Academy
- ○ University of the Arts
- ○ The University of British Columbia
- ○ The University of Montana— Western
- ○ University of Rochester
- ○ University of Toronto
- ○ Wadhams Hall Seminary College
- ○ Washington College
- ○ Whitworth College
- ○ Wilmington College (DE)

On The Rise

Schools that are growing in resources and popularity

- Dallas Baptist University
- Elon University
- Babson College
- Bentley College
- Chapman University
- DePaul University
- Drexel University
- Elon University
- Emerson College
- Florida Southern College
- Goucher College
- Hendrix College
- James Madison University
- Juniata College
- Loyola College of Maryland
- McMaster University
- Monmouth University
- New College of Florida
- Rensselaer Polytechnic University
- Rollins College
- Saint Michael's College
- Santa Clara University
- Suffolk University
- Temple University
- University of California—Riverside
- University of Central Florida
- University of Cincinnati
- University of Denver
- University of Maine—Augusta
- University of Phoenix
- University of Toronto
- University of Washington
- Ursinus College
- Wells College
- Wentworth Institute of Technology
- Xavier University of Louisiana

part 2

Special Programs

Not Your Usual Schedule

Schools with 4-4-1 or 4-1-4 calendars

- Albright College
- Augustana College (SD)
- Austin College
- Baker University College of Arts and Sciences
- Barton College
- Berea College
- Bethany College (KS)
- Bethany College (WV)
- Bethel College (KS)
- Bethel University (MN)
- Biola University
- Birmingham-Southern College
- Bridgewater College
- Buena Vista University
- California State University—Stanislaus
- Calvin College
- Carthage College
- Centre College
- Chapman University
- Chatham College
- Clearwater Christian College
- Colby College
- The College of St. Catherine
- Concordia University Wisconsin
- Converse College
- Dallas Baptist University
- Dana College
- DePauw University
- Doane College
- Eastern Nazarene College
- Eckerd College
- Edgewood College
- Elmhurst College
- Elon University
- Endicott College

- Erskine College
- Franklin College
- Graceland University
- Greenville College
- Gustavus Adolphus College
- Hamline University
- Hampshire College
- Hartwick College
- Hastings College
- Hofstra University
- Hollins University
- Hope International University
- Huntington College
- Iowa Wesleyan College
- Johns Hopkins University
- Keuka College
- LaGrange College
- Linfield College
- Luther College
- Manchester College
- Marymount Manhattan College
- Maryville College
- Massachusetts Institute of Technology
- McDaniel College
- McPherson College
- Middlebury College
- Midland Lutheran College
- Millersville University of Pennsylvania
- Missouri Valley College
- Molloy College
- Mount Mercy College
- Mount Vernon Nazarene University
- New College of Florida
- Northland College
- Oberlin College
- Oklahoma Baptist University
- Pacific Lutheran University
- Pacific University
- Randolph-Macon College
- Rhode Island School of Design
- Saint Mary's College of California
- St. Olaf College
- Saint Thomas Aquinas College
- Salem College
- Salisbury University
- Samford University
- Samuel Merritt College
- Southwest Baptist University
- St. Ambrose University
- St. Olaf College
- State University of New York—Erie Community College, City Campus
- State University of New York—Erie Community College, North Campus

- State University of New York—Erie Community College, South Campus
- State University of New York—Fashion Institute of Technology
- Sterling College
- Sullivan County Community College
- Tabor College
- Taylor University
- Taylor University—Fort Wayne Campus
- University of Delaware
- University of La Verne
- University of Maryland—Baltimore County
- University of New Haven
- University of Saint Thomas (MN)
- University of San Diego
- University of San Francisco
- University of Sioux Falls
- University of Wisconsin—Stout
- Virginia Wesleyan College
- Washington & Jefferson College
- Westminster College
- Whittier College
- Whitworth College
- Williams College

- Wilson College
- Wofford College

Double The Degree, Double Your Fun, Take 1

Great 3+2 programs (i.e., programs in which you receive a bachelor's after three years and a master's after an additional two years)

- Assumption College (engineering)
- Augustana College (SD) (engineering)
- Austin College (engineering)
- Bradley Univesity (engineering)

FUN FACT

Austin College's mascot is the kangaroo—hence the sports teams' nicknames, the "'Roos" and the "Lady 'Roos."

- Clark University (engineering)
- Colorado College (engineering)
- Centre College (engineering)

43

- ○ Columbia University (engineering)
- ○ Corcoran School of Art & Design (fine arts/art education)
- ○ DePauw University (engineering)
- ○ Dickinson College (engineering)
- ○ Eckerd College (engineering)
- ○ Embry Riddle Aeronautical University (engineering)
- ○ Erskine College (engineering)
- ○ Eugene Lang College—The New School for Liberal Arts (fine arts)
- ○ Florida A&M University (business administration)
- ○ Florida State University (engineering)
- ○ Hobart & William Smith Colleges (engineering)
- ○ Illinois Institute of Technology (engineering)
- ○ Illinois Wesleyan University (engineering)
- ○ Jacksonville University (engineering)
- ○ Kalamazoo College (engineering)
- ○ Lewis & Clark University (engineering)
- ○ Miami University (computer science)
- ○ Michigan Technology University (engineering)
- ○ Muhlenberg College (engineering)
- ○ New York University (liberal arts)
- ○ Northern Michigan University (engineering)
- ○ Northwestern University (engineering)
- ○ Occidental College (engineering)
- ○ Oregon Graduate Institute, School of Science & Engineering (engineering)
- ○ Reed College (engineering)
- ○ Ripon College (engineering)
- ○ Rutgers, The State University of New Jersey—New Brunswick/Piscataway (business administration, education, public health)
- ○ Skidmore College (engineering)
- ○ Southwestern University (engineering)
- ○ Spelman College (engineering)
- ○ St. Joseph's College of Maine (engineering)
- ○ St. Mary's College of California (engineering)
- ○ St. Olaf College (engineering)
- ○ State University of New York at Binghamton (engineering, computer science, individualized study programs)
- ○ State University of New York—Plattsburg (engineering)

- State University of New York—Stony Brook University (education)
- State University of New York—University at Albany (business administration)
- Trinity College (CT) (engineering)
- Trinity University (Washington, DC) (education)
- Union College (engineering)
- University of California—Berkeley (engineering)
- University of California—San Diego (computer science)
- University of California—Santa Cruz (engineering)
- University of Colorado—Boulder (liberal arts, business administration, engineering)
- University of Denver (engineering)
- University of Maryland—College Park (individualized study programs)
- University of Massachusetts—Lowell (engineering, education)
- University of Rochester (liberal arts)
- The University of Scranton (education)
- University of Southern California (engineering)
- University of Virginia (engineering)
- Villanova University (engineering)
- Washington University in St. Louis (engineering)
- Willamette University (engineering)
- Whitman College (engineering)

Double The Degree, Double Your Fun, Take 2

Great 4+1 programs (i.e., programs in which you receive a bachelor's after four years and a master's after an additional year)

- Abilene Christian University (psychology)
- American University (individualized study programs)
- Brown University (literature)
- Bucknell University (engineering)
- Clark University (education)

FUN FACT

The **University of Southern California**'s list of alumni is rather star-struck—John Wayne, Tom Selleck, George Lucas, Cybill Shepherd, and Will Ferrell to name a few.

- ○ Clarkson University (economics and business)
- ○ Florida State University (liberal arts, criminal justice, education, human science)
- ○ Johns Hopkins University (biology)
- ○ Kettering University (physics)
- ○ Lehigh University (engineering)
- ○ Manhattanville College (English and communication)
- ○ Northwestern University (engineering and music)
- ○ Rochester Institute of Technology (economics and business)
- ○ Stanford University (engineering)
- ○ State University of New York— College at Oneonta (economics and business)
- ○ University of Chicago (biological sciences)
- ○ University of Colorado—Boulder (engineering)
- ○ University of Denver (engineering)
- ○ University of Florida (engineering, business administration, Sciences, education, liberal arts)
- ○ University of Michigan (engineering)
- ○ University of Richmond (engineering)

- ○ WPI University (science, engineering, business administration)

The Knowledge Syndicates

Outstanding consortium programs

Five Colleges, Inc.:

- ○ Amherst College
- ○ Hampshire College
- ○ Mount Holyoke College
- ○ Smith College
- ○ University of Massachusetts— Amherst

Five Colleges of Ohio:

- ○ The College of Wooster
- ○ Denison University
- ○ Kenyon College
- ○ Oberlin College
- ○ Ohio Wesleyan University

Tri-College Consortium:

- ○ Bryn Mawr College
- ○ Haverford College
- ○ Swarthmore College

The Claremont Colleges:

- ○ Claremont Graduate University
- ○ Claremont McKenna College
- ○ Harvey Mudd College
- ○ Keck Graduate Institute

- ○ Pitzer College
- ○ Pomona College
- ○ Scripps College

Colleges of Worcester, Inc.:

- ○ Anna Maria College
- ○ Assumption College
- ○ Atlantic Union College
- ○ Becker College
- ○ Clark University
- ○ College of the Holy Cross
- ○ Massachusetts College of Pharmacy and Health Sciences
- ○ Nichols College
- ○ Quinsigamond Community College
- ○ Tufts Cummings School of Veterinary Medicine
- ○ University of Massachusetts Medical School
- ○ Worcester State College
- ○ Worcester Polytechnic Institute

Downtown College Consortium:

- ○ Oklahoma City Community College
- ○ Oklahoma State University—Oklahoma City
- ○ Redlands Community College
- ○ Rose State College
- ○ University of Central Oklahoma

Eco-League Consortium:

- ○ Antioch College
- ○ Alaska Pacific University
- ○ College of the Atlantic
- ○ Green Mountain College
- ○ Northland College
- ○ Prescott College

Spread the Wealth of Knowledge

Schools with great cross-registration programs

- ○ Amherst College (Hampshire College, Mount Holyoke College, Smith College, University of Massachusetts—Amherst)
- ○ Babson College (Bentley College, Boston College, Boston University, Brandeis University, Tufts University, Wellesley College)
- ○ Bentley College (Babson College, Boston College, Boston University, Brandeis University, Tufts University, Wellesley College)
- ○ Boston College (Babson College, Bentley College, Boston University, Brandeis University, Tufts University, Wellesley College)

47

- Boston University (Babson College, Bentley College, Boston College, Brandeis University, Tufts University, Wellesley College)
- Brandeis University (Babson College, Bentley College, Boston College, Boston University, Tufts University, Wellesley College)
- Capital University (Franklin University, The Ohio State University, Otterbein College)
- College of Notre Dame (Johns Hopkins University, Loyola College—Maryland, Towson University, University of Baltimore, University of Maryland—Baltimore County)
- College of Saint Scholastica (University of Minnesota—Duluth, University of Wisconsin—Superior)
- Eastern Oregon University (Oregon Heath Sciences University, Oregon State University, University of Oregon, Portland State University, Southern Oregon University, Western Oregon University)
- Franklin University (Capital University, The Ohio State University, Otterbein College)
- Hampshire College (Amherst College, Mount Holyoke College, Smith College, University of Massachusetts—Amherst)
- Harvard University (Massachusetts Institute of Technology)
- Johns Hopkins University (College of Notre Dame, Loyola College—Maryland, Towson University, University of Baltimore, University of Maryland—Baltimore County)
- Loyola College—Maryland (College of Notre Dame, Goucher College, Johns Hopkins University, Towson University, University of Baltimore, University of Maryland—Baltimore County)
- Massachusetts Institute of Technology (Harvard University)
- The Ohio State University (Capital University, Franklin University, Otterbein College)
- Oregon Heath Sciences University (Eastern Oregon University, Oregon State University, University of Oregon, Portland State University, Southern Oregon University, Western Oregon University)

- ○ Oregon State University (Eastern Oregon University, Oregon Health Sciences University, Portland State University, Southern Oregon University, University of Oregon, Western Oregon University)

- ○ Otterbein College (Capital University, Franklin University, The Ohio State University)

- ○ Portland State University (Eastern Oregon University, Oregon Health Sciences University, Oregon State University, Southern Oregon University, University of Oregon, Western Oregon University)

- ○ Smith College (Amherst College, Hampshire College, Mount Holyoke College, University of Massachusetts—Amherst)

- ○ Southern Oregon University (Eastern Oregon University, Oregon Health Sciences University, Oregon State University, Portland State University, University of Oregon, Western Oregon University)

- ○ Tufts University (Babson College, Bentley College, Boston College, Boston University, Brandeis University, Wellesley College)

- ○ University of Baltimore (College of Notre Dame, Johns Hopkins University, Loyola College—Maryland, Towson University, University of Maryland—Baltimore County)

- ○ University of California—Los Angeles (Any California community college, California State University, or University of California campus can apply and vice-versa)

- ○ University of Maryland—Baltimore County (College of Notre Dame, Loyola College—Maryland, Johns Hopkins University, Towson University, University of Baltimore)

- ○ University of Massachusetts—Amherst (Amherst College, Hampshire College, Mount Holyoke College, Smith College)

- ○ University of Minnesota—Duluth (College of Saint Scholastica, University of Wisconsin—Superior)

- ○ University of Nebraska—Kearney (University of Nebraska—Omaha, University of Nebraska—Lincoln)

- ○ University of Nebraska—Omaha (University of Nebraska—Kearney, University of Nebraska—Lincoln)

- ○ University of Nebraska—Lincoln (University of Nebraska—Kearney, University of Nebraska—Omaha)

○ University of Oregon (Eastern Oregon University, Oregon Health Sciences University, Oregon State University, Portland State University, Southern Oregon University, Western Oregon University)
○ University of Wisconsin—Superior (College of Saint Scholastica, University of Minnesota—Duluth)

FUN FACT

The **University of Arizona** does not currently give plus or minus grades for courses—only A, B, C, D, and E.

○ Wellesley College (Babson College, Bentley College, Boston College, Boston University, Brandeis University, Tufts University)
○ Western Oregon University (Eastern Oregon University, Oregon Health Sciences University, Oregon State University, Portland State University, Southern Oregon University, University of Oregon)

A Helping Hand

Schools with great learning disabilities services

○ Abilene Christian University
○ American University
○ Brown University
○ California State University—Northridge
○ Landmark College
○ Lehigh University
○ Mira Costa College
○ Oberlin College
○ Pennsylvania State University
○ Seton Hall University
○ Smith College
○ University of Arizona
○ University of California—Berkeley
○ University of Michigan
○ University of Minnesota
○ University of Northern Iowa
○ University of Southern California
○ Western Carolina University

Honorable Honors

Schools with outstanding honors programs

- ○ Augsburg College
- ○ The Catholic University of America
- ○ City University of New York
- ○ DePaul University
- ○ Louisiana State University
- ○ Marquette University
- ○ Rice University
- ○ Stanford University
- ○ Texas A&M University
- ○ University of California—Berkeley
- ○ University of California—Santa Cruz
- ○ University of Connecticut
- ○ University of Delaware
- ○ University of Georgia
- ○ University of Idaho
- ○ University of Iowa
- ○ University of Maryland
- ○ University of Missouri—Columbia
- ○ University of North Carolina
- ○ University of South Florida
- ○ The University of Texas
- ○ University of Virginia

No "A" For Effort

Schools that don't give grades

- ○ Alverno College
- ○ Antioch College
- ○ Bennington College
- ○ Brown University
- ○ Burlington College
- ○ California Institute of the Arts
- ○ The Evergreen State College
- ○ Fairhaven College (Western Washington University)
- ○ Hampshire College
- ○ Middlebury College
- ○ New College of Florida
- ○ Sarah Lawrence College

FUN FACT

Sarah Lawrence College operates the only formal American university program in Cuba.

- ○ St. John's College (MD)
- ○ St. John's College (NM)
- ○ University of California—Santa Cruz

You're the Boss

Great schools for designing your own major

- Antioch College
- Bard College
- Brown University
- Hampshire College
- New York University
- Rice University
- Sarah Lawrence College
- Stanford University
- University of California—Santa Cruz
- University of Chicago
- University of Southern California
- Washington University in St. Louis

The Undiscovered Major

Schools that offer unusual/unconventional majors

- American University (foreign language and communication media)
- Brown University (late antique cultures)
- Bryn Mawr College (growth and structure of cities)
- Cornell University (entomology)
- Earlham College (wilderness education)
- Harvard College (folklore and mythology)
- North Carolina State University (wood and paper science)
- Northland College (sustainable systems)
- Princeton University (robotics and intelligent systems)
- University of California—Berkeley (forestry and natural resources)
- University of California—Los Angeles (cybernetics)
- University of Chicago (fundamentals: issues and texts)
- University of North Carolina at Chapel Hill (exercise and sport science)
- University of North Texas (speech and hearing sciences)
- William Jewell College (bioethics)
- Yale University (humanities)

part 3

Campus Facilities

The Natural World

Schools with great on-campus arboreta

- Arizona State University
- Austin State University
- California State University—Fullerton
- Cornell University
- Georgian Court College
- Harvard College
- Haverford College
- Hesston College
- James Madison University
- Mississippi State University
- Missouri State University
- North Carolina State University
- Salisbury University
- State University of New York at Geneseo
- Swarthmore College
- University of California—Davis
- University of California—Santa Cruz
- University of Central Florida
- University of Hawaii—Manoa
- University of Kentucky—Lexington
- University of Michigan
- University of Minnesota
- University of Nebraska—Lincoln
- University of Pennsylvania
- University of Utah
- University of Virginia
- University of Washington
- University of Wisconsin—Madison

The Life Botanica
Schools with botanical gardens

- Iowa State University
- Michigan State University
- Mount Holyoke College
- Smith College
- University of California—Berkeley
- University of Delaware

FUN FACT

Founded as Mount Holyoke Female Seminary on November 8th, 1837, **Mount Holyoke College** is the oldest women's liberal arts college in the United States.

- University of Georgia
- University of Michigan
- University of Nebraska—Lincoln
- University of North Carolina
- University of Southern Florida
- University of Tennessee—Knoxville
- Utah State University
- Virginia Polytechnic and State University (Virginia Tech)

Books, Books, Everywhere
Schools with the most extensive library collections

- Columbia University (7.4 million volumes)
- Cornell University (6.8 million volumes)
- Duke University (5.1 million volumes)
- Harvard College (14.7 million volumes)
- Indiana University (6.4 million volumes)
- Michigan State University (4.4 million volumes)
- New York University (4.0 million volumes)
- Northwestern University (4.1 million volumes)
- The Ohio State University (5.5 million volumes)
- Pennsylvania State University (4.6 million volumes)
- Princeton University (6.0 million volumes)
- Rutgers, The State University of New Jersey (3.9 million volumes)
- Stanford University (7.5 million volumes)

- University of Arizona (4.8 million volumes)
- University of California—Berkeley (9.3 million volumes)
- University of California—Los Angeles (7.7 million volumes)
- University of Chicago (6.7 million volumes)
- University of Florida (3.9 million volumes)
- University of Georgia (3.8 million volumes)
- University of Illinois at Urbana-Champaign (9.7 million volumes)
- University of Iowa (4.2 million volumes)

I know what you're thinking: Philadelphia mass turbulance of 1947.

- University of Kansas (3.8 million volumes)
- University of Michigan (7.5 million volumes)
- University of Minnesota (6.0 million volumes)
- University of North Carolina at Chapel Hill (5.2 million volumes)
- University of Oklahoma (4.2 million volumes)
- University of Pennsylvania (5.0 million volumes)
- University of Pittsburgh (4.3 million volumes)
- University of Southern California (3.7 million volumes)
- The University of Texas at Austin (8.1 million volumes)
- University of Virginia (4.7 million volumes)
- University of Washington (6.2 million volumes)
- University of Wisconsin—Madison (6.1 million volumes)
- Yale University (10.7 million volumes)

On Exhibit

Schools with awe-inspiring on-campus museums

- Brigham Young University (Brigham Young University Museum of Art)
- Colby College (Colby College Museum of Art)
- DePaul University (DePaul University Art Museum)
- Duke University (Duke University Museum of Art)
- Florida State University (Florida State Museum of Fine Arts, John and Mable Ringling Museum of Art)
- Harvard College (Harvard College Art Museums, Harvard Museum of Natural History, Fisher Museum at the Harvard Forest, Peabody Museum of Archaeology and Ethnology, Warren Anatomical Museum)
- Iowa State University (Brunnier Art Museum, Farm House Museum, Art on Campus Collection, Christian Petersen Art Museum)
- Michigan State University (Michigan State University Museum)

- Pennsylvania Academy of the Fine Arts (Pennsylvania Academy of the Fine Arts Museum)
- Saint Louis University (Saint Louis University Museum of Art)
- Smith College (Smith College Museum of Art)
- Stanford University (Cantor Arts Center)
- University of California—Berkeley (Berkeley Art Museum and Pacific Film Archive, Berkeley Natural History Museums, Lawrence Hall of Science)
- University of California—Los Angeles (Hammer Museum, Fowler Museum)
- University of Colorado (University of Colorado Museum)
- University of Delaware (University Gallery Collection, Paul R. Jones Collection, Mineralogical Museum)
- University of Illinois (Krannert Art Museum and Kinkead Pavilion, World Heritage Museum, Museum of Natural History)
- University of Michigan (Exhibit Museum of Natural History, Kelsey Museum of Archaeology, Museum of Art, Museum of Anthropology, Museum of Paleontology, Museum of Zoology)
- University of Missouri (University of Missouri Museum of Art and Archaeology)
- University of New Mexico (University Art Museum, Jonson Gallery, Maxwell Museum of Anthropology, Tamarind Institute, Museum of Geology, Museum of Southwestern Biology)
- University of North Carolina at Chapel Hill (Ackland Art Museum)
- University of Oregon (Condon Museum of Geology, Jordan Schnitzer Museum of Art, Museum of Natural History, Oregon State Museum of Anthropology)
- University of Pennsylvania (University of Pennsylvania Museum of Archaeology and Anthropology)
- University of Richmond (Joel and Lila Harnett Museum of Art, Joel and Lila Harnett Print Study Center, Lora Robins Gallery of Design from Nature)
- University of Utah (Utah Museum of Fine Arts, Utah Museum of Natural History)
- Washington and Lee University (Lee Chapel Museum)
- Wellesley College (Davis Museum and Cultural Center)

○ Yale University (Yale University Center for British Art)

Put It On Wax

Schools with recording studios on campus

○ Baylor University
○ Belmont University
○ Bennington College
○ Berklee College of Music

FUN FACT

Berklee School of Music's list of famous alumni includes Quincy Davis, Diana Krall, and Branford Marsalis.

○ California Institute for the Arts
○ California State University—Chico
○ California State University—Dominguez Hills
○ Capital University
○ Carnegie Mellon University
○ Cleveland Institute of Music
○ Columbia University
○ Duke University

○ Duquesne University
○ Eastman School of Music
○ Emerson College
○ Georgia State University
○ Harvard College
○ Johns Hopkins University
○ Manhattan School of Music
○ Mannes College—The New School of Music
○ New York University
○ The Peabody Institute
○ San Francisco Conservatory of Music
○ San Francisco State University
○ Sonoma State University
○ State University of New York—University at Albany
○ State University of New York—University at Buffalo
○ University of California—Berkeley
○ University of California—Irvine
○ University of California—San Diego
○ University of Colorado at Denver
○ University of Illinois at Urbana-Champaign
○ University of Iowa
○ University of Massachusetts—Lowell

- ○ The University of Memphis
- ○ University of Miami
- ○ University of Michigan
- ○ University of Missouri—Kansas City
- ○ University of New Orleans
- ○ University of Rochester
- ○ University of Southern California
- ○ The University of Texas at Austin
- ○ University of Washington
- ○ Webster University
- ○ Wesleyan University

American Gladiators

Schools with the largest stadiums

- ○ Auburn University
  (Jordan-Hare Stadium: 85,612 capacity)
- ○ Clemson University
  (Memorial Stadium: 81,474 capacity)
- ○ Florida State University
  (Doak Campbell Stadium: 82,000 capacity)
- ○ Louisiana State University
  (Tiger Stadium: 91,600 capacity)
- ○ The Ohio State University
  (Ohio Stadium: 101,568 capacity)

- ○ Pennsylvania State University
  (Beaver Stadium: 107, 282 capacity)
- ○ Stanford University
  (Stanford Stadium: 85,500 capacity)
- ○ Texas A&M University
  (Kyle Field: 80,650 capacity)
- ○ University of Alabama
  (Bryant-Denny Stadium: 83,818 capacity)
- ○ University of Arkansas
  (Donald W. Reynolds Stadium: 71,000 capacity)
- ○ University of California—Los Angeles
  (Rose Bowl: 98,636 capacity)
- ○ University of Florida
  (Ben Hill Griffin Stadium: 90,716 capacity)
- ○ University of Georgia
  (Sanford Stadium: 92,000)
- ○ University of Iowa
  (Kinnick Stadium: 70,397 capacity)
- ○ University of Michigan
  (Michigan Stadium: 107,501 capacity)
- ○ University of Nebraska—Lincoln
  (Memorial Stadium: 74,031 capacity)
- ○ University of Notre Dame
  (Notre Dame Stadium: 80,232 capacity)

- University of Oklahoma
  (Gaylord Family-Memorial Stadium: 82,112 capacity)
- University of Southern California
  (Los Angeles Memorial Coliseum: 92,000 capacity)
- University of Southern Carolina
  (Williams-Brice Stadium: 80,250 capacity)
- University of Tennessee—Knoxville
  (Neyland Stadium: 104,079 capacity)
- University of Wisconsin
  (Camp Randall Stadium: 80,321 capacity)

Right-Click Me!

Schools with computer labs that have the greatest PC-to-Mac ratios

- Agnes Scott College
- Albertson College of Idaho
- Albion College
- Augusta State University
- Baker College—Auburn Hills
- Bridgewater College
- California State University—Sacramento
- Carroll College (MT)

- Catawba College
- Cedarville University
- Central Christian College of the Bible
- Colorado Christian University
- Colorado School of Mines
- Concordia College (NY)
- DePaul University
- Embry Riddle Aeronautical University (FL)
- Fairleigh Dickinson University—College at Florham
- Fairleigh Dickinson University—Metropolitan Campus
- Gettysburg College
- Limestone College
- Metropolitan College of New York
- Mississippi University for Women
- Missouri Southern State University—Joplin
- Montana Tech of the University of Montana
- Mount Mercy College
- Muhlenberg College
- Newberry College
- Nova Southeastern University
- Oklahoma Christian University
- Rensselaer Polytechnic Institute
- Roanoke College

- Rust College
- Southeast Missouri State University
- Southeastern College of the Assemblies of God
- Southeastern Louisiana University
- Southeastern Oklahoma State University
- Southwest Baptist University
- St. Lawrence University
- Sterling College
- Sul Ross State University
- Texas A&M University—Galveston
- Texas Wesleyan University
- The Franciscan University
- University of Alabama—Huntsville
- Thomas College
- University of Maine—Augusta
- University of North Alabama
- Ursinus College
- Valdosta State University
- Vaughn College of Aeronautics and Technology
- Westminster College
- Worcester Polytechnic Institute

An Apple A Day

Schools with computer labs that have the greatest Mac-to-PC ratios

- Alma College
- American Conservatory of Music
- The Art Institute of California— San Diego
- Bennington College
- Brown University
- California College of the Arts
- City University of New York— Borough of Manhattan Community College
- The College of Wooster

FUN FACT

Depending on which athletic team you're referring to at **Rensselaer Polytechnic Institute**, you might find yourself cheering for either the "Engineers" or the "Red Hawks."

- Collins College
- Corcoran College of Art and Design

- Eastman School of Music—University of Rochester
- Hampshire College
- Harvard College
- Kansas City Art Institute
- Lesley College
- Lewis & Clark College
- Maine College of Art
- Maryland Institute College of Art
- Medical University of South Carolina
- Milwaukee Institute of Art and Design
- Minneapolis College of Art and Design
- Montserrat College of Art
- Moore College of Art & Design
- Nova Scotia College of Art and Design
- Oberlin College
- Oregon College of Art and Craft
- Otis College of Art & Design
- Pacific Northwest College of Art
- Reed College
- Rhode Island School of Design
- Ringling School of Art & Design
- School of the Art Institute of Chicago
- School of the Museum of Fine Arts
- School of Visual Arts
- Simpson College (IA)
- State University of New York—Potsdam
- Sweet Briar College
- University of the Arts
- University of California—San Diego
- Vandercook College of Music
- Vassar College
- Whittier College

FUN FACT

Become a "Double Eagle" by graduating from both Boston College High School and **Boston College**. If you think you're up for a triple, head to Boston College Law School.

Where There Isn't Smoke...

Schools with the highest fire safety ratings

- Adelphi University
- Aurora University

- Bloomfield College
- Boise State University
- Boston College
- Brenau University, The Women's College
- Bryant University
- California College of the Arts
- Canisius College
- Carlow University
- Clark University
- College of Saint Elizabeth
- College of St. Joseph in Vermont
- Corban College
- City University of New York—Hunter College
- Dominican College
- Elmhurst College
- Emerson College
- Emmanuel College
- Endicott College
- Fairleigh Dickinson University—College at Florham
- Franklin W. Olin College of engineering
- Goshen College
- Grace College and Seminary
- Hobart and William Smith Colleges
- Iona College
- Kennesaw State University
- King's College (PA)
- Lake Region State College
- Lock Haven University of Pennsylvania
- Loyola University—New Orleans
- Manhattan School of Music
- Mansfield University of Pennsylvania
- Massachusetts College of Pharmacy and Health Science
- Merrimack College
- Michigan Technological University
- Montana State University—Billings
- Montclair State University
- Morrisville State College
- Muhlenberg College
- Murray State University
- Neumann College
- New England College
- Prairie View A&M University
- Providence College
- Randolph-Macon College
- Rensselaer Polytechnic Institute
- Richard Stockton College of New Jersey
- Rochester Institute of Technology
- Roger Williams University

- Rowan University
- Sacred Heart University
- Saint Joseph College (CT)
- Saint Joseph's University (PA)
- Sarah Lawrence College
- School of the Art Institute of Chicago
- School of Visual Arts
- Shawnee State University
- Siena College
- Soka University of America
- Southern Illinois University—Edwardsville
- Spring Hill College
- State University of New York—The College at Old Westbury
- Stevens Institute of Technology
- Suffolk University
- Syracuse University
- Talladega College
- Texas Woman's University
- Thiel College
- Tufts University
- Union University
- University of Alabama at Birmingham
- University of Alaska—Fairbanks
- University of Bridgeport

- University of California—Santa Barbara
- University of Cincinnati
- University of Colorado—Boulder
- University of Connecticut
- University of the Cumberlands
- University of Dubuque
- University of Minnesota—Crookston
- The University of Montana
- University of North Carolina at Asheville
- University of Notre Dame
- University of Science and Arts of Oklahoma
- University of Southern California
- University of St. Thomas (TX)
- University of Washington
- Ursinus College
- Virginia Intermont College
- Wake Forest University
- Walsh University
- West Virginia University
- Western Kentucky University
- Westminster College
- Williams College
- Wright State University

part 4

Nontraditional Paths

Knowledge From Afar

Schools with outstanding distance learning programs

- American Intercontinental University
- Arcadia University
- Baker College
- Bellevue University
- Boston University
- Brigham Young University
- Colorado Technical University
- DeVry University
- Florida Metropolitan University
- Goucher College
- Grand Canyon University
- Grantham University
- Liberty University (nursing, business, and psychology)
- Mountain State University
- Pepperdine University (management)
- Portland State University (criminology and criminal justice)
- Sam Houston State University
- St. Leo University
- State University of New York
- Strayer University
- Thomas Edison State College
- University of California—Irvine
- University of California—Los Angeles (Extension Center)
- University of Houston
- University of Idaho (engineering)

FUN FACT

Grand Canyon University is the first for-profit Christian university in the United States.

○ University of Massachusetts
○ University of Phoenix
○ The University of Texas
○ University of Wisconsin—Stout
○ Utica College
○ Villanova University

A Sense Of Community
Great community colleges

○ Blinn College
○ Chaffey College
○ College of the Redwoods
○ Collin County Community Colleges
○ Community College of Denver
○ Cy-Fair College

FUN FACT
Cooper Union, Franklin W. Olin College of engineering, and Webb Institute are of but a few American schools that do not charge tuition.

○ Kilgore College
○ Kingwood College
○ Miami Dade Community College

○ Minneapolis Community and Tech College
○ North Harris College
○ Orange Coast College
○ Pasadena City College
○ Rochester Community College
○ Saddleback College
○ Santa Monica College
○ Sheridan College
○ Simon's Rock College of Bard

Technically Speaking
Great technical colleges

○ Benjamin Franklin Institute of Technology
○ California Institute of Technology
○ Capitol College
○ Colorado School of Mines
○ The Cooper Union for the Advancement of Science and Art
○ DeVry University
○ Dunwoody Institute
○ Franklin W. Olin College of Engineering
○ Henry Cogswell College
○ Ketterling University
○ Milwaukee School of Engineering

- ○ Massachusetts Institute of Technology
- ○ Montana Tech of the University of Montana
- ○ New Jersey Institute of Technology
- ○ New York Institute of Technology
- ○ Oregon Institute of Technology
- ○ Rensselaer Polytechnic Institute
- ○ Rose-Hulman Institute of Technology
- ○ South Dakota School of Mines and Technology
- ○ Southern Polytechnic State University
- ○ Vaughn College of Aeronautics and Technology
- ○ Vermont Technical College
- ○ Webb Institute
- ○ Wentworth Institute of Technology
- ○ Western Wisconsin Technical College

chapter 2

Teaching and Advising

Professors, advisors, and other staff can bring your college experience to life. They can engage you, challenge you, and support you. They can transform a set of buildings, offices, and classrooms into a true campus. Or they can do none of those things. Ultimately, they are the faces, voices, and opinions— for better or for worse—that set one school apart from another.

For that reason, you should research the teaching and advising paradigms at your prospective schools. This chapter will tell you which schools have the lowest student-to-faculty ratios (and which have the highest), where you'll find the greatest proportions of professors with PhDs, where you'll be more likely to have classes with female and minority professors, and where you can sign up for courses taught by Nobel laureates.

When you visit a campus, take the time to meet at least one or two faculty members. Schedule an appointment with one of the advisors in your program of choice; make arrangements ahead of time to sit in on one of the classes you might take. Are the students roused to lively discussion, or do they use class time to catnap? Does the class make you wish you could tune in to the next session, or does it remind you a little too much of high school?

While you're at it, ask the students how they feel about their classes.

It's much easier to be a dedicated, passionate student when you have dedicated, passionate instructors. Get the information you need now to find the advisors and mentors who will promote your intellectual growth in college. Ask tough questions (good professors will ask them of you, too!), and expect nuanced answers. Your experience will be all the richer for it.

I'm sorry to bother you, but I'm afraid I took a wrong turn somewhere back there, and I was hoping you could direct me back to the English building.

Resting on their Laurels

Highest number of Nobel laureates currently on the faculty

- California Institute of Technology (5)
- Columbia University (9)
- Cornell University (3)
- Harvard College (12)
- Massachusetts Institute of Technology (12)
- Princeton University (9)
- Stanford University (16)
- University of California—Berkeley (6)
- University of California—Santa Barbara (5)
- University of Chicago (6)
- University of Illinois at Urbana-Champaign (2)
- University of Pennsylvania (4)
- University of Washington (5)
- Yale University (1)

FUN FACT

Beneath **Columbia University** runs a series of tunnels that lead to and from every building on campus. They have been used for things as varied as phone tapping, coal transportation, and access to the Manhattan Project's lair.

Women on the Faculty

Highest proportion of female faculty members

- Adams State College
- Agnes Scott College
- Allen College
- Alverno College
- American Academy for Dramatic Arts—West
- Aquinas College (TN)
- Baker College of Auburn Hills
- Barnard College
- Blessing-Rieman College of Nursing
- Brenau University—The Women's College
- Carlow University
- Chatham College
- Chestnut Hill College

- Clarke College
- Clarkson College
- College of Mount St. Joseph
- College of Notre Dame of Maryland
- College of Saint Elizabeth
- College of Saint Mary
- The College of Saint Scholastica
- The College of St. Catherine
- Columbia College (SC)
- Daemen College
- Dominican College
- Dominican University of California
- Elms College
- Fontbonne University
- Georgia Baptist College of Nursing
- Grand Canyon University
- Gratz College
- Holy Names College
- Huron University
- Indiana University East
- John F. Kennedy University
- Lasell College
- Laura and Alvin Siegal College of Judaic Studies
- Lourdes College
- Marymount Manhattan College
- Marymount University

- Massachusetts College of Pharmacy and Health Science
- Medcenter One College of Nursing
- Medical University of South Carolina
- Meredith College
- Metropolitan College of Court Reporting
- Midway College
- Mills College
- Molloy College
- Moore College of Art & Design
- Mount Aloysius College
- Mount Mary College
- Mount Saint Vincent University
- Nebraska Methodist College
- Notre Dame College
- Peace College
- Pine Manor College
- Queens University of Charlotte
- Randolph College
- Regis College
- Rivier College
- Russell Sage College
- Saint Joseph College (CT)
- Saint Mary-of-the-Woods College
- Saint Mary's College (IN)
- Saint Xavier University

- ○ Scripps College
- ○ Simmons College
- ○ Spelman College
- ○ St. John's College, Department of Nursing (IL)
- ○ Stephens College
- ○ Trinity University (Washington, DC)
- ○ University of Texas Medical Branch at Galveston
- ○ Ursuline College
- ○ West Suburban College of Nursing

Diverse Faculty

Highest proportions of faculty belonging to a minority group

- ○ Alabama State University
- ○ Alcorn State University
- ○ Antioch Southern California—Los Angeles
- ○ Bethune-Cookman College
- ○ Beulah Heights Bible College
- ○ Bloomfield College
- ○ Chaminade University of Honolulu
- ○ Chicago State University
- ○ City University of New York—Hostos Community College
- ○ City University of New York—LaGuardia Community College

- ○ City University of New York—Lehman College
- ○ City University of New York—Medgar Evers College
- ○ City University of New York—New York City College of Technology
- ○ City University of New York—York College
- ○ Claflin University
- ○ Columbia Union College
- ○ Dillard University
- ○ East-West University
- ○ Emmanuel Bible College
- ○ Fayetteville State University
- ○ Florida A&M University
- ○ Florida International University
- ○ Grambling State University
- ○ Howard University
- ○ Huston-Tillotson University

▼ Highest proportions of faculty belonging to a minority group

FUN FACT

Founded in 1871, **Alcorn State University** was the United States' first state-supported institute of higher education for African-Americans.

- International Academy of Design & Technology—Tampa
- Jarvis Christian College
- Lane College
- Lincoln University (PA)
- Livingstone College
- Lynn University
- Miles College
- Mississippi Valley State University
- Morris College
- The New School for Jazz & Contemporary Music
- Norfolk State University
- Nyack College
- Philander Smith College
- Rust College
- Saint Augustine's College
- Saint Paul's College
- Shaw University
- Soka University of America
- Southeastern University
- Southern California College of Optometry
- Southern University and A&M College
- Spelman College
- St. John's College, Department of Nursing (IL)
- St. Thomas University
- Talladega College
- Tougaloo College
- Trinity University (Washington, DC)
- Tuskegee University
- University of Arkansas—Pine Bluff
- University of Hawaii—Hilo
- University of Maryland—Eastern Shore
- University of South Carolina—Spartanburg
- The University of Texas at El Paso
- The University of Texas—Pan American
- University of the Virgin Islands
- Vaughn College of Aeronautics and Technology
- Virginia State University
- Voorhees College
- Xavier University of Louisiana

The Doctor Is In

Schools at which the greatest proportions (98-plus percent) of full-time faculty hold PhDs

- Alliant International University
- Appalachian State University
- Bowdoin College
- Cambridge Online Learning
- Carlos Albizu University
- Carnegie Mellon University
- The College of Saint Thomas More
- The College of Wooster
- Colorado State University
- Columbia University
- Davidson College
- Dominican School of Philosophy and Theology
- Elmira College
- Emmanuel Bible College
- Emory University
- Grace University
- Gratz College
- Harvard College
- Harvey Mudd College
- Haverford College
- Hendrix College
- Heritage Bible College
- Hollins University
- Hood College
- Husson College
- Jewish Theological Seminary— Albert A. List College
- Lafayette College
- Lawrence University
- Lehigh University
- Minneapolis College of Art and Design
- New College of Florida
- New Jersey Institute of Technology
- New Mexico Institute of Mining & Technology
- New World School of the Arts
- Northwestern University
- The Ohio State University— Columbus
- The Ohio State University— Newark
- Ohio Wesleyan University
- Pitzer College

FUN FACT

The most popular method of getting around **Harvey Mudd College** includes walking, skateboarding, and unicycling.

- ○ Purdue University—West Lafayette
- ○ Rose-Hulman Institute of Technology
- ○ Rutgers, The State University of New Jersey—Camden
- ○ Rutgers, The State University of New Jersey—New Brunswick/Piscataway
- ○ Scripps College
- ○ Southern California College of Optometry
- ○ Southwestern University
- ○ St. Lawrence University
- ○ Stanford University
- ○ Swarthmore College
- ○ Sweet Briar College
- ○ Thomas More College of Liberal Arts
- ○ Trinity University (Washington, DC)
- ○ Trinity University
- ○ University of Arizona
- ○ University of Arkansas—Pine Bluff
- ○ University of California—Davis
- ○ University of California—Los Angeles
- ○ University of California—San Diego
- ○ University of Colorado at Colorado Springs

- ○ University of Houston—Victoria
- ○ University of Pennsylvania
- ○ University of West Los Angeles
- ○ Washington University at St. Louis
- ○ Wheaton College (MA)
- ○ Whittier College
- ○ Williams College
- ○ York University

Don't Call Me Doctor

Schools at which the smallest proportions (25 percent or less) of full-time faculty hold PhDs

- ○ Academy of Art University (formerly The San Francisco Academy)
- ○ Allen College
- ○ Art Institute of Colorado
- ○ The Art Institute of Dallas
- ○ Baker College of Port Huron
- ○ Beulah Heights Bible College
- ○ Central Wyoming College
- ○ College of the Siskiyous
- ○ Colorado Mountain College—Alpine
- ○ Colorado Mountain College—Timberline Campus
- ○ The Culinary Institute of America
- ○ Davenport University
- ○ Eastern Oregon University

- ○ Humphreys College
- ○ The Illinois Institute of Art—Schaumburg
- ○ Inter American University of Puerto Rico—Aguadilla
- ○ Johnson & Wales University at Denver
- ○ Johnson & Wales University at Charleston
- ○ Johnson & Wales University at North Miami
- ○ Kendall College of Art and Design of Ferris State University
- ○ Keystone College
- ○ Lake Region State College
- ○ Landmark College
- ○ Life Pacific College
- ○ Minot State University—Bottineau Campus
- ○ Morrisville State College
- ○ Neumont University
- ○ Northwood University—Texas Campus
- ○ Ozark Christian College
- ○ Robert Morris College (IL)
- ○ Rowan University
- ○ San Francisco Conservatory of Music
- ○ Southwestern Christian University
- ○ St. John's College, Department of Nursing (IL)
- ○ State University of New York—Canton
- ○ State University of New York—Mohawk Valley Community College
- ○ State University of New York—Schenectady County Community College
- ○ State University of New York—Ulster Community College
- ○ University of Montana—Helena College of Technology
- ○ University of Phoenix
- ○ Westwood College of Technology

Part-Timer Paradise

Schools at which 75-plus percent of the faculty are part-time employees

- ○ Academy of Art University (formerly The San Francisco Academy)
- ○ Albertus Magnus College
- ○ American Academy for Dramatic Arts—West
- ○ American Conservatory of Music
- ○ Anna Maria College
- ○ Antioch Southern California—Los Angeles
- ○ Art Center College of Design
- ○ The Art Institute of California—San Francisco

- Athabasca University
- Baker College of Auburn Hills
- Baker College of Port Huron
- Barclay College
- Bellevue University
- Benedictine University
- Bloomfield College
- Boston Architectural Center
- Burlington College
- California College of the Arts
- Calumet College of Saint Joseph
- Capella University
- Capitol College
- Cardinal Stritch College
- Carlos Albizu University
- Centenary College
- Central Wyoming College
- Charter Oak State College
- City University
- Cleary University
- College for Creative Studies
- College of St. Joseph in Vermont
- Columbia College—Chicago
- The Cooper Union for the Advancement of Science and Art
- Corcoran College of Art and Design
- Dallas Baptist University

- Davenport University
- DeVry University—Colorado Springs
- DeVry University—West Hills
- Dowling College
- Eastern University
- East-West University
- Emmanuel Bible College
- Eugene Lang College—The New School for Liberal Arts
- Fontbonne University
- Franklin University
- Global University
- Globe Institute of Technology
- Goddard College
- Golden Gate University
- Gratz College
- Griggs University
- Holy Names College
- Hope International University
- Indiana Institute of Technology
- International Academy of Design & Technology—Tampa
- John F. Kennedy University
- Jones International University
- Laboratory Institute of Merchandising
- LeTourneau University

- Luther Rice Bible College and Seminary
- Mannes College—The New School for Music
- Marylhurst University
- Marymount Manhattan College
- Mercy College
- Metropolitan College of New York
- Mountain State University
- Naropa University
- National American University (NM)
- National University
- The New School for Jazz & Contemporary Music
- New World School of the Arts
- New York School of Interior Design
- North Carolina Wesleyan College
- Northcentral University
- Oakland City University
- Otis College of Art & Design
- Pacific States University
- Park University
- Parsons—The New School for Design
- Pennsylvania College of Art & Design
- Philadelphia University
- Post University
- Pratt Institute
- Rosemont College
- Saint Mary's College of Ave Maria University (MI)
- Saint Mary's University of Minnesota
- School of Visual Arts
- Shasta Bible College
- Southeastern University
- Southern Maine Community College
- Southern Wesleyan University
- Strayer University
- State University of New York—Empire State College
- Trinity International University
- Troy University Montgomery
- University of Great Falls
- University of Judaism
- University of Maryland University College
- University of New Hampshire at Manchester
- University of the Arts
- University of West Los Angeles
- Walsh College of Accountancy and Business Administration
- William Tyndale College
- Woodbury University

Pro Pluribus Unum

Schools with the highest student-to-faculty ratios

- Argosy University—Orange County
- Arizona State University—Tempe
- Baptist Bible College and Seminary of Pennsylvania
- Bellevue University
- Berkeley College
- Berkeley College—New York City
- Berkeley College—Westchester
- Black Hills State University
- Brigham Young University (ID)
- California State Polytechnic University—Pomona
- California State University—Dominguez Hills
- California State University—Sacramento
- California State University—San Bernardino
- California University of Pennsylvania
- Central Michigan University
- Central Washington University
- City University of New York—Kingsborough Community College
- Clayton College & State University
- Collins College
- Colorado Technical University
- Concord University—Athens
- Crown College
- DeVry University—Kansas City, MO
- DeVry University—Phoenix
- DeVry University—Tinley Park
- Eastern Oregon University
- Eastern Washington University
- Emily Carr Institute of Art and Design
- Florida A&M University
- Florida Metropolitan University—Orlando North
- Florida State University
- Herkimer County Community College
- Hope International University
- Johnson & Wales University at Norfolk
- Johnson Bible College
- Jones International University
- Louisiana Tech University
- Metropolitan State College of Denver
- Minnesota State University—Mankato

- Minnesota State University—Moorhead
- Mississippi Valley State University
- Mountain State University
- Nicholls State University
- Northeastern State University
- Northern Michigan University
- Northwestern Michigan College
- Northwood University—Florida Campus
- Northwood University—Texas Campus
- Oakland University
- The Ohio State University—Mansfield
- The Ohio State University—Marion
- Philander Smith College
- Reedley College
- Robert Morris College (IL)
- Sam Houston State University
- Simon Fraser University
- Sonoma State University
- Southeastern College of the Assemblies of God
- Southeastern Louisiana University
- Southern Utah University
- State University of New York—Canton
- Tennessee State University
- Texas State University—San Marcos
- University of Central Florida
- University of Florida
- University of Guelph
- University of Louisiana at Lafayette
- University of Maryland—University College
- University of Minnesota—Duluth
- University of North Florida
- University of Northern Colorado
- University of Oklahoma
- University of Regina
- The University of Texas at Arlington
- The University of Texas at San Antonio
- University of Toronto
- University of Windsor
- University of Wisconsin—Green Bay

FUN FACT

Old Sorrel, the horse that helped **Southern Utah University** builders get lumber in record-high snowdrifts, is memorialized by an on-campus statue.

- University of Wisconsin—La Crosse
- University of Wisconsin—River Falls
- Walsh College of Accountancy and Business Administration
- Weber State University
- Wentworth Institute of Technology
- West Texas A&M University
- West Virginia University
- Winona State University

Closer to Equal

Schools with the lowest student-to-faculty ratios

- Alaska Bible College
- American Conservatory of Music
- American Indian College of the Assemblies of God, Inc.
- Bennington College
- Boston Conservatory
- Bryn Athyn College of the New Church
- California Institute of the Arts
- California Institute of Technology
- Cambridge Online Learning
- Cleveland Institute of Music
- College of Santa Fe

- The College of Saint Thomas More
- Columbia College—Hollywood
- Columbia University
- Conception Seminary College
- The Cooper Union for the Advancement of Science and Art
- Corcoran College of Art and Design
- Deep Springs College
- DeVry University—Philadelphia
- DeVry University—Westminster
- Divine Word College
- Dominican School of Philosophy and Theology
- Emory University
- Gallaudet University
- Griggs University
- Holy Apostles College and Seminary
- Jewish Theological Seminary—Albert A. List College
- Landmark College
- Lexington College
- Lyme Academy of Fine Arts
- Marlboro College
- Marylhurst University
- Medcenter One College of Nursing
- Medical University of South Carolina

I helped Southern Utah University builders haul lumber in record-high snowdrifts, and all I got was this stupid statue.

- ○ San Francisco Conservatory of Music
- ○ Sarah Lawrence College
- ○ School of Visual Arts
- ○ St. Charles Borromeno Seminary
- ○ St. John's College (NM)
- ○ St. John's College, Department of Nursing (IL)
- ○ Stanford University
- ○ Sterling College (VT)
- ○ United States Military Academy
- ○ United States Naval Academy

FUN FACT

The Chicago El-train that runs through Evanston is named the Purple Line in honor of **Northwestern University**'s school color.

- ○ University of Chicago
- ○ University of Colorado at Denver and Health Sciences Center
- ○ University of Judaism
- ○ University of Pennsylvania
- ○ Wadhams Hall Seminary College
- ○ Washington University in St. Louis

- ○ Williams College
- ○ Yale University

TAs Rule the School

School at which 10-plus percent of classes are taught by teaching assistants

- ○ Andrews University
- ○ Auburn University
- ○ Bowling Green State University
- ○ Brown University
- ○ The Catholic University of America
- ○ Dominican School of Philosophy and Theology
- ○ Eastman School of Music— University of Rochester
- ○ Emory University
- ○ Eugene Lang College—The New School for Liberal Arts
- ○ Florida Atlantic University
- ○ Florida Metropolitan University— Melbourne
- ○ Florida State University
- ○ George Mason University
- ○ Indiana University—Bloomington
- ○ Iowa State University
- ○ Iowa State University of Science and Technology

- Kansas State University
- LeMoyne-Owen College
- Louisiana State University
- McNeese State University
- Miami University
- Missouri Baptist College
- Nova Scotia College of Art and Design
- Ohio University—Athens
- Oklahoma State University
- Rutgers, The State University of New Jersey—New Brunswick/Piscataway
- Southern Illinois University—Carbondale
- State University of New York—University at Albany
- State University of New York—University at Buffalo
- Texas A&M University—College Station
- Texas A&M University—Commerce
- Texas A&M University—Corpus Christi
- Texas Tech University
- University of Alabama—Tuscaloosa
- University of Arizona
- University of Arkansas—Fayetteville
- University of California—San Diego
- University of Colorado—Boulder
- University of Connecticut
- University of Georgia
- University of Houston
- University of Idaho
- University of Illinois at Chicago
- University of Illinois at Urbana-Champaign
- University of Kansas
- University of Kentucky
- University of Maine
- University of Maryland—College Park
- University of Massachusetts—Amherst
- University of Missouri—Rolla
- University of Nebraska—Lincoln
- University of Nevada—Las Vegas
- University of North Texas
- University of Northern Colorado
- University of Oklahoma
- University of Oregon
- University of South Carolina—Columbia
- University of South Florida
- University of Tennessee—Knoxville

- University of Utah
- University of Virginia
- University of West Florida
- University of Wisconsin—Madison
- Washington Bible College

- Wichita State University
- Wofford College
- Wright State University

chapter 3

Academic Opportunities— Inside and Outside the Classroom

Many high school students begin their college search with just a single criterion: overall academic reputation. This can be an excellent starting point—but there are hundreds of schools that don't get the airplay that the Ivies do, yet are nevertheless academically top-notch.

Peruse the lists of requirements that your potential schools are going to expect you to fulfill before you graduate. While some schools don't have a set general curriculum, others have such rigid course requirements that their students are lucky to get in any electives at all.

The academic environment of a school also encompasses internship, research, and study abroad opportunities as well as all manner of outside-the-classroom learning options. Northeastern's longstanding tradition of co-ops allows students access to career-strengthening paid work experiences as part of the curriculum, and Goucher College gives all students a voucher of at least $1,200 to help cover study abroad travel expenses. These are just the tip of the academic iceberg. Opportunities for intellectual growth are often plentiful—you just have to look.

part 1

Academic Programs Inside and Outside the Classroom

Never Take [You Name It!] Again

Schools with no general education/distribution requirements

- ○ Amherst College
- ○ Brown University
- ○ Hampshire College
- ○ Mount Holyoke College
- ○ New College of Florida
- ○ Smith College

No Foreign Tongues Necessary

Schools that do not have a foreign language requirement

- ○ Albion College
- ○ Aurora University
- ○ Benedictine University
- ○ Bradley University
- ○ Brown University
- ○ Chicago State University
- ○ Cleary University
- ○ Columbia College—Chicago
- ○ DePaul University
- ○ Drake University

- ○ Eastern Illinois University
- ○ Ferris State University
- ○ Governors State University
- ○ Illinois Institute of Technology
- ○ Kansas State University
- ○ Kettering University
- ○ Lewis University
- ○ Lindenwood University (recommended, not required)
- ○ Missouri Baptist University (recommended, not required)
- ○ Northeastern Illinois University
- ○ Northwood University
- ○ Oakland University
- ○ Robert Morris University
- ○ Roosevelt University
- ○ Southern Illinois University—Edwardsville (recommended, not required)
- ○ University of Kansas
- ○ Western Illinois University

FUN FACT

The asteroid 516 Amherstia was dubbed so in honor of **Amherst College** by alumni Raymond Smith Dugan.

- ○ Wichita State University

Indispensable Internships
Schools that require internships

- ○ Alverno College
- ○ Antioch College
- ○ College of the Atlantic
- ○ Endicott College
- ○ Northeastern University
- ○ Salem College
- ○ Temple University

Thesis = Diploma
Schools that require a thesis

- ○ Claremont McKenna College
- ○ Harvey Mudd College (thesis or Clinic Program participation required)
- ○ Haverford College (thesis, comprehensive exam, and/or designated courses required)
- ○ Kettering University
- ○ New College of Florida
- ○ Princeton University
- ○ Reed College
- ○ Scripps College
- ○ Shimer College

part 2

Research Opportunities Outside the Classroom

A Penny for Your Thoughts

Schools with great grant programs for independent study

- Clark University
- Columbia University
- Duke University
- Georgetown University
- Harvard College
- Johns Hopkins University
- Knox College
- Pennsylvania State University—Erie, The Behrend College
- Princeton University
- Stanford University
- University of California—Berkeley
- University of California—Irvine
- University of Michigan
- University of Minnesota
- University of Pennsylvania
- University of Southern California
- University of Wisconsin—Madison
- Yale University

Building Rapport

Schools with great opportunities to conduct research with professors

- Abilene Christian University
- Amherst College
- Brandeis University
- California Institute of Technology
- Carleton College
- Clark University
- College of the Atlantic
- Cornell College
- Cornell University
- Davidson College
- Franklin & Marshall College
- Franklin W. Olin College of Engineering
- Hampden-Sydney College
- Harvard College
- Harvey Mudd College
- Haverford College
- Johns Hopkins University
- Lawrence University
- Marlboro College
- Massachusetts Institute of Technology
- Northwestern University
- Oberlin College
- Rhodes College
- Sewanee—The University of the South
- Smith College
- St. John's College (NM)
- Sweet Briar College
- United States Air Force Academy
- United States Military Academy
- United States Naval Academy
- University of California—San Diego
- University of Chicago
- University of Southern California
- The University of Texas at Austin
- University of Wisconsin—Eau Claire
- University of Wisconsin—Madison
- Yale University
- Wabash College
- Washington and Lee University

FUN FACT

Fictional FBI agent Dale Cooper studied at **Haverford College** before being assigned to the Laura Palmer case in Twin Peaks, Washington.

- Webb Institute
- Wellesley College

Appearing Soon in Print

Schools that have a track record of publishing under-graduate papers

- Brigham Young University
- California Institute of Technology
- Carleton University
- Colby College
- Dartmouth College
- Denison University
- Hampshire College
- Hiram College
- Johns Hopkins University
- Loyola University—Chicago
- Princeton University
- Rose-Hulman Institute of Technology
- Saint Anselm College
- Saint Mary's University
- San Diego State University
- Sewanee—The University of the South
- Skidmore College
- Stanford University

- Texas A&M University
- Union College
- University of California—Berkeley
- University of California—Davis
- University of California—Los Angeles
- University of Florida
- University of Michigan
- University of New Hampshire
- University of Pennsylvania
- University of Pittsburgh
- University of San Francisco
- University of South Carolina
- University of Southern Maine
- Villanova University
- Yale University

Splitting the Atom

Schools with on-campus nuclear reactors

- Georgia Institute of Technology
- Kansas State University
- Massachusetts Institute of Technology
- North Carolina State University
- The Ohio State University
- Oregon State University

- ○ Pennsylvania State University
- ○ Purdue University
- ○ Reed College
- ○ Rensselaer Polytechnic Institute
- ○ Texas A&M University
- ○ University of California—Berkeley
- ○ University of California—Irvine
- ○ University of Cincinnati
- ○ University of Florida
- ○ University of Maryland—College Park
- ○ University of Michigan—Ann Arbor
- ○ University of Missouri—Rolla
- ○ University of New Mexico
- ○ University of Tennessee—Knoxville
- ○ University of Wisconsin—Madison

FUN FACT

Besides having the oldest engineering program in the Ivies and the only undergraduate "History of Mathematics" department in the world, **Brown University** can also boast its library that contains three books bound in human skin.

Kelly, Watch the Stars
Schools with observatories

- ○ Amherst College
- ○ Boston University
- ○ Bridgewater State College
- ○ Brown University
- ○ California Institute of Technology
- ○ California State University—Fresno
- ○ California State University—Northridge
- ○ Case Western Reserve University
- ○ Central Connecticut State University
- ○ Colgate University
- ○ Concordia College
- ○ Cornell University
- ○ Creighton University
- ○ Francis Marion University
- ○ Georgia State University
- ○ Gettysburg College
- ○ Grinnell College
- ○ Hampshire College
- ○ Harvard College
- ○ Indiana University
- ○ Iowa State University
- ○ Macalester College
- ○ Massachusetts Institute of Technology

- Mississippi State University
- Mount Holyoke College
- New Mexico State University
- Oberlin College
- Pennsylvania State University—Erie, The Behrend College
- Saint Ambrose University
- San Diego State University
- Sewanee—The University of the South
- Smith College
- Swarthmore College
- Texas A&M University
- University of Alaska
- University of Arizona
- University of California—Berkeley
- University of California—Santa Cruz
- University of Central Florida
- University of Colorado—Boulder
- University of Delaware
- University of Denver
- University of Maine
- University of Massachusetts—Amherst
- University of Mississippi
- University of Missouri—Columbia
- University of New Hampshire
- University of New Mexico
- University of Oklahoma
- University of Oregon
- University of Rochester
- The University of Texas at Austin
- University of Virginia
- University of Wisconsin—Eau Claire
- University of Wyoming
- Vanderbilt University
- Vassar College
- Washburn University
- Washington State University
- Wellesley College
- Wesleyan University
- West Virginia University
- Western Connecticut State University
- Wheaton College
- Williams College
- Yale University

When You Wish Upon a Star
Schools with planetaria

- Amherst College
- Ball State University

- Bates College
- Berea College
- Bowling Green State University
- Brigham Young University
- Butler University
- California State University—Fresno
- California State University—Northridge
- Central Connecticut State University
- Dickerson College
- Eastern Connecticut State University
- Eastern Kentucky University
- Emporia State University
- Florida State University
- Georgetown College

- Georgia Southern University
- Gettysburg College
- Henderson State University
- Idaho State University
- Illinois State University
- Jacksonville State University
- Keene State College
- Kent State University
- Louisiana Tech University
- Michigan State University
- Minnesota State University—Moorhead
- Montana State University
- The Ohio State University
- Oklahoma Baptist University
- Pittsburgh State University
- Saint Cloud State University
- Samford University
- San Francisco State University
- Southern Connecticut State University
- State University of New York—Cortland
- State University of New York—New Paltz
- Texas A&M University
- Towson University
- Troy State University

FUN FACT

University of California—Berkeley
is the oldest school in the UC system and can claim the isolation of the human polio virus, the invention of the cyclotron, and the discovery of 17 chemical elements to its credit.

- United States Air Force Academy
- University of Arizona
- University of Arkansas—Monticello
- University of California—Berkeley
- University of California—Los Angeles
- University of Colorado
- University of Connecticut
- University of Georgia
- University of Maine
- University of Michigan—Ann Arbor
- University of Minnesota—Duluth
- University of Nebraska—Lincoln
- University of Nebraska—Omaha
- University of Nevada—Reno
- University of New Mexico
- University of North Alabama
- University of North Carolina at Chapel Hill
- University of North Texas
- University of Rhode Island
- University of Saint Francis
- University of Southern Maine
- Western Kentucky University
- Wayne State College
- Wheaton College
- Williams College

E-I-E-I-O

Schools with organic farms

- Bennington College
- California State University—Chico
- California State Polytechnic University—Pomona
- California State Polytechnic University—San Luis Obispo
- Carleton College
- The College of the Atlantic
- The College of the Ozarks
- Colorado State University
- Cornell University
- Dartmouth College
- Dickinson College
- Earlham College
- Evergreen State University
- Hampshire College
- Humboldt State University
- Iowa State University
- Maharishi University of Management
- Michigan State University
- Middlebury College
- New Mexico State University
- North Carolina State University
- Oberlin College
- Oregon State University

- ○ Pomona College
- ○ St. Olaf College
- ○ Stanford University
- ○ University of California—Davis
- ○ University of California—Santa Cruz
- ○ University of Idaho
- ○ University of Maine—Orono
- ○ University of Minnesota—Twin Cities
- ○ University of Montana
- ○ University of New Hampshire
- ○ University of Vermont
- ○ University of Wisconsin—Madison
- ○ Vassar College
- ○ Warren Wilson College
- ○ Washington State University
- ○ Yale University

FUN FACT

Arcadia University—originally called "Beaver College"—has an actual castle on campus, Grey Towers, a National Historic Landmark.

The World Is Yours

Schools with great study abroad programs

- ○ Agnes Scott College
- ○ American University
- ○ Arcadia University
- ○ Austin College
- ○ Bates College
- ○ Boston College
- ○ Brandeis University
- ○ Carleton College
- ○ Centre College
- ○ Claremont McKenna College
- ○ Covenant College
- ○ Colby College
- ○ Dickinson College
- ○ Duke University
- ○ Eckerd College
- ○ Elon University
- ○ Emory University
- ○ Georgetown University
- ○ The George Washington University
- ○ Gonzaga University
- ○ Goucher College
- ○ Grace College and Seminary
- ○ Hobart and William Smith Colleges

- ○ Kalamazoo College
- ○ Lafayette University
- ○ Lee University
- ○ Lewis & Clark College
- ○ Lynn University
- ○ Macalester College
- ○ Middlebury College
- ○ Michigan State University
- ○ New York University
- ○ Pennsylvania State University
- ○ Pomona College
- ○ Saint Louis University

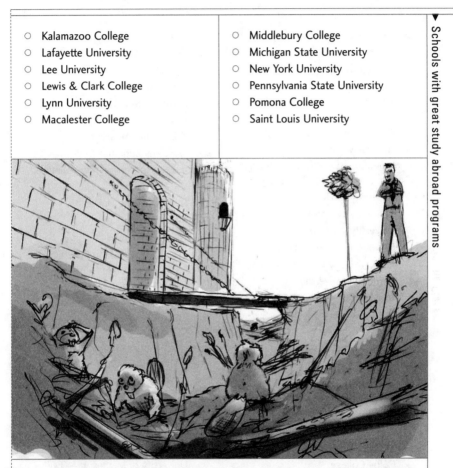

Seriously. If you guys can't stop damming up this moat, we may have to go with someone else.

- ○ San Diego State University
- ○ Southwestern University
- ○ St. Olaf College
- ○ Sarah Lawrence University
- ○ State University of New York—Brockport
- ○ Syracuse University
- ○ Tufts University
- ○ University of California (all campuses have the UC EAP program)
- ○ University of Delaware
- ○ University of Denver
- ○ University of Notre Dame
- ○ University of Portland
- ○ The University of Texas at Austin
- ○ Vanderbilt University
- ○ Wofford College
- ○ Yeshiva University

Leaving on a Jet Plane

Schools with the greatest proportion of students who study abroad

- ○ Arizona State University
- ○ Boston University
- ○ Brigham Young University
- ○ Colby College
- ○ Colgate University

- ○ DePauw University
- ○ Dickinson College
- ○ Duke University
- ○ Eckerd College
- ○ Emory University
- ○ Georgetown University
- ○ The George Washington University
- ○ Gustavus Adolphus College
- ○ Indiana University—Bloomington
- ○ Lee University
- ○ Michigan State University
- ○ Middlebury College
- ○ New York University
- ○ The Ohio State University
- ○ Pennsylvania State University—University Park
- ○ Saint Louis University
- ○ Smith College
- ○ St. Olaf College
- ○ Texas A&M University
- ○ Tufts University
- ○ Union College (NY)
- ○ University of Arizona
- ○ University of Georgia
- ○ University of Illinois at Urbana-Champaign
- ○ University of Minnesota—Twin Cities

- ○ University of North Carolina at Chapel Hill
- ○ University of Notre Dame
- ○ University of Pennsylvania
- ○ The University of Texas at Austin
- ○ University of Southern California
- ○ University of Wisconsin—Madison
- ○ Vanderbilt University
- ○ Yeshiva University

Source: *The Chronicle of Higher Education*

Destination: Unknown
Schools that require students to study abroad

- ○ Goucher College

FUN FACT
The **University of Denver** is one of the few schools in the United States that interviews every undergraduate applicant.

An Offer You Can't Refuse
Schools that offer great financial incentives to study abroad

- ○ Brandeis University
- ○ The George Washington University
- ○ Goucher College
- ○ St. Cloud State University
- ○ Syracuse University
- ○ University of Denver
- ○ University of Wisconsin—Platteville

▼ Schools that require students to study abroad

chapter 4

Majors

The major you choose is, to some degree, very important. It can determine the difference between a career in banking and one in medicine, a job as a forest ranger and one as a violinist. It can be overwhelming to consider the strengths of an entire institution, but it's manageable to weigh the pros and cons of a specific field of study. A lot of schools may be particularly strong in one area—journalism, for example—but average in another—biomedical engineering, perhaps. If you're an aspiring *New York Times* op-ed columnist, you probably won't much care whether your college grooms the next generation of rocket or other scientists, but you will care whether you'll get incomparable preparation in your field of study.

For this reason, you can search for schools by program of study in this chapter. As we mentioned earlier, the lists are accurate but not necessarily exhaustive. You may be able to find a tremendous archaeology program not listed here—so if you're interested in archaeology, ask about on your college visits!—but you won't find any school listed here that doesn't have an outstanding program in the area listed.

Throughout your search, please do keep in mind that other factors besides your potential future major should come into play in your college search. As you change over the next few years, so could your major. (Fact: According to the National Research Center of College and University Admissions, more than half of all college students switch majors at least once.) If you do have a strong sense of what you want to study, it probably doesn't make sense to spend a lot of time looking at schools that don't even offer a program in forensic science, music therapy, wildlife management, or whatever else excites your mind. We recommend focusing on a number of schools that offer solid programs in your primary area(s) of interest—but don't let that preliminary list rule your final decision without making sure your other needs are met, too. If you have no idea about what you'd like to pursue, then let your other college preferences direct you in your search; as a rule of thumb, a liberal arts school almost always promises to be a fine choice.

While many schools will ask you for an intended major from the get-go, most don't require you to declare a major on your application, acceptance form, or even during your first year. You will probably have time to do a bit of soul-searching once you arrive on campus. We recommend that you start researching now, and then be open to where your passions might lead you.

part 1

Academic Programs— Outstanding Programs By Major

Goodnight and Good Luck

Schools with great broadcast journalism programs

- American University
- Boston University
- Bowling Green State University
- California State University—Long Beach
- Central Washington University
- Chatham College
- The College of the Ozarks
- Delaware State University
- Emerson College
- Florida Southern College
- Hampton University
- Northwestern University
- Ohio University
- State University of New York— Plattsburgh
- Suffolk University
- University of California—Los Angeles
- University of Georgia
- University of Miami
- University of Nebraska—Lincoln
- University of Nebraska—Omaha
- University of Oklahoma

- ○ University of Southern California
- ○ Washington State University

Hello, Hello?

Schools with great communications programs

- ○ Augsburg College
- ○ Baylor College
- ○ Boise State University
- ○ Bradley University
- ○ City University of New York—Hunter College
- ○ Clemson University
- ○ College of Charleston
- ○ Cornell University
- ○ Denison University
- ○ DePaul University
- ○ Duquesne University
- ○ Eckerd College
- ○ Emerson College
- ○ Fairfield University
- ○ Fordham University
- ○ Gonzaga University
- ○ Gustavus Adolphus College
- ○ Hollins University
- ○ Indiana University—Bloomington
- ○ Iowa State University
- ○ Ithaca College
- ○ James Madison University
- ○ Lake Forest College
- ○ Loyola University—New Orleans
- ○ Michigan State University
- ○ Muhlenberg College
- ○ New York University
- ○ Northwestern University
- ○ Pepperdine University
- ○ Ripon College
- ○ Salisbury University
- ○ Seton Hall University
- ○ St. John's University (NY)
- ○ Suffolk University
- ○ Syracuse University
- ○ University of California—San Diego
- ○ University of California—Santa Barbara
- ○ University of Iowa
- ○ University of Maryland—College Park
- ○ The University of Texas—Austin
- ○ University of Utah

Investigative Undergraduate
Schools with great journalism programs

- ○ American University
- ○ Boston University
- ○ Carleton University
- ○ Hampton University
- ○ Howard University
- ○ Indiana University
- ○ Loyola University—New Orleans
- ○ Middle Tennessee State University
- ○ Northwestern University
- ○ Ohio University—Athens
- ○ Pennsylvania State University
- ○ Samford University
- ○ St. Bonaventure University
- ○ Temple University
- ○ University of Florida
- ○ University of Missouri—Columbia
- ○ The University of North Carolina at Chapel Hill
- ○ University of Oregon
- ○ The University of Texas at Austin
- ○ University of Wisconsin—Madison

It's a Long Way From Atari
Schools with great video game design programs

- ○ Art Institute of Phoenix
- ○ Carnegie Mellon University
- ○ Columbia College Chicago
- ○ DePaul University
- ○ DigiPen Institute of Technology
- ○ Georgia Institute of Technology
- ○ The Illinois Institute of Art
- ○ Massachusetts Institute of Technology
- ○ New York University
- ○ Rensselaer Polytechnic Institute
- ○ Shawnee State University
- ○ Sheridan College
- ○ University of California—Irvine
- ○ University of Central Florida
- ○ University of Colorado
- ○ University of Denver

FUN FACT

The **University of Oregon** is the only school in the United States to have a popular cartoon character as its mascot—Donald Duck.

- ○ University of Illinois at Chicago
- ○ University of North Texas
- ○ University of Pennsylvania
- ○ University of Southern California
- ○ University of Washington

You Talkin' To Me?
Schools with great acting/theater programs

- ○ Agnes Scott College
- ○ Alfred University
- ○ Amherst College
- ○ Auburn University
- ○ Bard College
- ○ Boston University
- ○ Brigham Young University
- ○ California State University—Long Beach
- ○ Carnegie Mellon University
- ○ Columbia College—Chicago
- ○ DePaul University
- ○ Emerson College
- ○ Florida State University
- ○ Harvard College
- ○ The Juilliard School
- ○ The New School for Drama
- ○ New York University

- ○ Northwestern University
- ○ Oberlin College
- ○ Occidental College
- ○ Rutgers, The State University of New Jersey
- ○ University of California—Los Angeles
- ○ University of California—San Diego
- ○ University of Chicago
- ○ University of Maryland—Baltimore County
- ○ University of Miami
- ○ University of Southern California
- ○ University of Utah
- ○ University of Wisconsin—Green Bay
- ○ University of Wisconsin—Milwaukee
- ○ West Virginia University
- ○ Yale University

From Blueprint to Flying Buttress
Schools with great architecture programs

- ○ Academy of Art University (formerly The San Francisco Academy)

- California Polytechnic State University—San Luis Obispo
- Carnegie Mellon University
- The Cooper Union for the Advancement of Science and Art
- Cornell University
- Harvard College
- Massachusetts Institute of Technology
- New Jersey Institute of Technology
- New York Institute of Technology
- North Carolina State University
- Smith College
- Texas A&M University—College Station
- University of California—Berkeley
- University of California—Los Angeles
- University of Cincinnati
- University of Illinois at Urbana-Champaign
- University of Michigan
- University of Minnesota
- University of Pennsylvania
- University of Southern California
- The University of Texas at Austin
- University of Wisconsin—Madison
- Washington University in St. Louis
- Yale University

Art Saves
Schools with great art therapy programs

- Alfred University
- Antioch University
- DePaul University
- Drexel University
- Florida State University
- The George Washington University
- Loyola Marymont University
- New York University
- Oberlin College
- Ringling School of Art & Design
- Seton Hill University
- Southern Illinois University—Edwardsville
- Southwestern College
- Tufts University
- University of Illinois at Chicago

Bon Appetit!
Schools with great culinary arts programs

- California School of Culinary Arts
- The Culinary Institute of America
- Johnson & Wales
- Kendall College

- Le Cordon Bleu College of Culinary Arts
- New England Culinary Institute
- Newbury College
- Orlando Culinary Academy
- Pasadena School of Culinary Arts
- Saint Louis University

- Kilgore University
- New York University
- State University of New York—Purchase College
- Texas Christian University
- University of Miami
- University of Utah
- Viterbo University

FUN FACT

Inside the Actor's Studio, hosted by television's most bearded host, James Lipton, is filmed at **The New School**, where Lipton is the dean emeritus of The Actors Studio Drama School.

Fire on the Dance Floor
Schools with great dance programs

- Brenau University—The Women's College
- Brigham Young University
- Columbia College—Chicago
- Connecticut College
- The Juilliard School

The Learned Fashionista
Schools with great fashion design programs

- Academy of Art University (formerly The San Francisco Academy)
- American InterContinental University
- The Art Institute of Chicago
- Berkeley College
- Brooks College
- Parsons—The New School for Design
- Pratt Institute
- Rhode Island School of Design
- State University of New York—Fashion Institute of Technology
- University of Wisconsin—Stout

Lights, Camera, Action!

Schools with terrific film programs

- Bowling Green State University
- Brigham Young University
- California Institute of the Arts
- California State University—Fullerton
- California State University—Long Beach
- Carnegie Mellon University
- Chapman University
- City University of New York—Brooklyn College
- Emerson College
- Florida State University
- Harvard College
- James Madison University
- New York University
- North Carolina School of the Arts
- San Francisco Art Institute
- San Francisco State University
- Savannah College of Art and Design
- School of Visual Arts
- Seton Hall University
- State University of New York—University at Buffalo
- Syracuse University
- University of Arizona
- University of California—Berkeley
- University of California—Irvine
- University of California—Los Angeles
- University of California—Santa Barbara
- University of California—Santa Cruz
- University of Chicago
- University of Colorado—Boulder
- University of Florida
- University of Miami
- University of North Carolina at Greensboro
- University of Southern California
- The University of Texas at Austin

FUN FACT

What do Spike Lee, Jim Jarmusch, and M. Night Shyamalan have in common? They're all directors, and they all graduated from **New York University**'s Tisch School of the Arts.

- University of Utah
- Wesleyan University

Designs On You
Schools with great graphic design programs

- Academy of Art University (formerly The San Francisco Academy)
- Arizona State University
- Auburn University
- Bowling Green State University
- California Institute of the Arts
- California State University—Sacramento
- Corcoran College of Art & Design
- East Carolina University
- Florida State University
- Georgia State University
- Kean University
- Mississippi State University
- North Carolina State University
- Otis College of Art & Design
- Parsons—The New School for Design
- Pratt Institute
- Rhode Island School of Design
- San Jose State University

- School of Visual Arts
- State University of New York—Fashion Institute of Technology
- Syracuse University

Extreme Makeover
Schools with great interior design programs

- Academy of Art University (formerly The San Francisco Academy)
- American InterContinental University
- Arizona State University
- Auburn University
- Brenau University—The Women's College
- Brooks College
- California State University—Fresno
- California State University—Northridge
- California State University—Sacramento
- Colorado State University
- Corcoran College of Art & Design
- Endicott College
- Florida State University
- The Illinois Institute of Art

- Meredith College
- Parsons—The New School for Design
- Pratt Institute
- Rhode Island School of Design
- School of Visual Arts
- State University of New York—Fashion Institute of Technology
- University of Alabama
- University of Arkansas
- University of Florida
- University of North Carolina at Greensboro
- The University of Texas at Austin
- University of Wisconsin—Stout

Maintain Your Composure

Schools with great music composition programs

- Berklee College of Music
- Boston University
- Bowling Green State University
- Carnegie Mellon University
- California State University—Long Beach
- Chapman University
- College of Charleston
- Columbia College—Chicago
- Eastman School of Music
- Elmhurst College
- Florida State University
- The Juilliard School
- Manhattan School of Music
- Mannes College—The New School of Music
- New England Conservatory
- New York University
- Oberlin College
- San Francisco Conservatory of Music
- Stanford University
- University of California—Santa Barbara
- University of Miami

FUN FACT

Besides its main campus in Pittsburgh, **Carnegie Mellon University** also has schools in Australia, California, Greece, New York, and Qatar.

- University of Michigan
- University of Rochester
- University of Southern California

○ University of Tennessee
○ Vanderbilt University

Music Appreciation 101
Schools with great music education programs

○ Appalachian State University
○ Berklee College of Music
○ Boston College
○ Carnegie Mellon University
○ Chapman University
○ Columbia College—Chicago
○ DePaul University
○ Eastman School of Music
○ Elmhurst College
○ Elon University
○ Florida State University
○ Humboldt State University
○ New York University
○ Northwestern University
○ The Peabody Institute
○ University of Hawaii—Manoa
○ University of Miami
○ The University of North Carolina at Chapel Hill
○ University of North Carolina at Greensboro

○ University of North Texas
○ University of Rochester
○ University of Wisconsin—Stevens Point
○ Viterbo University

Symphony Space
Schools with great music performance programs

○ Appalachian State University
○ Berklee College of Music
○ California State University—Fullerton
○ Chapman University
○ Columbia College—Chicago
○ Eastern Michigan University
○ The Juilliard School
○ Manhattan School of Music
○ Mannes College—The New School of Music
○ New England Conservatory
○ New York University
○ Northwestern University
○ The Peabody Institute
○ Texas A&M University—Corpus Christi
○ University of California—Berkeley

- University of California—Los Angeles
- University of Miami
- University of North Carolina at Greensboro
- The University of North Carolina at Chapel Hill
- University of South Florida
- University of Southern California
- The University of Texas at Austin
- University of Wisconsin—Stevens Point
- Viterbo University

Lens of the Beholder

Schools with great photography programs

- Academy of Art University (formerly The San Francisco Academy)
- The Art Institute of Chicago
- Bard College
- Bennington College
- Bradley University
- Brigham Young University
- The College of the Atlantic
- Corcoran College of Art & Design
- Drexel University

- Hampshire College
- Harvard College
- Hofstra University
- Hollins University
- Marlboro College
- Miami University
- New York University
- Ohio University—Athens
- Pacific Northwest College of Art
- Rochester Institute of Technology
- School of Visual Arts
- Seattle University
- Simon's Rock College of Bard
- St. John's University (NY)
- State University of New York—Fashion Institute of Technology
- State University of New York—Purchase College

FUN FACT

Legendary forger and conman Frank Abagnale, Jr. claims to have taught sociology for a semester at **Brigham Young University**, though the school says it has no record of his hiring.

- ○ Syracuse University
- ○ Texas Christian University
- ○ Temple University
- ○ Tulane University
- ○ University of Delaware
- ○ University of Georgia
- ○ University of Illinois at Urbana-Champaign
- ○ University of Iowa
- ○ University of Miami
- ○ University of Michigan—Ann Arbor
- ○ University of Oregon
- ○ Warren Wilson College
- ○ Washington University in St. Louis

Bring Your Art Alive

Schools with great studio art programs

- ○ Academy of Art University (formerly The San Francisco Academy)
- ○ The Art Institute of Chicago
- ○ Carnegie Mellon University
- ○ City University of New York—Hunter College
- ○ DePauw University
- ○ Indiana University—Bloomington
- ○ New York University

- ○ Otis College of Art & Design
- ○ Parsons—The New School for Design
- ○ Pennsylvania Academy of the Fine Arts (certificate program; BFA available in coordination with the University of Pennsylvania)
- ○ Pratt Institute
- ○ Rhode Island School of Design
- ○ Rutgers, The State University of New Jersey—Camden
- ○ Savannah College of Art and Design
- ○ School of the Museum of Fine Arts
- ○ School of Visual Arts
- ○ State University of New York at Binghamton
- ○ Temple University
- ○ University of California—Berkeley
- ○ University of Pennsylvania
- ○ University of Tennessee
- ○ The University of Texas at Austin
- ○ University of the Arts
- ○ University of Wisconsin—Madison
- ○ Viterbo University

Know Your Fellow Humans

Schools with great anthropology programs

- American University
- Amherst College
- Auburn University
- Bard College
- Beloit College
- Boston University
- Case Western Reserve University
- Colby College
- Colgate University
- College of Charleston
- Colorado State University
- Columbia University
- Cornell University
- Dartmouth College
- Davidson College
- DePauw University
- Duke University
- Eckerd College
- Emory University
- Florida State University
- Fordham University
- Georgetown University
- Harvard College
- Illinois Wesleyan University
- Indiana University—Bloomington
- Iowa State University
- James Madison University
- Johns Hopkins University
- Lewis & Clark College
- Mount Holyoke College
- New York University
- Northeastern University
- Northwestern University
- Princeton University
- Reed College
- Rice University
- Seton Hall University
- Stanford University
- State University of New York—Purchase College
- Syracuse University
- Temple University
- Texas A&M University—College Station
- Tulane University

FUN FACT

Dartmouth College is the smallest school in the Ivy League and the ninth-oldest college in the United States.

- University of Arkansas
- University of California—Berkeley
- University of California—Irvine
- University of California—Los Angeles
- University of California—Riverside
- University of California—San Diego
- University of California—Santa Cruz

Paging Dr. Jones...

Schools with great archaeology programs

- Bard College
- Baylor University
- Boston University
- Bowdoin College
- Brown University
- Bryn Mawr College
- City University of New York—Brooklyn College
- City University of New York—Hunter College
- Columbia University
- Cornell University
- Dickinson College
- Harvard College

- New York University
- Oberlin College
- Southern Methodist University
- Stanford University
- Texas A&M University—College Station
- Tufts University
- University of California—Los Angeles
- University of California—San Diego
- University of Hawaii—Manoa
- University of Michigan—Ann Arbor
- The University of Texas at Austin
- Washington and Lee University
- Washington University in St. Louis
- Wesleyan University
- Wheaton College
- Yale University

Lifting the Prints

Schools with great criminology programs

- American University
- Auburn University
- City University of New York—John Jay College of Criminal Justice
- North Carolina State University

- The Ohio State University—Columbus
- Ohio University—Athens
- Quinnipiac University
- Suffolk University
- University of Delaware
- University of Denver
- University of Maryland—College Park
- University of Miami
- University of New Hampshire
- University of South Florida
- University of Utah
- Valparaiso University

Speaking in General Terms

Schools with great general studies programs

- Adelphi University
- American University (liberal studies; for adult students returning to school)
- Columbia University (for nontraditional students and adult students returning to school)
- New York University
- Stanford University (interdisciplinary studies in humanities)
- University of Arizona South (interdisciplinary studies)
- University of Pennsylvania (for adult students returning to school)
- University of Southern California

An Eye On the Past

Schools with great history programs

- Bowdoin College
- Brown University
- Centre College
- Colgate University
- College of the Holy Cross
- Columbia University
- Furman University
- Grinnell College
- Hampden-Sydney College
- Harvard College
- Haverford College
- Hillsdale College
- Kenyon College
- Oberlin College
- Princeton University
- Trinity College (CT)
- Tulane University
- Wabash College

○ Washington and Lee University
○ Yale University

Be a Jetsetter
Schools with great international relations programs

○ American University
○ Brown University
○ Bryn Mawr College
○ Claremont McKenna College
○ George Mason University
○ The George Washington University
○ Georgetown University

FUN FACT

Since 1989, every President of the United States has been an alumnus of **Yale University**.

○ Harvard College
○ Johns Hopkins University
○ Lewis & Clark College
○ Pepperdine University
○ Sweet Briar College
○ Tufts University

○ University of California—Los Angeles
○ University of Pennsylvania
○ University of Southern California

Your Pal Socrates
Schools with great philosophy programs

○ Bard College
○ Bates College
○ Brown University
○ Carnegie Mellon University
○ Claremont McKenna College
○ Columbia University
○ Gettysburg College
○ Harvard College
○ Princeton University
○ Rice University
○ University of California—Berkeley
○ University of Chicago
○ University of North Carolina
○ University of Pennsylvania
○ Yale University

Politicking

Schools with great political science programs

- Amherst College
- Bates College
- Bowdoin College
- Brigham Young University
- Bryn Mawr College
- Carleton College
- Claremont McKenna College
- College of the Holy Cross
- Columbia University
- Davidson College
- Dickinson College
- Drew University
- Furman University
- George Mason University
- Georgetown University
- Gettysburg College
- Gonzaga University
- Kenyon College
- Macalester College
- Princeton University
- Stanford University
- Swarthmore College
- Syracuse University
- University of Arizona
- University of California—Berkeley
- University of California—Los Angeles
- University of Washington
- Vassar College
- Yale University

The Social Life

Schools with great social work programs

- Baylor University
- Columbia University
- North Carolina State University
- Ohio University
- San Diego State University
- San Francisco State University
- Smith College
- University of California—Berkeley
- University of California—Los Angeles
- University of Iowa
- University of Michigan
- University of North Carolina at Greensboro
- University of Southern California
- University of St. Thomas
- University of Wisconsin—Milwaukee

○ Washington University in St. Louis
○ Western Illinois University
○ Western Michigan University
○ Winona State University

In God We Trust
Schools with great theology programs

○ Abilene Christian University
○ Bard College
○ Boston College
○ Calvin College
○ The Catholic University of America
○ College of Saint Benedict/ Saint John's University
○ College of William & Mary (religious studies)
○ Duquesne University
○ Fordham University
○ Franciscan University of Steubenville
○ Gonzaga University
○ Loyola Marymount University
○ Loyola University—Chicago
○ McGill University
○ Oral Roberts University
○ Providence College
○ Saint Anselm College

○ Saint Michael's College
○ Southern Methodist University
○ St. Bonaventure University
○ Texas Christian University
○ University of Dallas
○ University of Notre Dame
○ University of San Francisco
○ Ursuline College

The Word's the Thing
Schools with great creative writing programs

○ Brown University
○ Carnegie Mellon University
○ Columbia University
○ Emerson College
○ Hollins University
○ New York University
○ Princeton University
○ San Francisco State University
○ University of California—Riverside
○ University of Florida
○ University of Houston
○ University of Iowa
○ The University of North Carolina at Chapel Hill
○ University of Oregon

- University of Southern California
- University of Utah
- University of Virginia
- University of Wisconsin—Madison
- Vanderbilt University
- Vassar College
- Yale University

The Company of a Thousand Good Books

Schools with great English literature and language programs

- Amherst College
- Auburn University
- Bard College
- Barnard College
- Bennington College
- Boston College
- Brown University
- City University of New York—Hunter College
- Claremont McKenna College
- Clemson University
- Colby College
- Colgate University
- Columbia University
- Cornell University
- Dartmouth College
- Denison University
- Duke University
- Emory University
- Fordham University
- George Mason University
- Gettysburg College
- Harvard College
- The New School University
- Pitzer College
- Princeton University
- Rice University
- Stanford University
- Syracuse University
- Tufts University
- University of California—Berkeley
- University of Chicago
- University of Michigan—Ann Arbor
- University of Utah
- Vassar College
- Washington University in St. Louis
- Wellesley College
- Yale University

It's a Sign
Schools with great sign language programs

- Boston University (not a degree program)
- College of the Holy Cross
- Columbia College—Chicago
- Gallaudet University
- Lenoir-Rhyne College (not a degree program)

FUN FACT

Baylor University's Armstrong Browning Library is home to the world's largest collection of work from the poets Robert and Elizabeth Barrett Browning.

- Ohlone College (certificate)
- Towson University
- University of Arizona
- University of Pittsburgh (certificate)
- University of Rochester
- The University of Texas at Austin

So Long, Abacus
Schools with great accounting programs

- Alfred University
- Auburn University
- Baylor University
- Birmingham—Southern College
- Boston College
- Boston University
- Brigham Young University
- Bucknell University
- Calvin College
- Claremont McKenna College
- Clemson University
- College of Charleston
- DePaul University
- Drexel University
- Duquesne University
- Elon University
- Emory University
- Fordham University
- Georgetown University
- Indiana University—Bloomington
- Iowa State University
- James Madison University
- Lehigh University
- Michigan State University

- ○ New York University
- ○ Northeastern University
- ○ Pepperdine University
- ○ Rider University
- ○ Rochester Institute of Technology
- ○ Seton Hall University
- ○ Suffolk University
- ○ Temple University
- ○ Texas A&M University—College Station
- ○ University of Illinois at Urbana-Champaign

The Real World

Schools with great applied mathematics programs

- ○ American University
- ○ Auburn University
- ○ Barnard College
- ○ Baylor University
- ○ Brown University
- ○ California Institute of Technology
- ○ Carnegie Mellon University
- ○ Case Western Reserve University
- ○ City University of New York—Queens College
- ○ Clarkson University

- ○ The College of the Atlantic
- ○ Columbia University
- ○ Georgia Institute of Technology
- ○ Gettysburg College
- ○ Hampton University
- ○ Harvard College
- ○ Hofstra University
- ○ Iowa State University
- ○ Loyola College—Maryland
- ○ McGill University
- ○ Michigan State University
- ○ New Jersey Institute of Technology
- ○ North Carolina State University
- ○ Northwestern University
- ○ Ohio Wesleyan University
- ○ Rice University
- ○ Stevens Institute of Technology
- ○ Tufts University
- ○ Tulane University

FUN FACT

The unmanned spacecraft that NASA uses is built and operated by the Jet Propulsion Laboratory, which is owned and managed by the **California Institute of Technology**.

- University of Alabama
- University of California—Berkeley
- University of California—Los Angeles
- University of California—Riverside
- University of California—San Diego
- University of California—Santa Cruz
- University of Connecticut
- The University of Texas at Austin
- University of Tulsa
- Yale University

They Mean Business

Schools with great business/finance programs

- Bentley College
- Boston College
- Carnegie Mellon University
- DePaul University
- Emory University
- Florida State University
- Harvard College
- Iowa State University
- Lehigh University
- Massachusetts Institute of Technology

- Miami University
- Michigan State University
- New York University
- Rice University
- Seattle University
- University of California—Berkeley
- University of California—Los Angeles
- University of Florida
- University of Michigan
- University of Pennsylvania
- University of Southern California
- The University of Texas at Austin
- Washington University in St. Louis

From Foundation to Completion

Schools with great construction management programs

- California State University—Chico
- California State University—Fresno
- Dean Institute of Technology
- East Carolina University
- New Mexico State University—Carlsbad
- North Dakota State University
- Northern Michigan University

- ○ Pittsburgh State University
- ○ Pratt Institute
- ○ Purdue University—West Lafayette
- ○ Southern Utah University

Business, the Universal Language

Schools with great schools for international business studies

- ○ American University
- ○ Auburn University
- ○ Baylor University
- ○ Boston University
- ○ Bradley University
- ○ Clemson University
- ○ College of Charleston
- ○ Cornell College
- ○ Dickinson College
- ○ Drexel University
- ○ Duquesne University
- ○ Elon University
- ○ Florida State University
- ○ Georgetown University
- ○ Gettysburg College
- ○ Gustavus Adolphus College
- ○ Iowa State University
- ○ Ithaca College

- ○ James Madison University
- ○ Loyola Marymount University
- ○ New York University
- ○ Pepperdine University
- ○ Quinnipiac University
- ○ Rochester Institute of Technology
- ○ Suffolk University
- ○ University of Denver
- ○ University of Hawaii—Manoa
- ○ University of Iowa
- ○ University of Maryland—College Park
- ○ University of Oregon
- ○ University of Pennsylvania
- ○ University of Utah
- ○ Wofford College

FUN FACT

Pepperdine University was originally located near Watts, California, but after the 1965 riots, the campus was moved to its present location in Malibu.

Know Your Customer
Schools with great marketing and sales programs

- Baylor University
- Bentley College
- Duquesne University
- Fairfield University
- Hofstra University
- Indiana University—Bloomington
- Iowa State University
- James Madison University
- Miami University
- Providence College
- Seattle University
- Siena College
- Syracuse University
- University of Central Florida
- University of Mississippi
- University of South Florida

Interested in Integers?
Schools with great mathematics programs

- American University
- Amherst College
- Boston College
- Brown University
- California Institute of Technology
- Columbia University
- Cornell University
- Duke University
- Georgetown University
- Harvard College
- Illinois Institute of Technology
- Massachusetts Institute of Technology
- Middlebury College
- New York University
- Northwestern University
- Pepperdine University
- Princeton University
- Reed College
- Rice University
- Rider University
- Smith College
- Stanford University
- Suffolk University
- Texas A&M University—College Station
- United States Naval Academy
- University of California—Berkeley
- University of Chicago
- The University of Texas at Austin

Do Not Disturb

Schools with great tourism and hotel management programs

○ Boston University
○ College of Charleston
○ Cornell University
○ Florida State University
○ James Madison University
○ Michigan State University
○ New York University
○ The Ohio State University—Columbus
○ Purdue University—West Lafayette
○ Rochester Institute of Technology
○ St. John's University (NY)
○ Temple University
○ University of Alabama
○ University of Central Florida
○ University of Delaware
○ University of Denver
○ University of Illinois at Urbana-Champaign
○ University of Kentucky
○ University of Louisiana at Lafayette
○ University of Massachusetts—Amherst
○ University of Nevada—Las Vegas
○ University of New Hampshire
○ University of New Orleans
○ University of North Texas
○ University of South Carolina—Columbia
○ University of South Florida
○ Virginia Institute of Technology

Teaching the Teachers

Schools with great undergraduate programs in education

○ Adelphi University
○ Alma College
○ Arcadia University
○ Ashland University
○ Auburn University
○ Augsburg College
○ Barnard College
○ Bethany College (WV)
○ Bryn Athyn College of the New Church
○ Bucknell University
○ California State University—Sacramento
○ Carthage College
○ Clark University (minor)
○ City University of New York—Brooklyn College
○ City University of New York—Hunter College

129

- Colgate University
- College of William & Mary
- Columbia College (MO)
- Columbia University
- Cornell College
- Cornell University
- Duquesne University
- Elon University
- Franklin Pierce College
- Gonzaga University
- Goucher College
- Hardin-Simmons University
- Hillsdale College
- Indiana University—Bloomington
- Jewish Theological Seminary—Albert A. List College
- LaSalle University
- Loyola Marymount University
- Marquette University
- McGill University
- Miami University
- Montana State University—Bozeman
- Nazareth College of Rochester
- New York Institute of Technology
- New York University
- Northeastern University
- Northwestern University

- The Ohio State University—Columbus
- San Francisco State University
- Simmons College
- Smith College
- State University of New York—New Paltz
- Trinity University (Washington, DC)
- Trinity University
- University of California—Santa Cruz (minor)
- University of Maine
- The University of Montana
- University of St. Thomas (TX)
- University of Toledo
- Villanova College
- Wagner College
- Wellesley College
- Xavier University (OH)

The Perfect Smile

Schools with great pre-dental studies and advising

- American University
- Arcadia University
- Ball State University
- Beloit College
- Claremont McKenna College

- Hardin-Simmons University
- Hillsdale College
- Hofstra University
- Ithaca College
- Kent State University—Kent
- Lewis & Clark College
- Manhattan College
- Marquette University
- Miami University
- New York University
- Northwestern University
- Notre Dame College
- Oberlin College
- Pittsburg State University
- Purdue University—West Lafayette
- Roberts Wesleyan College
- Seton Hall University
- South Dakota State University
- State University of New York at Geneseo
- State University of New York—University at Albany
- State University of New York—University at Buffalo
- Temple University
- Texas A&M University—Commerce
- Towson University
- Trinity University

- University of Alabama—Tuscaloosa
- University of Miami
- University of Notre Dame
- University of the Pacific
- University of Vermont
- University of Washington
- Ventura College
- Villanova University
- Wofford College
- Worcester State College
- Yeshiva University

Petition the Court

Schools with great pre-law studies and advising

- Alfred University
- Boston University
- Brigham Young University
- Columbia University
- Drew University
- Duke University
- Emory University
- Georgetown University
- Harvard College
- Loyola University—Chicago
- Montana State University—Billings
- New York University

○ Northwestern University
○ Rice University
○ Southern Methodist University
○ Stanford University
○ University of California—Berkeley
○ University of California—Los Angeles
○ University of Chicago
○ University of Illinois at Urbana-Champaign
○ University of Massachusetts—Amherst
○ University of Missouri
○ The University of Texas
○ Washington University in St. Louis
○ Wesleyan University
○ Yale University

FUN FACT

When the Soviet Union could not locate the first issue of *Pravda*—Trotsky's communist newspaper—in any of its libraries, it asked the Hoover Institution on War, Revolution, and Peace at **Stanford University** for a copy.

132

What's the Prognosis?

Schools with great premedical studies and advising

○ Brandeis University
○ California Institute of Technology
○ Columbia University
○ Cornell University
○ Drew University
○ Duke University
○ Georgia Institute of Technology
○ Harvard College
○ Haverford College
○ Johns Hopkins University
○ Massachusetts Institute of Technology
○ Northwestern University
○ Pepperdine University
○ Princeton University
○ Stanford University
○ Texas A&M University—College Station
○ Tufts University
○ University of California—Berkeley
○ University of California—Los Angeles
○ University of Chicago
○ University of Michigan
○ University of Pennsylvania

- University of Southern California
- The University of Texas
- University of Utah
- University of Wisconsin—Madison
- Washington University in St. Louis
- Xavier University of Louisiana
- Yale University

Fluffy Will Thank You

Schools with great pre-veterinary studies and advising

- Arizona State University
- Auburn University
- Colorado State University
- Cornell University
- Indiana State University
- Michigan State University
- North Carolina State University
- Reed College
- South Dakota State University
- St. John's University (NY)
- Texas A&M University—College Station
- University of Alabama
- University of Florida
- University of Georgia
- University of Iowa

- University of Maryland—College Park
- University of Minnesota
- University of Missouri
- University of New Orleans
- University of St. Thomas

Risk Assessment

Schools with great actuarial science programs

- Bradley University
- Brigham Young University
- City University of New York—Queens College
- Florida State University
- Hofstra University
- New York University
- The Ohio State University—Columbus
- Ohio University—Athens
- Quinnipiac University
- Rider University
- St. John's University (NY)
- State University of New York—University at Albany
- Temple University
- University of Central Florida
- University of Connecticut

- University of Illinois at Urbana-Champaign
- University of Pennsylvania
- University of Wisconsin—Madison
- Valparaiso University
- Worcester Polytechnic Institute

Take Flight
Schools with great aviation programs

- Central Washington University

FUN FACT

In keeping with local legumes, **Delta State University**'s mascot is the "Fighting Okra," which looks like what you'd expect—only with boxing gloves.

- Delaware State University
- Delta State University
- Embry Riddle Aeronautical University
- Florida Institute of Technology
- Kent State University

- Minnesota State University—Mankato
- The Ohio State University—Columbus
- Ohio University—Athens
- Purdue University—West Lafayette
- United States Air Force Academy
- University of North Dakota

Better Living Through Biochemistry
Schools with great biochemistry programs

- American University
- Bard College
- Bates College
- Baylor University
- Boston University
- Calvin College
- Claremont McKenna College
- Colorado State University
- Cornell University
- Drexel University
- Eckerd College
- Florida State University
- Georgetown University
- Gettysburg College
- Harvard College

- Iowa State University
- Ithaca College
- Lehigh University
- Lewis & Clark College
- Michigan State University
- Muhlenberg College
- New York University
- Pitzer College
- Pomona College
- Rice University
- Rochester Institute of Technology
- Seton Hall University
- Smith College
- St. Bonaventure University
- Swarthmore College
- Syracuse University
- Tulane University
- University of California—Los Angeles
- University of California—Riverside
- University of California—San Diego
- University of California—Santa Barbara
- University of Denver
- University of Georgia
- The University of Texas at Austin

Biological Impulse
Schools with great biology programs

- Agnes Scott College
- Albion College
- Austin College
- Baylor University
- Brandeis University
- Colby College
- Cornell University
- Drexel University
- Harvard College
- Haverford College
- Howard University
- Illinois Wesleyan University
- Indiana University—Bloomington
- Louisiana State University
- Loyola University—Chicago
- Massachusetts Institute of Technology
- Mount Holyoke College
- The Ohio State University—Columbus
- Pomona College
- Reed College
- Rice University
- Siena College
- Swarthmore College

- ○ Temple University
- ○ Texas A&M University—College Station
- ○ University of California—Davis
- ○ University of Chicago
- ○ University of Dallas
- ○ University of Delaware
- ○ University of Denver
- ○ University of New Mexico
- ○ University of the Pacific
- ○ Wofford College
- ○ Xavier University of Louisiana

FUN FACT

The **Lafayette College** Phi Kappa Psi fraternity house held the Guinness Record for a few years for being the largest house ever moved after the school decided to build a library in its place. The administration footed the bill, and the entire house was transported to its present location.

And Now For Something More Complicated...

Schools with great biomedical engineering programs

- ○ Boston University
- ○ Brown University
- ○ Bucknell University
- ○ Carnegie Mellon University
- ○ Case Western Reserve University
- ○ Drexel University
- ○ Duke University
- ○ Georgia Institute of Technology
- ○ Harvard College
- ○ Hofstra University
- ○ Johns Hopkins University
- ○ Lafayette College
- ○ Lehigh University
- ○ Louisiana State University
- ○ Michigan State University
- ○ New Jersey Institute of Technology
- ○ Northwestern University
- ○ The Ohio State University—Columbus
- ○ Rice University
- ○ Rochester Institute of Technology
- ○ Syracuse University
- ○ Temple University

- Texas A&M University—College Station
- Tufts University
- Tulane University
- University of California—Berkeley
- University of California—Los Angeles
- University of California—Riverside
- University of California—Santa Cruz
- University of Southern California
- University of Utah
- University of Washington
- Washington University in St. Louis
- Yale University

All About the Chemistry
Schools with great chemistry programs

- California Institute of Technology
- Columbia University
- Cornell University
- Indiana University—Bloomington
- Johns Hopkins University
- Massachusetts Institute of Technology
- New Jersey Institute of Technology
- Northwestern University
- The Ohio State University
- Pennsylvania State University
- Purdue University—West Lafayette
- Princeton University
- Rice University
- Texas A&M University—College Station
- University of California—Berkeley
- University of California—Irvine
- University of California—Los Angeles
- University of California—San Diego
- University of California—Santa Barbara
- University of Chicago
- University of Illinois at Urbana-Champaign
- University of Michigan—Ann Arbor
- University of Minnesota—Twin Cities
- The University of North Carolina at Chapel Hill
- University of Pennsylvania
- University of Rochester
- The University of Texas at Austin
- University of Washington
- University of Wisconsin—Madison

○ Xavier University of Louisiana
○ Yale University

Building the Next Hal 9000
Schools with great computer engineering programs

○ Auburn University
○ Boston University
○ Bradley University
○ Brown University
○ California Institute of Technology
○ Clemson University
○ Drexel University
○ Florida State University

FUN FACT

Michigan State University first admitted women in 1870, though since there were no female dorms at the time, most had to journey by stagecoach to class.

○ George Mason University
○ Georgia Institute of Technology
○ Gonzaga University
○ Hampton University

○ Iowa State University
○ Johns Hopkins University
○ Lehigh University
○ Massachusetts Institute of Technology
○ Michigan State University
○ New Jersey Institute of Technology
○ Northeastern University
○ Northwestern University
○ Princeton University
○ Rice University
○ Rochester Institute of Technology
○ Seattle University
○ State University of New York at Binghamton
○ State University of New York—University at Buffalo
○ Texas A&M University—College Station
○ United States Air Force Academy
○ University of Arizona
○ University of California—Berkeley
○ University of California—Los Angeles
○ University of California—Riverside
○ University of Massachusetts—Amherst

I Sing the Body Electric

Schools with great electrical engineering programs

- Alfred University
- Auburn University
- Baylor University
- Boston University
- Brown University
- Bucknell University
- California Institute of Technology
- Clemson University
- Colorado State University
- The Cooper Union for the Advancement of Science & Art
- Cornell University
- Duke University
- Florida State University
- Georgia Institute of Technology
- Hampton University
- Harvard College
- Illinois Institute of Technology
- Iowa State University
- Louisiana State University
- Massachusetts Institute of Technology
- Michigan State University
- Northwestern University
- Ohio University—Athens
- Princeton University
- Rice University
- Rochester Institute of Technology
- Syracuse University
- Temple University
- Texas A&M University—College Station
- University of California—Berkeley
- University of California—Irvine
- University of California—Los Angeles
- University of California—San Diego
- University of California—Santa Barbara
- University of California—Santa Cruz
- University of Delaware
- University of Utah
- University of Vermont
- Yale University

Engineering Your Future

Schools with great engineering programs

- California Institute of Technology
- Carnegie Mellon University
- Columbia University

- Cornell University
- Duke University
- Georgia Institute of Technology
- Harvard College
- Johns Hopkins University
- Massachusetts Institute of Technology
- Princeton University
- Purdue University—West Lafayette
- Stanford University
- Texas A&M University—College Station
- University of California—Berkeley
- University of California—Los Angeles

FUN FACT

Founded in 1865, **Cornell University** is the youngest of the Ivy League schools.

- University of California—San Diego
- University of California—Santa Barbara
- University of Colorado—Boulder

- University of Illinois at Urbana-Champaign
- University of Michigan—Ann Arbor
- University of Southern California

A Bug's Life
Schools with great entomology programs

- The College of the Atlantic
- Colorado State University
- Cornell University
- Iowa State University
- McGill University
- Michigan State University
- The Ohio State University—Columbus
- Purdue University—West Lafayette
- Texas A&M University—College Station
- University of Arkansas
- University of California—Riverside
- University of Delaware
- University of Florida
- University of Georgia
- University of Hawaii—Manoa
- University of Illinois at Urbana-Champaign
- University of Kentucky

- University of Nebraska—Lincoln
- University of Wisconsin—Madison

Save the World

Schools with great environmental engineering programs

- California Institute of Technology
- Clarkson University
- Clemson University
- Colorado State University
- Cornell University
- Dartmouth College
- Drexel University
- Johns Hopkins University
- Lehigh University
- Louisiana State University
- Massachusetts Institute of Technology
- Michigan State University
- New Jersey Institute of Technology
- Northeastern University
- Rensselaer Polytechnic Institute
- Rice University
- State University of New York—University at Buffalo
- Suffolk University
- Syracuse University

- Tufts University
- Tulane University
- United States Military Academy
- University of California—Riverside
- University of Pennsylvania
- University of Utah
- Yale University

CSI University

Schools with great forensic science programs

- Baylor University
- City University of New York—John Jay College of Criminal Justice
- The College of the Ozarks
- Columbia College
- Loyola University
- Loyola University—Chicago
- Ohio Northern University
- Pace University
- Seattle University
- University of Baltimore
- University of Central Florida
- University of Mississippi
- University of North Dakota
- West Virginia University

Timber!

Schools with great forestry programs

- Auburn University
- Baylor University
- California Polytechnic State University—San Luis Obispo
- Clemson University
- Colorado State University
- Cornell University
- Gettysburg College
- Humboldt State University
- Iowa State University
- Louisiana Tech University
- Michigan State University
- North Carolina State University
- Northern Arizona University
- The Ohio State University—Columbus
- Oklahoma State University
- Oregon State University
- Pennsylvania State University
- Purdue University—West Lafayette
- Sewanee—The University of the South
- Southern Illinois University
- State University of New York—College of Environmental Science and Forestry
- Texas A&M University—College Station
- University of Alaska—Fairbanks
- University of Arizona
- University of California—Berkeley
- University of Florida
- University of Georgia
- University of Maryland—College Park
- University of Massachusetts—Amherst
- University of Michigan—Ann Arbor
- University of New Hampshire
- University of Tennessee—Knoxville
- University of Vermont
- University of Washington
- Virginia Institute of Technology
- Wake Forest University
- West Virginia University

FUN FACT

Gatorade was created at the **University of Florida** in 1965 and named in honor of their football team. Legal battles aside, the royalties have been lucrative for the school.

Solid as a Rock

Schools with great geology programs

- Auburn University
- Bakersfield College
- Boston College
- Boston University
- Brown University
- California Institute of Technology
- California State University—Long Beach
- City University of New York—City College
- Colby College
- Colgate University
- College of Charleston
- The College of the Atlantic
- College of William & Mary
- Colorado State University
- Columbia University
- Cornell University
- Dartmouth College
- DePauw University
- Duke University
- Florida State University
- Franklin & Marshall College
- George Mason University
- Gustavus Adolphus University
- Hardin-Simmons University
- Hartwick College
- Hobart and William Smith Colleges
- Iowa State University
- James Madison University
- Johns Hopkins University
- Lawrence University
- Lehigh University
- Massachusetts Institute of Technology
- Michigan State University
- Middlebury College
- Oberlin College
- Occidental College
- Pomona College
- Saint Louis University
- Salisbury University
- Skidmore College
- State University of New York at Binghamton
- State University of New York—University at Buffalo
- Syracuse University
- Tufts University
- University of California—Los Angeles
- University of California—Riverside
- University of Dayton

- ○ University of Oregon
- ○ University of Pennsylvania
- ○ University of Utah
- ○ Washington University in St. Louis
- ○ Wellesley College
- ○ Wheaton College (IL)
- ○ Yale University

The Life Aquatic
Schools with great marine biology programs

- ○ California Lutheran University
- ○ Missouri Southern State University—Joplin
- ○ Samford University
- ○ Stanford University
- ○ Texas State University—San Marcos
- ○ University of California—Los Angeles

FUN FACT

The **Colorado School of Mines** has the United States's second oldest mountainside monument—an "M" emblazoned on Mount Zion's side.

- ○ University of Hawaii—Hilo
- ○ University of Miami
- ○ University of New England
- ○ University of New Haven

A Question of Mechanics
Schools with great mechanical engineering programs

- ○ Bradley University
- ○ California Institute of Technology
- ○ Clarkson University
- ○ Colorado School of Mines
- ○ Drexel University
- ○ Franklin W. Olin College of Engineering
- ○ Georgia Institute of Technology
- ○ Iowa State University
- ○ Lehigh University
- ○ Massachusetts Institute of Technology
- ○ New Jersey Institute of Technology
- ○ North Carolina State University
- ○ Purdue University—West Lafayette
- ○ Rose-Hulman Institute of Technology
- ○ State University of New York— University at Buffalo
- ○ Stevens Institute of Technology

- United States Military Academy
- University of Michigan—Ann Arbor
- University of Missouri—Rolla
- Worcester Polytechnic Institute

In the Laboratory
Schools with great medical technology programs

- Auburn University
- Baylor University
- Bradley University
- Brigham Young University
- City University of New York—Hunter College
- Clemson University
- The College of the Ozarks
- DePaul University
- Drexel University
- George Mason University
- Lafayette College
- Miami University
- Michigan State University
- North Carolina State University
- The Ohio State University—Columbus
- Purdue University—West Lafayette
- Salisbury University

- Seattle University
- St. John's University (NY)
- State University of New York—Stony Brook University
- State University of New York—University at Buffalo
- University of Arizona
- University of Central Florida
- University of Connecticut
- University of Delaware
- University of Hawaii—Manoa
- University of Iowa
- University of Kentucky
- University of Mississippi
- The University of Texas at Austin
- University of Utah
- West Virginia University

Sounds Rather Grave...
Schools with great mortuary science programs

- Black Hills State University
- Briarwood College
- Cypress College
- Ferris State University
- Gannon University
- Lindenwood University
- Point Park University

145

- ○ San Antonio College
- ○ St. John's University (NY)
- ○ Wayne State University

Future Florence Nightengales
Schools with great nursing programs

- ○ Albany State University
- ○ Alderson-Broaddus College
- ○ Allen College
- ○ Alverno College
- ○ Auburn University—Montgomery
- ○ Augustana College (SD)
- ○ Bethel College (IN)
- ○ Bethel University (MN)
- ○ Brenau University—The Women's College
- ○ California State University—Sacramento
- ○ Carroll College (MT)
- ○ Cedarville University
- ○ College Misericordia
- ○ College of Mount Saint Vincent
- ○ The College of Saint Scholastica
- ○ Dominican University of California
- ○ Duquesne University
- ○ East Carolina University

- ○ Edgewood College
- ○ Excelsior College
- ○ Hartwick College
- ○ Hawaii Pacific University
- ○ Indiana Wesleyan University
- ○ Jacksonville University
- ○ Jamestown College
- ○ Kennesaw State University
- ○ Kent State University—Kent
- ○ King College (TN)
- ○ Lewis University
- ○ Loyola University—Chicago
- ○ Lynchburg College
- ○ Malone College
- ○ Marian College
- ○ Marquette University
- ○ Medical University of South Carolina
- ○ Messiah College
- ○ Milligan College
- ○ Mississippi College
- ○ Molloy College
- ○ Mount Saint Mary College
- ○ Oklahoma Baptist University
- ○ Pacific Union College
- ○ Rockhurst University
- ○ Saint Joseph's College of Maine
- ○ Saint Louis University

- Samford University
- Seattle University
- Seton Hall University
- Simmons College
- Spring Hill College
- St. John's College, Department of Nursing (IL)
- Trinity Christian College
- The University of Akron
- University of Alabama—Huntsville
- University of Alabama—Tuscaloosa
- University of Connecticut
- University of Indianapolis
- University of Louisiana at Lafayette
- University of Mary Hardin—Baylor
- University of Massachusetts—Boston
- University of Missouri—Saint Louis
- University of Nebraska Medical Center
- The University of North Carolina at Chapel Hill
- The University of North Carolina at Greensboro
- University of North Dakota
- University of Pennsylvania
- University of Pittsburgh—Bradford
- University of Portland
- University of Rhode Island
- University of San Francisco
- The University of Texas at Tyler
- University of Texas Medical Branch at Galveston
- University of Virginia
- Valdosta State University
- Valparaiso University
- Vanderbilt University
- Villanova University
- Weber State University
- Westminster College (UT)
- William Jewell College
- York College of Pennsylvania

Eat Your Vegetables

Schools with great nutrition programs

- City University of New York—Brooklyn College
- City University of New York—Hunter College

FUN FACT

Seton Hall University was named for Elizabeth Ann Seton, aunt to Theodore Roosevelt and first American-born Catholic saint.

- College of Saint Benedict/Saint John's University
- Colorado State University
- Cornell University
- Florida State University
- Iowa State University
- James Madison University
- McGill University
- Miami University
- Michigan State University
- New York University
- The Ohio State University—Columbus
- Ohio University—Athens
- Purdue University—West Lafayette
- Samford University
- Simmons College
- Syracuse University
- Texas A&M University—College Station
- University of Dayton
- University of Delaware
- University of Georgia
- University of Maryland—College Park
- University of New Mexico
- The University of North Carolina at Chapel Hill
- University of Rhode Island
- The University of Texas at Austin
- University of Utah

Set Your Caged Bird Free

Schools with great occupational therapy programs

- Boston University
- Calvin College
- Colorado State University
- Duquesne University
- Ithaca College
- Lafayette College
- McGill University
- The Ohio State University—Columbus
- Quinnipiac University
- State University of New York—University at Buffalo
- Temple University
- University of Florida
- University of North Dakota
- University of Puget Sound
- The University of South Dakota
- University of Southern California
- University of Tennessee—Knoxville
- University of Utah
- West Virginia University
- Western Michigan University

Check Your Prescription

Schools with great pharmacy programs

- Auburn University
- Fisk University
- Northeastern University
- Ohio Northern University
- The Ohio State University—Columbus
- Purdue University—West Lafayette
- St. John's University (NY)
- Temple University
- University of Connecticut
- University of Iowa
- University of Kentucky
- University of Mississippi
- The University of Texas at Austin
- University of Utah
- Xavier University of Louisiana

Laws You Don't Want to Break

Schools with great physics programs

- Bennington College
- California Institute of Technology
- Columbia University

- Cornell University
- Harvard College
- Harvey Mudd College
- Indiana University—Bloomington
- Johns Hopkins University
- Massachusetts Institute of Technology
- New Jersey Institute of Technology
- Northwestern University
- The Ohio State University
- Pennsylvania State University
- Princeton University
- Purdue University—West Lafayette
- Rice University
- Texas A&M University—College Station
- University of California—Berkeley
- University of California—Irvine
- University of California—Los Angeles

FUN FACT

Amelia Earheart served as a Counselor on Careers for Women at **Purdue University** from 1935 until her disappearance in 1937.

- University of California—San Diego
- University of California—Santa Barbara
- University of Chicago
- University of Illinois at Urbana-Champaign
- University of Michigan—Ann Arbor
- University of Minnesota—Twin Cities
- The University of North Carolina at Chapel Hill
- University of Pennsylvania
- University of Rochester
- The University of Texas at Austin
- University of Washington
- University of Wisconsin—Madison
- Yale University

Exploring the Mind

Schools with great psychology programs

- Albion College
- Bates College
- Carnegie Mellon University
- Colorado State University
- Columbia University
- Cornell University

- Dartmouth College
- Duke University
- George Mason University
- Gettysburg College
- Harvard College
- James Madison University
- Lewis & Clark College
- Loyola University—Chicago
- New York University
- Pitzer College
- Princeton University
- Smith College
- Stanford University
- University of California—Davis
- University of California—Los Angeles
- University of California—Riverside
- University of California—Santa Barbara
- University of California—Santa Cruz
- University of Michigan—Ann Arbor
- University of Southern California
- The University of Texas at Austin
- University of Utah
- Yale University

Zoo Station

Schools with great zoology programs

- Auburn University
- Bennington College
- Clemson University
- The College of the Atlantic
- Colorado State University
- Connecticut College
- Humboldt State University
- Indiana University—Bloomington
- Juniata College
- Miami University
- Michigan State University
- North Carolina State University
- Ohio Wesleyan University
- Oklahoma State University
- Oregon State University
- San Diego State University
- San Francisco State University
- State University of New York—College of Environmental Science and Forestry
- Texas A&M University—College Station
- University of Alaska—Fairbanks
- University of Florida
- University of Hawaii—Manoa
- University of Maine
- University of Michigan—Ann Arbor
- The University of Montana
- University of New Hampshire
- University of Oklahoma
- University of Rhode Island
- The University of Texas at Austin
- University of Wisconsin—Madison
- University of Wyoming

The Science of Sports

Schools with great athletic training programs

- Brigham Young University
- California State University—Fullerton
- California State University—Northridge
- Chapman University
- Colorado State University
- Illinois State University
- Iowa State University
- San Diego State University
- Smith College
- University of Alabama
- University of Connecticut
- University of Florida

○ University of Georgia
○ University of Hawaii—Manoa
○ University of Idaho
○ University of Michigan
○ The University of Montana—Missoula
○ University of New Mexico
○ The University of Texas at Austin
○ University of the Pacific
○ University of Utah

FUN FACT

Chapman University owns a five-ton piece of the Berlin Wall, which is displayed next to a statue of Ronald Reagan.

Whoa, Nelly
Schools with great equine studies programs

○ Alfred University
○ California State Polytechnic University—Pomona
○ Centenary College
○ Colorado State University
○ Oregon State College

○ Stephens College
○ Truman State University
○ University of Findlay
○ University of Maryland—College Park
○ University of Minnesota—Crookston
○ The University of Montana—Western
○ University of New Hampshire
○ West Texas A&M University

Green Acres
Schools with great farming/agriculture programs

○ Colorado State University
○ Cornell University
○ Hampshire College
○ Iowa State University
○ McGill University
○ North Carolina State University
○ Purdue University—West Lafayette
○ Texas A&M University—College Station
○ University of Connecticut
○ University of Delaware
○ University of Louisiana at Lafayette
○ University of Nebraska—Lincoln

- University of Tennessee—Knoxville
- University of Vermont
- Virginia Institute of Technology
- West Virginia University

Laying Down the Law
Schools with great turfgrass science programs

- Clemson University
- Colorado State University
- North Carolina State University
- North Dakota State University
- The Ohio State University—Columbus
- Oregon State University
- Pennsylvania State University
- Texas A&M University—College Station
- University of Connecticut
- University of Georgia
- University of Illinois at Urbana-Champaign
- University of Maryland—College Park

Safari-Bound
Schools with great outdoor leadership/adventure education programs

- Bowdoin College
- Brevard College
- Bucknell University
- Idaho State University
- Lewis & Clark College
- Prescott College
- University of Colorado
- Warren Wilson College
- Western Carolina University

Courtside Every Night
Schools with great sports management/sports entertainment programs

- Albertson College of Idaho
- Catawba College

FUN FACT

Harriet Beecher Stowe began writing *Uncle Tom's Cabin* in Appleton Hall at **Bowdoin College**.

- Drexel University
- Elon University
- Flagler College
- Florida State University
- Gettysburg College
- Guilford College
- Hampton University
- Ithaca College
- Miami University
- New York University
- North Carolina State University
- Ohio Northern University
- Ohio University—Athens
- Samford University
- Seton Hall University
- St. John's University (NY)
- Syracuse University

- University of Central Florida
- University of Dayton
- University of Delaware
- University of Georgia
- University of Iowa
- University of Massachusetts—Amherst
- University of Miami
- University of Michigan—Ann Arbor
- University of San Francisco
- University of South Carolina—Columbia
- University of Tennessee—Knoxville
- The University of Texas at Austin
- Valparaiso University

part 2

Enrollment—Highest Proportional Enrollments by Major

Biology

Schools with high enrollments in biology

- Agnes Scott College
- Albertson College of Idaho
- Albion College
- Augusta State University
- Austin College
- Baker University—College of Arts & Sciences
- Baylor University
- Bowling Green State University
- Brandeis University
- Bridgewater College
- Bucknell University
- Buena Vista University
- Butler University
- Canisius College
- Case Western Reserve University
- Centenary College
- Centenary College of Louisiana
- Chatham College
- Christian Brothers University
- Claflin University
- Clark University
- Coe College
- Colby College

- College of Charleston
- Colorado College
- Colorado State University
- Cornell University
- Drake University
- Drexel University
- Earlham College
- Emmanuel College
- Erskine College
- Freed-Hardeman University
- George Fox University

FUN FACT

At **Hendrix College**, no fraternities or sororities are allowed on campus. Instead, all social events are organized by residence halls.

- Hanover College
- Hardin-Simmons University
- Haverford College
- Hendrix College
- Hillsdale College
- Hood College
- Houston Baptist University
- Howard University

- Illinois Wesleyan University
- Indiana University—Bloomington
- Jarvis Christian College
- Judson College (AL)
- Juniata College
- Lawrence University
- Le Moyne College
- Louisiana State University
- Loyola University—Chicago
- Loyola University—New Orleans
- Luther College
- Lycoming College
- Lyon College
- Mars Hill College
- Marymount University
- Maryville College
- Millsaps College
- Morningside College
- Morris College
- Mount Holyoke College
- North Carolina State University
- North Georgia College & State University
- Northwestern College (IA)
- The Ohio State University—Columbus
- Pomona College
- Prairie View A&M University
- Presbyterian College

- Providence College
- Randolph College
- Reed College
- Regis College
- Rhodes College
- Rice University
- Rutgers, The State University of New Jersey—New Brunswick/Piscataway
- Saint Olaf College
- Saint Vincent College
- Shorter College
- Siena College
- South Dakota State University
- Southeastern Louisiana University
- Southern University and A&M College
- Spring Hill College
- Stanford University
- State University of New York at Geneseo
- State University of New York—Stony Brook University
- Susquehanna University
- Swarthmore College
- Talladega College
- Temple University
- Thiel College
- Transylvania University
- Truman State University
- University of Alabama at Birmingham
- University of Alaska—Fairbanks
- University of California—Davis
- University of California—Irvine
- University of California—Riverside
- University of Chicago
- University of Colorado at Denver and Health Sciences Center
- University of Dallas
- University of Delaware
- University of Denver
- University of Georgia
- University of Illinois at Urbana-Champaign
- University of Kansas
- University of New Mexico
- The University of North Carolina at Chapel Hill
- University of St. Francis
- University of Tennessee at Martin
- The University of Texas at San Antonio
- University of the Pacific
- University of the Sciences in Philadelphia
- University of West Georgia

- University of Wisconsin—Superior
- Valdosta State University
- Virginia Commonwealth University
- Virginia Polytechnic and State University (Virginia Tech)
- Wagner College
- Wartburg College
- Washington University in St. Louis
- Westminster College (MO)
- Westminster College (PA)
- Willamette University
- Wingate University
- Wofford College

FUN FACT

California State Polytechnic University—Pomona is one of two schools in Southern California to offer an agricultural program (the University of California—Riverside is the other).

Computer/Information

Schools with high enrollments in computer/information science

- Acadia University
- Alabama State University
- Brandon University
- California State Polytechnic University—Pomona
- Capella University
- Central Pennsylvania College
- City University
- City University of New York—Baruch College
- City University of New York—New York Institute of Technology
- The College of Saint Scholastica
- Colorado Technical University
- Columbus State University
- Concordia University (QC)
- Dakota State University
- Dalhousie University
- Daniel Webster College
- East-West University
- Franklin University
- Gibbs College
- Globe Institute of Technology
- Grantham University

- ○ Harvey Mudd College
- ○ Huston-Tillotson University
- ○ Illinois Institute of Technology
- ○ Inter American University of Puerto Rico—Aguadilla
- ○ Jarvis Christian College
- ○ Kentucky State University
- ○ Lane College
- ○ Livingstone College
- ○ Marygrove College
- ○ Mayville State University
- ○ Mercy College
- ○ Monroe College
- ○ Montana State University, College of Technology—Great Falls
- ○ Morehouse College
- ○ New Jersey Institute of Technology
- ○ New Mexico Institute of Mining & Technology
- ○ Norfolk State University
- ○ North Carolina Wesleyan College
- ○ Northeastern Illinois University
- ○ Oklahoma Panhandle State University
- ○ Pace University—Pleasantville/Briarcliff
- ○ Polytechnic University—Brooklyn
- ○ Rensselaer Polytechnic Institute
- ○ Rockford College
- ○ Rust College
- ○ Saint Augustine's College
- ○ Salem International University
- ○ Stanford University
- ○ State University of New York—Institute of Technology at Utica/Rome
- ○ Stevens Institute of Technology
- ○ Texas A&M University—Commerce
- ○ Thomas College
- ○ Troy University Dothan
- ○ The University of British Columbia
- ○ University of California—Irvine
- ○ University of Houston—Clear Lake
- ○ University of Maryland—College Park
- ○ University of North Texas
- ○ University of Northern British Columbia
- ○ University of Phoenix
- ○ University of Regina
- ○ The University of Texas at Dallas
- ○ The University of Tulsa
- ○ University of Waterloo
- ○ University of West Florida
- ○ Valley City State University
- ○ Waldorf College

○ Webster University
○ Wentworth Institute of Technology
○ Worcester Polytechnic Institute

FUN FACT

Colby College is one of many campuses to have a Gravity Research Foundation monument, in honor of an organization—now sadly defunct—that sought to find ways to reduce or even eliminate the effects of gravity on everyday life.

Economics
Schools with high enrollments in economics

○ Albion College
○ Amherst College
○ Bates College
○ Bowdoin College
○ Brandeis University
○ Carleton College
○ Centre College
○ Claremont McKenna College

○ Colby College
○ Colgate University
○ College of the Holy Cross
○ Colorado College
○ Columbia University
○ Cornell College
○ Dartmouth College
○ Denison University
○ DePauw University
○ Doane College
○ Drew University
○ Duke University
○ Emory University
○ Emory University—Oxford College
○ Grinnell College
○ Hamilton College
○ Hampden-Sydney College
○ Harvard College
○ Hobart and William Smith Colleges
○ Johns Hopkins University
○ Kalamazoo College
○ Macalester College
○ Middlebury College
○ Northwestern University
○ Occidental College
○ Pomona College
○ Rice University
○ Rollins College

- South Dakota State University
- St. Mary's College of Maryland
- State University of New York—University at Buffalo
- Swarthmore College
- The University of Texas at Austin
- Trinity College (CT)
- Tufts University
- Union College (NY)
- United States Naval Academy
- University of California—Davis
- University of California—Irvine
- University of California—Los Angeles
- University of California—Santa Barbara
- University of Chicago
- University of Michigan—Ann Arbor
- University of Pennsylvania
- University of Utah
- University of Virginia
- University of Washington
- Ursinus College
- Washington and Lee University
- Wellesley College
- Westmont College
- Wheaton College (MA)
- Willamette University
- Williams College
- Yale University

Education

Schools with high enrollments in education

- Adelphi University
- Alma College
- Alverno College
- Arcadia University
- Ashland University
- Auburn University
- Augsburg College
- Bemidji State University
- Bethany College (WV)
- Bishop's University
- Brewton-Parker College
- Briar Cliff University
- Capital University
- Cardinal Stritch College
- Carroll College (WI)
- Carthage College
- Central College
- Central Missouri State University
- City University of New York—Brooklyn College
- Columbia College (MO)

- ○ Concordia College (NY)
- ○ Concordia University—Wisconsin
- ○ Converse College
- ○ Cornell College
- ○ Cornerstone University
- ○ Dana College
- ○ Drury University
- ○ D'Youville College
- ○ Edgewood College
- ○ Elms College
- ○ Elon University

FUN FACT

President James Garfield was a student, teacher, and principal at **Hiram College**, back when it was called the Western Reserve Eclectic Institute.

- ○ Fitchburg State College
- ○ The Franciscan University
- ○ Franklin Pierce College
- ○ Fresno Pacific University
- ○ Goddard College
- ○ Grace University
- ○ Grand View College

- ○ Greensboro College
- ○ Gwynedd-Mercy College
- ○ Hannibal-LaGrange College
- ○ Hardin-Simmons University
- ○ Hastings College
- ○ Heidelberg College
- ○ High Point University
- ○ Hiram College
- ○ Howard Payne University
- ○ Huston-Tillotson University
- ○ Jones International University
- ○ Juniata College
- ○ LaSalle University
- ○ LeMoyne-Owen College
- ○ Manchester College
- ○ Mansfield University of Pennsylvania
- ○ Marian College
- ○ Marietta College
- ○ Maryville College
- ○ Missouri Southern State University—Joplin
- ○ Molloy College
- ○ Monmouth College (IL)
- ○ Monmouth University
- ○ Montana State University—Bozeman
- ○ Mount Marty College

- Mount Mercy College
- Mount Saint Mary College
- Mount Union College
- Nazareth College of Rochester
- North Central University
- Northern Michigan University
- Northland College
- Northwest Nazarene University
- Northwestern College (IA)
- Ohio Northern University
- Oklahoma Panhandle State University
- Olivet Nazarene University
- Otterbein College
- Our Lady of Holy Cross College
- Pacific Lutheran University
- Peru State College
- Ripon College
- Rockford College
- Russell Sage College
- Salem State College
- Southern Adventist University
- Spring Arbor University
- State University of New York—New Paltz
- Tarleton State University
- Tennessee Wesleyan College
- The University of Montana
- Union Institute & University
- University of Alberta
- University College of the Cariboo
- University of Central Arkansas
- University of Charleston
- University of Houston—Clear Lake
- University of the Incarnate Word
- University of Indianapolis
- University of Maine
- University of Michigan—Flint
- University of South Carolina—Aiken
- University of South Carolina—Spartanburg
- University of St. Thomas (TX)
- University of Toledo
- Vanguard University of Southern California
- Walsh University
- Warner Southern College
- Washington State University
- Western Oregon University
- Westminster College
- Westminster College (PA)
- William Penn University
- William Woods University

- Wilmington College (DE)
- Xavier University (OH)

English

Schools with highest enrollments in English

- Adrian College
- Agnes Scott College
- Allegheny College
- The American University of Paris
- Amherst College
- Assumption College
- Augustana College (IL)

FUN FACT

Bryn Mawr College is named after the Welsh term for "big hill."

- Bard College
- Barnard College
- Bennington College
- Boston College
- Brigham Young University (UT)
- Bryn Athyn College of the New Church

- Bryn Mawr College
- Central Michigan University
- Centre College
- Chatham College
- Christopher Newport University
- City University of New York— Hunter College
- Colby College
- Colgate University
- The College of New Jersey
- The College of Wooster
- Colorado College
- Columbia University
- Connecticut College
- Covenant College
- Davidson College
- Denison University
- Dickinson College
- Fairfield University
- Fordham University
- Georgetown University
- Gordon College
- Goucher College
- Grove City College
- Haverford College
- Hendrix College
- Hobart and William Smith Colleges
- Hollins University

- ○ Hope College
- ○ Kenyon College
- ○ Macalester College
- ○ Marlboro College
- ○ Middlebury College
- ○ Monmouth College (IL)
- ○ Mount Holyoke College
- ○ Naropa University
- ○ Oberlin College
- ○ Occidental College
- ○ Oglethorpe University
- ○ Pitzer College
- ○ Pomona College
- ○ Princeton University
- ○ Randolph College
- ○ Reed College
- ○ Rhodes College
- ○ Rice University
- ○ Roanoke College
- ○ Rosemont College
- ○ Saint Michael's College
- ○ Saint Olaf College
- ○ Skidmore College
- ○ Spring Arbor University
- ○ St. Andrews Presbyterian College
- ○ St. Lawrence University
- ○ St. Thomas University (CA)

- ○ State University of New York at Binghamton
- ○ State University of New York—University at Albany
- ○ Tufts University
- ○ University College of the Cariboo
- ○ University of California—Berkeley
- ○ University of Chicago
- ○ University of Colorado—Boulder
- ○ University of Dallas
- ○ University of Iowa
- ○ University of King's College
- ○ University of Mary Washington
- ○ University of Massachusetts—Boston
- ○ University of Michigan—Ann Arbor
- ○ University of Montevallo
- ○ University of New Hampshire
- ○ University of North Carolina at Asheville
- ○ University of North Carolina at Wilmington
- ○ University of Puget Sound
- ○ University of Richmond
- ○ University of Tennessee—Knoxville
- ○ University of Toronto
- ○ University of Wisconsin—Madison
- ○ Ursinus College

- ○ Vassar College
- ○ Wabash College
- ○ Washington & Jefferson College
- ○ Wellesley College
- ○ Wells College
- ○ Wheaton College (IL)
- ○ Wheaton College (MA)
- ○ Whitman College
- ○ Whittier College
- ○ Whitworth College

FUN FACT

Bowdoin College's newspaper, *The Bowdoin Orient*, was established in 1871 and has been in print ever since. It is, as such, the oldest continuously-published college weekly in the United States.

History

Schools with high enrollments in history

- ○ Bowdoin College
- ○ Brown University
- ○ Bryn Athyn College of the New Church

- ○ Central Michigan University
- ○ Centre College
- ○ Christendom College
- ○ Colgate University
- ○ College of the Holy Cross
- ○ The College of Wooster
- ○ Columbia University
- ○ Covenant College
- ○ Furman University
- ○ Grinnell College
- ○ Hampden-Sydney College
- ○ Haverford College
- ○ Hillsdale College
- ○ Hobart and William Smith Colleges
- ○ Judson College (AL)
- ○ Kenyon College
- ○ Mississippi Valley State University
- ○ Muskingum College
- ○ Oberlin College
- ○ Princeton University
- ○ Rhode Island College
- ○ Saint Vincent College
- ○ Trinity College (CT)
- ○ University of King's College
- ○ The University of Texas of the Permian Basin
- ○ Virginia Military Institute
- ○ Wabash College

- ○ Washington and Lee University
- ○ Yale University

Physics

Schools with high enrollments in physics

- ○ California Institute of Technology
- ○ Harvey Mudd College
- ○ New Mexico Institute of Mining & Technology

Political Science/Government

Schools with high enrollments in political science/government

- ○ Allegheny College
- ○ Amherst College
- ○ Bates College
- ○ Bowdoin College
- ○ Brigham Young University (UT)
- ○ Bryn Mawr College
- ○ Carleton College
- ○ The Catholic University of America
- ○ Christendom College
- ○ The Citadel—The Military College of South Carolina
- ○ Claremont McKenna College

- ○ Clark University
- ○ College of the Holy Cross
- ○ College of William & Mary
- ○ Columbia University
- ○ Connecticut College
- ○ Davidson College
- ○ Dickinson College
- ○ Drew University
- ○ Franklin & Marshall College
- ○ Furman University
- ○ George Mason University
- ○ Georgetown University
- ○ Gettysburg College
- ○ Gonzaga University
- ○ Hamilton College
- ○ Hamline University

FUN FACT

In 1779, at the insistence of Thomas Jefferson, **The College of William & Mary** appointed George Wythe as a Professor of Law, the first ever in the United States. Not surprisingly, the school also has the oldest law program in the country.

- ○ Hampden-Sydney College
- ○ Hartwick College
- ○ Harvard College
- ○ Kenyon College
- ○ Macalester College
- ○ McGill University
- ○ Merrimack College
- ○ The Ohio State University—Columbus
- ○ Presbyterian College
- ○ Princeton University
- ○ Scripps College
- ○ Smith College
- ○ Spelman College
- ○ St. Lawrence University
- ○ St. Mary's College of Maryland
- ○ St. Mary's University
- ○ Swarthmore College
- ○ Syracuse University
- ○ Trinity College (CT)
- ○ Union College (NY)
- ○ United States Coast Guard Academy
- ○ United States Naval Academy
- ○ University of Arizona
- ○ University of California—Berkeley
- ○ University of California—Los Angeles
- ○ University of Connecticut
- ○ University of Maryland—College Park
- ○ University of Richmond
- ○ The University of Texas at Austin
- ○ University of Washington
- ○ University of Wisconsin—Madison
- ○ Vassar College
- ○ Wabash College
- ○ Wake Forest University
- ○ Whitman College
- ○ Willamette University
- ○ Williams College
- ○ Wofford College
- ○ Yale University
- ○ Yeshiva University

Psychology

Schools with high enrollments in psychology

- ○ Abilene Christian University
- ○ Agnes Scott College
- ○ Albertson College of Idaho
- ○ Albion College
- ○ Allegheny College
- ○ Alliant International University
- ○ Alma College
- ○ Alverno College

- Appalachian State University
- Arcadia University
- Argosy University—Orange County
- Arizona State University—Tempe
- Arizona State University—West
- Asbury College
- Assumption College
- Athabasca University
- Augusta State University
- Austin College
- Avila University
- Baldwin-Wallace College
- Barnard College
- Bates College
- Bay Path College
- Baylor University
- Beloit College
- Benedictine University
- Bethany College (WV)
- Biola University
- Bloomfield College
- Bowling Green State University
- Brandeis University
- Brandon University
- Brenau University—The Women's College
- Brewton-Parker College
- Bridgewater State College
- Brigham Young University (UT)
- Brigham Young University (HI)
- Bucknell University
- Caldwell College
- California Baptist University
- California Polytechnic State University—San Luis Obispo
- California State University—Bakersfield
- California State University—Long Beach
- California State University—San Bernardino
- California State University—Stanislaus
- Canisius College
- Carroll College (MT)
- Cascade College
- Castleton State College
- The Catholic University of America
- Central Connecticut State University
- Central Michigan University
- Chaminade University of Honolulu
- Charleston Southern University
- Chatham College
- Chestnut Hill College
- Christian Brothers University
- Christopher Newport University

- City University of New York—Brooklyn College
- City University of New York—City College
- City University of New York—The College of Staten Island
- City University of New York—Hunter College
- City University of New York—Medgar Evers College
- City University of New York—Queens College
- City University of New York—York College
- Clark University
- Clarke College
- Coe College
- Coker College
- Colby-Sawyer College
- College of Mount Saint Vincent
- The College of New Rochelle
- College of Saint Benedict/Saint John's University
- College of Saint Elizabeth
- College of St. Joseph in Vermont
- College of William & Mary
- Colorado State University
- Concordia University—Irvine
- Connecticut College

- Converse College
- Cornell College
- Cornerstone University
- Creighton University
- Crown College
- Dallas Baptist University
- Dartmouth College
- Dickinson College
- Dominican University
- Drew University
- Duke University
- Earlham College
- Eastern Mennonite University
- Eastern Michigan University
- Eastern New Mexico University
- Elmira College
- Emmanuel College (GA)
- Emory University
- Emory University—Oxford College
- Erskine College
- Eureka College
- Fairleigh Dickinson University—College at Florham
- Fairleigh Dickinson University—Metropolitan Campus
- Felician College
- Florida International University
- Florida State University

- Fort Lewis College
- Franklin & Marshall College
- Frostburg State University
- Gallaudet University
- George Mason University
- Georgetown College
- Georgia College & State University
- Georgia Southern University
- Georgia Southwestern State University
- Georgian Court University
- Gettysburg College
- Goddard College
- Gonzaga University
- Gordon College
- Goucher College
- Grand Valley State University
- Guilford College
- Gustavus Adolphus College
- Hamilton College
- Hamline University
- Hampton University
- Hanover College
- Hartwick College
- Harvard College
- Hastings College
- Henderson State University
- Hendrix College
- High Point University
- Hofstra University
- Hollins University
- Holy Names College
- Hood College
- Hope College
- Hope International University
- Houghton College
- Houston Baptist University
- Illinois Wesleyan University
- Iona College
- James Madison University
- Judson College (AL)
- Kalamazoo College
- Kean University
- Kent State University—Kent
- Knox College
- Lake Forest College
- Lasell College
- Lawrence University
- Le Moyne College
- Lebanon Valley College
- Lehigh University
- Lewis & Clark College
- Liberty University
- Linfield College
- Lipscomb University
- Longwood University

- ○ Louisiana College
- ○ Louisiana State University
- ○ Loyola College in Maryland
- ○ Loyola Marymount University
- ○ Loyola University—New Orleans
- ○ Loyola University—Chicago
- ○ Lycoming College
- ○ Lyon College
- ○ Manhattanville College
- ○ Marist College
- ○ Marshall University
- ○ Mary Baldwin College
- ○ Marywood University

FUN FACT

Moravian College has two campuses, and the space between is referred to as the "Moravian Mile."

- ○ McDaniel College
- ○ McGill University
- ○ Mercy College
- ○ Meredith College
- ○ Merrimack College
- ○ Messiah College
- ○ Michigan State University
- ○ MidAmerica Nazarene University

- ○ Middlebury College
- ○ Millsaps College
- ○ Missouri State University
- ○ Molloy College
- ○ Moravian College
- ○ Mount Allison University
- ○ Mount Holyoke College
- ○ Mount Union College
- ○ Muhlenberg College
- ○ Naropa University
- ○ Nazareth College of Rochester
- ○ Nebraska Wesleyan University
- ○ New College of Florida
- ○ Norfolk State University
- ○ North Carolina Wesleyan College
- ○ North Central College
- ○ Northern Arizona University
- ○ Northern Kentucky University
- ○ Northwestern College (MN)
- ○ Notre Dame College
- ○ Oak Hills Christian College
- ○ Oglethorpe University
- ○ The Ohio State University—Columbus
- ○ The Ohio State University—Lima
- ○ Ohio Valley University
- ○ Ohio Wesleyan University
- ○ Old Dominion University

- Palm Beach Atlantic University
- Pepperdine University
- Pikeville College
- Pine Manor College
- Pitzer College
- Point Loma Nazarene University
- Portland State University
- Purdue University—West Lafayette
- Quincy University
- Quinnipiac University
- Ramapo College of New Jersey
- Randolph-Macon College
- Randolph College
- Rhode Island College
- Richard Stockton College (NJ)
- Roanoke College
- Rockhurst University
- Rollins College
- Roosevelt University
- Rosemont College
- Russell Sage College
- Sacred Heart University
- Saint Anselm College
- Saint Francis College (NY)
- Saint Joseph College (CT)
- Saint Louis University
- Saint Michael's College
- Saint Olaf College
- Saint Vincent College
- San Diego State University
- San Francisco State University
- Santa Clara University
- Schreiner University
- Scripps College
- Seattle Pacific University
- Seton Hill University
- Shaw University
- Shawnee State University
- Siena College
- Simon Fraser University
- Simon's Rock College of Bard
- Simpson University
- Smith College
- Sonoma State University
- Southeastern College of the Assemblies of God
- Southeastern Oklahoma State University
- Southern Oregon University
- Southwest Baptist University
- Southwestern University
- Spelman College
- St. Ambrose University
- St. Edward's University
- St. John's University (NY)
- St. Lawrence University

- St. Mary's College of Maryland
- St. Mary's University
- State University of New York at Binghamton
- State University of New York—New Paltz
- State University of New York—Old Westbury
- State University of New York—Potsdam
- State University of New York—Purchase College

FUN FACT

Truman State University wasn't known by its current moniker until 1996--and this was its seventh name change in 129 years.

- State University of New York—Stony Brook University
- State University of New York—University at Albany
- State University of New York—University at Buffalo
- Stetson University
- Sweet Briar College

- Syracuse University
- Talladega College
- Taylor University—Fort Wayne Campus
- Temple University
- Texas Tech University
- Texas Wesleyan University
- Texas Woman's University
- Transylvania University
- Trent University
- Truman State University
- Union College (NY)
- University of Alabama at Birmingham
- University of Alaska—Fairbanks
- University of Alberta
- University of Arizona
- The University of British Columbia
- University of California—Davis
- University of California—Los Angeles
- University of California—Riverside
- University of California—Santa Barbara
- University of California—Santa Cruz
- University of Central Florida
- University of Colorado at Denver and Health Sciences Center

- University of Colorado—Boulder
- University of Connecticut
- University of Delaware
- University of Florida
- University of Georgia
- University of Hartford
- University of Hawaii—Hilo
- University of Hawaii—Manoa
- University of Hawaii—West Oahu
- University of Houston
- University of Illinois at Chicago
- University of Illinois at Springfield
- University of Illinois at Urbana-Champaign
- University of Iowa
- University of Judaism
- University of Kansas
- University of La Verne
- The University of Lethbridge
- University of Maine—Farmington
- University of Mary Hardin—Baylor
- University of Mary Washington
- University of Maryland—Baltimore County
- University of Massachusetts—Amherst
- University of Massachusetts—Dartmouth

- University of Minnesota—Morris
- University of Missouri—Kansas City
- The University of Montana
- University of Nebraska—Lincoln
- University of Nevada—Las Vegas
- University of New Hampshire
- University of New Mexico
- University of North Carolina at Asheville
- The University of North Carolina at Chapel Hill
- University of North Carolina at Charlotte
- University of North Carolina at Wilmington
- University of North Texas
- University of Oklahoma
- University of Oregon
- University of Pittsburgh—Greensburg
- University of Pittsburgh—Pittsburgh Campus
- University of Prince Edward Island
- University of Puget Sound
- University of Redlands
- University of Rhode Island
- University of Saint Mary (KS)
- University of San Francisco

- University of Science and Arts of Oklahoma
- The University of South Dakota
- University of Southern California
- University of Southern Indiana
- University of Southern Maine
- University of Tennessee—Chattanooga
- University of Tennessee—Knoxville
- The University of Texas at El Paso
- The University of Texas at San Antonio

FUN FACT

Notoriously ruthless in business and with his family, Cornelius Vanderbilt nevertheless donated $1 million to found **Vanderbilt University**.

- The University of Texas at Tyler
- University of Vermont
- University of Virginia
- University of Washington
- University of West Florida
- University of Wisconsin—Green Bay

- University of Wisconsin—Madison
- Ursinus College
- Ursuline College
- Valparaiso University
- Vanderbilt University
- Vanguard University of Southern California
- Vassar College
- Virginia Commonwealth University
- Wagner College
- Washington & Jefferson College
- Washington University in St. Louis
- Wayne State University
- Wellesley College
- Wells College
- Wesley College (DE)
- Wesleyan College
- West Chester University of Pennsylvania
- West Virginia University
- Western New England College
- Western Washington University
- Westminster College (MO)
- Wheaton College (IL)
- Wheaton College (MA)
- Whitman College
- Wichita State University
- Wilkes University

- William Jewell College
- William Paterson University
- William Penn University
- Winthrop University
- Wisconsin Lutheran College

- Worcester State College
- Wright State University
- Xavier University of Louisiana
- Yeshiva University

chapter 5

Career Prospects

Figuring out what you want to do before you get a job is a job in itself. How much direction you have in what you're looking for and how aggressively you go after it will largely determine where you'll be employed after graduation—and how much you're paid for your hours of hard work.

Attending a school with a well-connected, proactive Career Services office can never hurt when it comes time to send out your resume. Even while you're still in school, the staff may assist you with landing a sweet internship that relates to your major, or a summer research stint that awards a small stipend for you to learn while you work. The more you can do to support your career before you leave school—say, by participating in internships, independent research, practical classes, or resume workshops—the better off you'll be for your first job search.

Almost every college will offer some set of career services. These could range from primitive bulletin boards with tacked-up job listings to an interactive database of openings complete with an online application process. Many colleges host job fairs, at which potential employers visit campus and recruit bright-eyed-and-bushy-tailed students. Some even conduct interviews on campus. While the career-focused page of a school's website will boast about how many students have jobs upon graduation, or which highly regarded corporations look to their student body to find the next generation of leaders, it's tough to get a true read on the typical student experience with a school's Career Services office. If possible, talk to students on your college visits about it, and pop into the office and scope the scene for yourself. You should get career-minded now and maintain that mindset through college and beyond. Start by finding out where you'll get the best career preparation. If you ultimately don't attend a school with a stellar Career Services office, you can still take the initiative for your own career success—but remember that succeeding without the help of a reliable Career Services office will take additional initiative.

The lists in this chapter will clue you in to a lot of helpful career information. You will find out which schools offer the best career preparation for college students, which have the best resources for post-graduation planning, and which help you get the certification you'll need to land the job you want. If you stay committed, we promise that you will make your alma mater—and yourself—very, very proud.

part 1

Opportunities During School—Campus-Connected Enterprises

A Cooperative Manner

Schools with great co-op programs

- Antioch College
- California Polytechnic State University—San Luis Obispo
- Cornell University
- Drexel University
- Georgia Institute of Technology
- Johnson & Wales University
- Kettering University
- Long Island University
- Marquette University
- Miami Dade College
- Northeastern University
- Pace University
- Pennsylvania State University
- Rochester Institute of Technology
- State University of New York—University at Buffalo
- Texas Tech University
- The University of Akron
- University of Alabama—Huntsville
- University of Cincinnati
- University of Houston
- The University of Texas at Austin
- University of Washington

Paid To Learn

Schools with great fellowship opportunities

- ○ Amherst College
- ○ Bates College
- ○ Boston College
- ○ Brown University
- ○ Bryn Mawr College
- ○ Harvard College
- ○ Massachusetts Institute of Technology
- ○ Stanford University
- ○ Swarthmore College
- ○ University of Chicago
- ○ University of Pittsburgh
- ○ University of Virginia

FUN FACT

John D. Rockefeller founded **Rockefeller University** to combat the influx of contagious diseases that struck in the early twentieth century. He was driven in particular by his grandson's death from scarlet fever.

- ○ University of Washington
- ○ Yale University

Mo' Money (Sometimes) Means Mo' Opportunities

Schools with the largest endowments

- ○ Amherst College
- ○ Boston College
- ○ Brown University
- ○ California Institute of Technology
- ○ Case Reserve Western University
- ○ Columbia University
- ○ Cornell University
- ○ Dartmouth College
- ○ Duke University
- ○ Emory University
- ○ Grinnell College
- ○ Harvard College
- ○ Indiana University
- ○ Johns Hopkins College
- ○ Massachusetts Institute of Technology
- ○ Michigan State University
- ○ New York University
- ○ Northwestern University
- ○ The Ohio State University

- ○ Pennsylvania State University
- ○ Princeton University
- ○ Purdue University
- ○ Rice University
- ○ Rockefeller University
- ○ Stanford University
- ○ Swarthmore College
- ○ Texas A&M University
- ○ University of California (all campuses)
- ○ University of Chicago
- ○ University of Delaware
- ○ University of Illinois
- ○ University of Michigan
- ○ University of Minnesota
- ○ The University of North Carolina at Chapel Hill
- ○ University of Notre Dame
- ○ University of Pennsylvania
- ○ University of Pittsburgh
- ○ University of Richmond
- ○ University of Rochester
- ○ University of Southern California
- ○ The University of Texas
- ○ University of Virginia
- ○ University of Washington
- ○ University of Wisconsin
- ○ Vanderbilt University
- ○ Washington University in St. Louis

- ○ Wellesley College
- ○ Williams College
- ○ Yeshiva University

Major in the American Dream

Schools that offer entrepreneurship as a major

- ○ Alfred State College
- ○ Ashland University
- ○ Babson College
- ○ Baker College of Flint
- ○ Baylor University
- ○ Belmont University
- ○ Berkeley College
- ○ Black Hills State University
- ○ Boston University
- ○ Bradley University
- ○ Brock University
- ○ Buena Vista University
- ○ California State University—San Bernardino
- ○ Canisius College
- ○ Carlos Albizu University
- ○ Central Michigan University
- ○ Central Pennsylvania College
- ○ Cleary University

- The College of St. Catherine
- The College of the Atlantic
- Davenport University
- Drake University
- Drexel University
- Duquesne University
- Eastern Michigan University
- Fairleigh Dickinson University—Metropolitan Campus
- Ferris State University
- Gettysburg College
- Gonzaga University
- Grove City College
- Hampton University
- Hawaii Pacific University
- Hofstra University
- Houston Baptist University
- Jacksonville State University
- Johnson & Wales University
- Juniata College
- Mars Hill College
- McGill University
- Messiah College
- Mitchell College
- Montana State University, College of Technology—Great Falls
- Montana Tech of the University of Montana

- Mountain State University
- Newman University
- Northeastern University
- Northern Michigan University
- Northwood University
- Oregon Institute of Technology
- Pace University
- Palm Beach Atlantic University
- Purdue University—Calumet
- Quinnipiac University
- Reinhardt College
- Rhode Island College
- Robert Morris University
- Saint Cloud State University
- Salem State College
- San Diego State University
- Seton Hill University
- Sierra Nevada College
- Southampton College of Long Island University
- Southern Adventist University
- Southern Methodist University
- Southwestern College (KS)
- St. Edward's University
- St. Mary's University
- Stetson University
- Stevens Institute of Technology

- Suffolk University
- Susquehanna University
- Syracuse University
- Temple University
- Thomas Edison State College
- The University of Akron
- University of Arizona
- University of Baltimore
- University of Dayton
- University of Illinois at Urbana-Champaign
- University of Indianapolis
- University of Manitoba
- University of Massachusetts—Boston
- University of Massachusetts—Lowell
- University of New Hampshire
- University of Pittsburgh—Bradford
- University of Portland
- University of Saint Thomas (MN)
- University of South Florida
- University of Southern Indiana
- University of Toledo
- University of Windsor
- Washington State University
- Washington University in St. Louis
- Western Carolina University

- Wilkes University
- Xavier University (OH)

Learning to Fly

Schools designated "enlisted-friendly" by the AFROTC (U.S. Air Force)

- Angelo State University
- Charleston Southern University
- Embry-Riddle Aeronautical University—Fort Knox (KY)
- Embry-Riddle Aeronautical University—Grand Forks AFB (ND)
- Montana State University
- North Carolina Central University—Durham
- Park University—F. E. Warren Air Force Base (WY)
- Park University—Grand Forks Air Force Base (ND)
- Park University—Tinker Air Force Base (OK)
- Texas State University—San Marcos
- Troy University
- University of Central Florida
- University of Maryland—University College

- University of Minnesota—Crookston
- University of Nebraska—Lincoln
- University of Nebraska—Omaha
- University of Tennessee
- The University of Texas at San Antonio

In the Army Now

Schools with ROTC (U.S. Army) programs on campus

- Alabama A&M University
- Alcorn State University
- Appalachian State University
- Arizona State University

FUN FACT

Military cadets enrolled at **The Citadel** take classes during the day, while civilian undergraduate and graduate students take their classes at night.

- Arkansas State University
- Atlanta Metropolitan College
- Auburn University

- Auburn University—Montgomery
- Augusta State University
- Austin Peay State University
- Ball State University
- Boise State University
- Boston University
- Bowie State University
- Bowling Green State University
- Brigham Young University
- Bucknell University
- California Polytechnic State University—San Luis Obispo
- California State University—Fresno
- California State University—Fullerton
- Cameron University
- Campbell University
- Canisius College
- Capital University
- Carson-Newman College
- Central Michigan University
- Central Missouri State University
- Central State University
- Central Washington University
- The Citadel—The Military College of South Carolina
- Claremont-McKenna College
- Clarkson University

- Clemson University
- College of William & Mary
- Colorado State University
- Columbus State University
- Cornell University
- Creighton University
- Dickinson College
- Drexel University
- Duke University
- East Carolina University
- East Tennessee State University
- Eastern Illinois University
- Eastern Kentucky University
- Eastern Michigan University
- Eastern Washington University
- Edinboro University of Pennsylvania
- Elizabeth City State University
- Embry-Riddle Aeronautical University
- Embry-Riddle Aeronautical University (AZ)
- Florida Agricultural & Mechanical University
- Florida Institute of Technology
- Florida International University
- Florida Southern College
- Florida State University
- Fordham University
- Fort Valley State University
- Furman University
- Gannon University
- George Mason University
- Georgetown University
- Georgia Institute of Technology
- Georgia Military College
- Georgia Southern University
- Georgia State University
- Gonzaga University
- Grambling State University
- Hampton University
- Hofstra University
- Howard University
- Illinois State University
- Indiana University—Purdue University at Indianapolis (IUPUI)
- Indiana University—Bloomington
- Indiana University of Pennsylvania
- Iowa State University
- Jackson State University
- Jacksonville State University
- James Madison University
- John Carroll University
- The Johns Hopkins University
- Kansas State University
- Kent State University
- Lehigh University

- Lincoln University
- Lock Haven University of Pennsylvania
- Louisiana State University
- Loyola College
- Marion Military Institute
- Marquette University
- Marshall University
- Massachusetts Institute of Technology
- McDaniel College
- Metropolitan Community College
- Michigan State University
- Michigan Technological University
- Middle Tennessee State University
- Minnesota State University—Mankato
- Mississippi State University
- Missouri State University
- Missouri Western State College
- Montana State University
- Morehead State University
- Morgan State University
- New Mexico Military Institute
- New Mexico State University
- Niagara University
- Norfolk State University
- North Carolina A&T State University
- North Carolina State University
- North Dakota State University
- North Georgia College & State University
- Northeastern State University
- Northeastern University
- Northern Arizona University
- Northern Illinois University
- Northern Michigan University
- Northwestern State University
- Norwich University
- Ohio University
- Oklahoma State University
- Old Dominion University
- Oregon State University
- Pacific Lutheran University
- Pennsylvania State University
- Pittsburg State University
- Prairie View A & M University
- Presbyterian College
- Princeton University
- Providence College
- Purdue University
- Rochester Institute of Technology
- Rose-Hulman Institute of Technology
- Rush University

- Rutgers, The State University of New Jersey
- Saint Augustine's College
- Saint Mary's University
- Sam Houston State University
- San Diego State University
- Santa Clara University
- Seattle University
- Seton Hall University
- Shippensburg University
- Siena College
- Slippery Rock University
- South Carolina State University
- South Dakota School of Mines & Technology
- South Dakota State University
- Southern Illinois University—Carbondale
- Southern Illinois University—Edwardsville
- Southern University and A&M College
- Southern Vermont College
- Southwest Texas State University
- St. Bonaventure University
- St. John's University (MN)
- St. John's University (NY)
- State University of New York—Brockport
- Stephen F. Austin State University
- Syracuse University
- Tarleton State University
- Texas Christian University
- Temple University
- Tennessee Tech University
- Texas A&M University—College Station
- Texas A&M University—Kingsville
- Texas Tech University
- Truman State University
- Tulane University
- Tuskegee University
- The University of Akron
- University of Alabama
- University of Alabama at Birmingham
- University of Alaska—Fairbanks
- University of Arizona
- University of Arkansas
- University of Arkansas—Pine Bluff
- University of California—Berkeley
- University of California—Davis
- University of California—Los Angeles
- University of California—Santa Barbara
- University of Central Arkansas
- University of Central Florida

189

- University of Central Oklahoma
- University of Cincinnati
- University of Colorado—Boulder
- University of Colorado at Colorado Springs
- University of Connecticut
- University of Dayton
- University of Delaware
- University of Florida
- University of Georgia
- University of Guam
- University of Hawaii—Manoa
- University of Houston
- University of Idaho
- University of Illinois at Chicago
- University of Illinois at Urbana-Champaign
- University of Iowa
- University of Kansas
- University of Kentucky
- University of Louisville
- University of Maine
- University of Maryland—College Park
- University of Massachusetts
- The University of Memphis
- University of Michigan

- University of Minnesota—Twin Cities
- University of Mississippi
- University of Missouri—Columbia
- University of Missouri—Rolla
- The University of Montana
- University of Nebraska—Lincoln
- University of Nevada—Reno
- University of New Hampshire
- University of New Mexico
- University of North Alabama
- The University of North Carolina at Chapel Hill
- University of North Carolina at Charlotte
- University of North Dakota
- University of Northern Iowa
- University of Notre Dame
- University of Oklahoma
- University of Oregon
- University of Pittsburgh
- University of Portland
- University of Puerto Rico—Mayaguez
- University of Puerto Rico—Rio Piedras
- University of Rhode Island
- University of Richmond

- University of San Francisco
- The University of Scranton
- University of South Alabama
- University of South Carolina
- The University of South Dakota
- University of South Florida
- University of Southern California
- University of Southern Mississippi
- University of Tampa
- University of Tennessee—Knoxville
- University of Tennessee at Martin
- The University of Texas at Arlington
- The University of Texas at Austin
- The University of Texas at El Paso
- The University of Texas—Pan American
- The University of Texas at San Antonio
- University of Toledo
- University of Utah
- University of Vermont
- University of Virginia
- University of Washington
- University of West Florida
- University of Wisconsin—La Crosse
- University of Wisconsin—Madison
- University of Wisconsin—Oshkosh
- University of Wisconsin—Stevens Point
- University of Wyoming
- Valley Forge Military College
- Vanderbilt University
- Virginia Military Institute
- Virginia State University
- Virginia Polytechnic and State University (Virginia Tech)
- Wake Forest University
- Washington State University
- Washington University
- Weber State University
- Wentworth Military Academy
- West Virginia State University
- West Virginia University
- Western Illinois University
- Western Kentucky University
- Western Michigan University
- Wheaton College
- Widener University
- Wofford College
- Worcester Polytechnic Institute
- Wright State University
- Xavier University (OH)

Sail the Seven Seas

Schools with NROTC (U.S. Navy/Marine Corps) programs on campus

○ Auburn University (nursing program available)
○ Boston University
○ Carnegie Mellon University
○ The Citadel
○ College of the Holy Cross
○ Cornell University
○ Duke University
○ Embry-Riddle Aeronautical University
○ Florida A&M University (nursing program available)
○ The George Washington University
○ Georgia Institute of Technology
○ Hampton University (nursing program available)
○ Illinois Institute of Technology
○ Iowa State University
○ Jacksonville University (nursing program available)
○ Maine Maritime Academy
○ Marquette University (nursing program available)
○ Massachusetts Institute of Technology

○ Miami University
○ Morehouse College
○ Norfolk State University (nursing program available)
○ North Carolina State University
○ Northwestern University
○ Norwich University (nursing program available)
○ The Ohio State University (nursing program available)
○ Old Dominion University (nursing program available)
○ Oregon State University
○ Pennsylvania State University (nursing program available)
○ Prairie View A&M University (nursing program available)
○ Purdue University (nursing program available)
○ Rensselaer Polytechnic Institute
○ Rice University
○ San Diego State University (nursing program available)
○ Savannah State University
○ Southern University and A&M College (nursing program available)
○ State University of New York—Maritime College

- Texas A&M University—College Station
- Tulane University
- University of Arizona (nursing program available)
- University of California—Berkeley
- University of California—Los Angeles
- University of Colorado
- University of Florida (nursing program available)
- University of Idaho
- University of Illinois (nursing program available)
- University of Kansas
- The University of Memphis (nursing program available)
- University of Michigan (nursing program available)
- University of Minnesota (nursing program available)
- University of Mississippi
- University of Missouri (nursing program available)
- University of Nebraska (nursing program available)
- University of New Mexico (nursing program available)
- University of North Carolina (nursing program available)
- University of Notre Dame
- University of Oklahoma (nursing program available)
- University of Pennsylvania (nursing program available)
- University of Rochester
- University of San Diego
- University of South Carolina (nursing program available)
- University of South Florida (nursing program available)
- University of Southern California
- The University of Texas (nursing program available)
- University of Utah (nursing program available)
- University of Virginia (nursing program available)
- University of Washington (nursing program available)
- University of Wisconsin (nursing program available)
- Vanderbilt University
- Villanova University (nursing program available)
- Virginia Military Institute
- Virginia Polytechnic Institute

All Aboard!

Schools that offer subsidies to students who use public transportation

- ○ Brown University
- ○ California Institute of Technology
- ○ California Polytechnic State University—San Luis Obispo
- ○ California State University—Dominguez Hills
- ○ California State University—Northridge
- ○ Emory University
- ○ Massachusetts Institute of Technology
- ○ Pennsylvania State University
- ○ Rice University
- ○ Stanford University

- University of California—Berkeley
- University of California—Davis
- The University of North Carolina at Chapel Hill
- West Virginia University
- Williams College

Off-Campus Forays

Schools at which students have great opportunities for off-campus employment

- American University
- Boston University
- California State University—Los Angeles
- Columbia University
- Georgia Institute of Technology
- Harvard College
- New York University
- Rice University
- San Francisco State University
- Temple University
- University of Alabama
- University of Arizona
- University of California—Berkeley
- University of California—Los Angeles

- University of California—San Diego
- University of Central Florida
- University of Chicago
- University of Denver
- University of Houston
- University of Miami
- University of Nevada—Las Vegas
- University of Pennsylvania
- University of Portland
- University of Southern California
- The University of Texas at Austin
- University of Utah
- University of Washington

FUN FACT

Emory University's unofficial mascot is Dooley—often called the "Spirit of Emory"—who happens to be a skeleton.

Get a Job? Not In This Town!

Schools at which students have less-than-optimal opportunities for off-campus employment

○ Alcorn State University
○ Alfred University
○ Bethany College (WV)
○ Bucknell University
○ California University of Pennsylvania
○ Graceland University
○ Henry Cogswell College
○ Houghton College
○ Judson College (AL)
○ Langston University
○ Lincoln University (MO)
○ Mississippi Valley State University
○ Mount Aloysius College
○ New Mexico Institute of Mining & Technology
○ Newberry College
○ Oakland City University
○ St. Lawrence University
○ Sul Ross State University
○ Voorhees College

part 2

Post-Graduation Opportunities

Affairs of the State

Schools at which the State Department typically recruits

- Arizona State University
- American University
- Florida A&M University
- George Mason University
- The George Washington University
- Georgetown University
- New Mexico State University
- San Francisco State University
- Tufts University
- University of Denver
- University of Miami
- The University of Texas at Austin

Bank On It

Schools at which JPMorgan Chase typically recruits

- Barnard College
- Boston College
- Brown University
- California Institute of Technology
- Carnegie Mellon University
- City University of New York— Baruch College
- Columbia University
- Cornell University
- Dartmouth College
- DePaul University
- DeVry University
- Duke University
- Fairfield University

- Florida A&M University
- Fordham University
- Georgetown University
- Harvard College
- Hofstra University
- Howard University
- Illinois State University
- Indiana University
- Johns Hopkins University
- Lehigh University
- Marquette University
- Miami University
- Michigan State University
- Massachusetts Institute of Technology
- Morehouse College
- Northeastern University
- Northern Illinois University
- Northwestern University
- New York University
- The Ohio State University
- Pace University
- Pennsylvania State University
- Princeton University
- Purdue University
- Rice University
- Rochester Institute of Technology
- Spelman College
- Stanford University
- St. John's University (NY)
- Syracuse University
- Temple University
- Texas A&M University
- Tufts University
- University of California—Berkeley
- University of Chicago
- University of Delaware
- University of Illinois at Chicago
- University of Illinois at Urbana-Champaign
- University of Maryland
- University of Michigan
- University of Michigan—Ross
- University of Pennsylvania
- The University of Texas at Arlington
- The University of Texas at Austin
- University of Virginia
- Valparaiso University
- Wellesley College
- Western Michigan University
- Williams College
- Yale University

On-Campus Consultation

Schools at which McKinsey typically recruits

- Amherst College
- Arizona State University
- Babson College
- Barnard College
- Bates College
- Bowdoin College
- Brandeis University
- Brigham Young University
- Brown University
- Bryn Mawr College
- California Institute of Technology
- Carleton College
- Carnegie Mellon University
- Case Western Reserve University
- Claremont McKenna College
- Clark Atlanta University
- Colby College
- Colgate University
- College of William & Mary
- Columbia University
- Cornell University
- Dartmouth College
- Davidson College
- Duke University
- Emory University
- Florida A&M University
- Franklin & Marshall College
- Georgetown University
- Georgia Institute of Technology
- Grinnell College
- Hamilton College
- Harvard College
- Haverford College
- Harvey Mudd College
- Howard University
- Indiana University—Bloomington
- Johns Hopkins University
- Kenyon College
- Macalaster College
- Massachusetts Institute of Technology
- Miami University
- Michigan State University
- Middlebury College
- Morehouse College
- Mount Holyoke College
- New York University
- North Carolina State University
- Northwestern University
- Oberlin College
- The Ohio State University
- Pennsylvania State University

- Pomona College
- Princeton University
- Purdue University
- Rice University
- Rose-Hulman Institute of Technology
- Rutgers, The State University of New Jersey
- Scripps College
- Smith College
- Southern Methodist University
- Spelman College
- St. Olaf College
- Stanford University
- Swarthmore College
- Texas A&M University
- Tufts University
- University of Arizona
- University of California—Berkeley
- University of California—Los Angeles
- University of California—San Diego
- University of Chicago
- University of Colorado—Boulder
- University of Florida
- University of Georgia

- University of Illinois at Urbana-Champaign
- University of Massachusetts—Amherst
- University of Michigan
- University of Minnesota—Twin Cities
- The University of North Carolina at Chapel Hill
- University of Notre Dame
- University of Pennsylvania
- University of Richmond
- University of Southern California
- The University of Texas at Austin
- University of Virginia
- University of Washington
- University of Wisconsin—Madison
- Vanderbilt University
- Vassar College
- Wabash College
- Wake Forest University
- Washington and Lee University
- Washington University in St. Louis
- Wellesley College
- Wesleyan University
- Williams College
- Yale University

Peace Incorporated

Schools from which the highest proportion of graduates join the Peace Corps

- American University
- Boston College
- Boston University
- Brown University
- College of William & Mary
- Colorado College
- Colorado State University
- Cornell University
- Dartmouth College
- The Evergreen State College
- Georgetown University
- The George Washington University
- Gonzaga University
- Grinnell College
- Indiana University—Bloomington
- James Madison University
- Kalamazoo College
- Michigan State University
- Middlebury College
- Montana State University—Bozeman
- Mount Holyoke College
- New York University
- Northwestern University
- Oberlin College
- Pennsylvania State University
- St. Olaf College
- Tufts University
- University of California—Berkeley
- University of California—Los Angeles
- University of California—Santa Cruz
- University of Chicago
- University of Colorado—Boulder
- University of Idaho
- University of Mary Washington
- University of Michigan—Ann Arbor
- University of Minnesota—Twin Cities
- The University of Montana
- The University of North Carolina at Chapel Hill
- University of Oregon
- University of Pennsylvania
- University of Puget Sound

FUN FACT

Evergreen State College forgoes giving students grades in favor of narrative evaluations.

- ○ The University of Texas at Austin
- ○ University of Virginia
- ○ University of Washington
- ○ University of Wisconsin—Madison
- ○ Wake Forest University
- ○ Wellesley College
- ○ Wesleyan University
- ○ Western Washington University

Source: Peace Corps

Come for the School, Stay for the City

Schools whose cities have promising job markets

- ○ Colorado College (Colorado Springs, CO)
- ○ Colorado Technical University (Colorado Springs, CO)
- ○ Drury University (Springfield, MO)
- ○ Duke University (Durham, NC)
- ○ Emory University (Atlanta, GA)
- ○ Georgia State University (Atlanta, GA)
- ○ Missouri State University (Springfield, MO)
- ○ New College of Florida (Sarasota, FL)
- ○ North Carolina State University (Raleigh, NC)
- ○ St. Mary's University (San Antonio, TX)
- ○ Texas Christian University (Fort Worth, TX)
- ○ Texas Wesleyan University (Fort Worth, TX)
- ○ Trinity University (San Antonio, TX)
- ○ United States Air Force Academy (Colorado Springs, CO)
- ○ University of Central Florida (Orlando, FL)
- ○ University of Colorado at Colorado Springs (Colorado Springs, CO)
- ○ University of Colorado at Denver (Denver, CO)
- ○ University of Denver (Denver, CO)
- ○ The University of North Carolina at Chapel Hill (Chapel Hill, NC)
- ○ The University of Texas at Austin (Austin, TX)
- ○ The University of Texas at San Antonio (San Antonio, TX)

Source: *Inc. Magazine*, "Top 25 Cities for Doing Business in America," by Joel Kotkin, March 2004.

Get Out of Town?

Schools whose cities have tough job markets

- Aquinas College (Grand Rapids, MI)
- Boston University (Boston, MA)
- Calvin College (Grand Rapids, MI)
- City University of New York—City College (New York, NY)
- City University of New York—Hunter College (New York, NY)
- Columbia University (New York, NY)
- Converse College (Spartanburg, SC)
- Drexel University (Philadelphia, PA)
- Fordham University (New York, NY)
- Furman University (Greenville, SC)
- Golden Gate University (San Francisco, CA)
- Harvard College (Boston, MA)
- Massachusetts Institute of Technology (Boston, MA)
- Milwaukee Institute of Art and Design (Milwaukee, WI)
- Milwaukee School of Engineering (Milwaukee, WI)
- Nazareth College of Rochester (Rochester, NY)
- New College of California (San Francisco, CA)
- New York University (New York, NY)
- Northeastern University (Boston, MA)
- Oregon Health Sciences University (Portland, OR)
- Philadelphia University (Philadelphia, PA)
- Portland State University (Portland, OR)
- Rochester Institute of Technology (Rochester, NY)
- San Francisco State University (San Francisco, CA)
- San Jose State University (San Jose, CA)
- Suffolk University (Boston, MA)
- Temple University (Philadelphia, PA)

FUN FACT

Furman University has a long-term exchange program with Kansai Gaidai University in Osaka, hence the impressive Japanese garden maintained on campus.

○ Tufts University (Boston, MA)
○ University of California—San Francisco (San Francisco, CA)
○ University of Connecticut (Hartford, CT)
○ University of Dayton (Dayton, OH)
○ University of Hartford (West Hartford, CT)
○ University of Massachusetts—Boston (Boston, MA)
○ University of Portland (Portland, OR)
○ University of Rochester (Rochester, NY)
○ University of San Francisco (San Francisco, CA)
○ University of South Carolina—Spartanburg (Spartanburg, SC)
○ University of Wisconsin—Milwaukee (Milwaukee, WI)
○ Wofford College (Spartanburg, SC)
○ Wright State University (Dayton, OH)

Source: *Inc. Magazine*, "Top 25 Cities for Doing Business in America: Ten Worst Metro Areas," by Joel Kotkin, March 2004.

Finding Love After Graduation

Schools in cities with high rates of single people

○ American University (Washington, DC)
○ Boston University (Boston, MA)
○ California State University—Los Angeles (Los Angeles, CA)
○ Chicago State University (Chicago, IL)
○ City University of New York—City College (New York, NY)
○ City University of New York—Hunter College (New York, NY)
○ Columbia University (New York, NY)
○ Emory University (Atlanta, GA)
○ Fordham University (New York, NY)
○ Gallaudet University (Washington, DC)
○ Georgetown University (Washington, DC)
○ The George Washington University (Washington, DC)
○ Georgia State University (Atlanta, GA)
○ Golden Gate University (San Francisco, CA)
○ Harvard College (Boston, MA)

- Loyola Marymount University (Los Angeles, CA)
- Loyola University—Chicago (Chicago, IL)
- Massachusetts Institute of Technology (Boston, MA)
- Naropa University (Boulder, CO)
- New College of California (San Francisco, CA)
- New York University (New York, NY)
- Northeastern University (Boston, MA)
- Northwestern University (Chicago, IL)
- San Diego State University (San Diego, CA)
- San Francisco State University (San Francisco, CA)
- Suffolk University (Boston, MA)
- Texas Christian University (Fort Worth, TX)
- Texas Wesleyan University (Fort Worth, TX)
- Tufts University (Boston, MA)
- University of California—Los Angeles (Los Angeles, CA)
- University of California—San Diego (San Diego, CA)
- University of California—San Francisco (San Francisco, CA)
- University of Chicago (Chicago, IL)
- University of Colorado—Boulder (Boulder, CO)
- University of Colorado at Denver (Denver, CO)
- University of Dallas (Dallas, TX)
- University of Denver (Denver, CO)
- University of Illinois at Chicago (Chicago, IL)
- University of Massachusetts—Boston (Boston, MA)
- University of Miami (Miami, FL)
- University of San Diego (San Diego, CA)
- University of San Francisco (San Francisco, CA)
- University of Southern California (Los Angeles, CA)
- The University of Texas at Austin (Austin, TX)
- The University of Texas at Dallas (Dallas, TX)

Source: *Forbes Magazine*. "Best Cities for Singles" by Lacey Rose and Leah Hoffmann, 25 July 2005.

chapter 6

Admissions
and Alumni

Newly-admitted students and alumni might at first seem not to have a lot in common. One group is on the verge of matriculating, while the other counts college as a (perhaps distant) memory. Yet the individuals going into and coming out of a school can reveal a lot about its ethos. You should keep that in mind as you make your campus visits, and ask questions like: Do the seniors seem just as excited about their college experience as the freshmen do? Are they just as impressive a group? What are the accomplishments of the entering freshman class? What have alumni gone on to accomplish?

This chapter can help you figure out whether the admissions profiles of current and former students are similar to your own. You'll find out which schools admit the highest percentages of applicants and which admit just a small fraction of those who want in. You'll also find out which schools have the highest and lowest yields—that is, percentages of accepted students who enroll. We reveal which schools have the priciest and which have the cheapest (as in *free*) tuition figures.

If the newly admitted students impress you and you're curious about alumni, keep reading. If you think you may want to be president some day, check out which schools have sent the greatest numbers of graduates to the Oval Office. If you want to be famous, check out where celebrities have tended to spend their undergraduate years. Schools with active alumni associations are also worth noting. It makes a difference if those who graduated have a fond attachment to their school, one that moves them to give something back. Many philanthropic graduates say they have their college to thank for setting them off in the right direction. You can use the lists in this chapter to identify schools that are likely to accept you, award you aid, and get you started in the right direction as well.

part 1

Admissions— Getting In

Transfer Here!

Schools with the highest proportions of incoming transfer students

○ Alaska Pacific University
○ Allen College
○ American InterContinental University
○ Antioch Southern California—Los Angeles
○ Aquinas College (TN)
○ Argosy University—Chicago
○ Argosy University—Orange County
○ The Art Institutes International—Minnesota
○ The Art Institutes International—Portland

○ Barat College of Depaul University
○ Bellevue University
○ Burlington College
○ Campbell University
○ Clarkson College
○ Dominican School of Philosophy and Theology
○ Excelsior College
○ Franklin University
○ Goldey-Beacom College
○ Governors State University
○ Gratz College
○ Massachusetts College of Pharmacy and Health Science
○ Medcenter One College of Nursing
○ Medical College of Georgia
○ Mercy College

- ○ Midway College
- ○ National American Unversity (NM)
- ○ Nebraska Methodist College
- ○ Oregon College of Art and Craft
- ○ Pacific Northwest College of Art
- ○ Pontifical College Josephinum
- ○ Rush University
- ○ Saint Anthony College of Nursing
- ○ Saint Francis Medical Center College of Nursing
- ○ San Francisco Art Institute
- ○ South College
- ○ St. John's College—Department of Nursing (IL)
- ○ State University of New York— Empire State College
- ○ State University of New York— Institute of Technology at Utica/Rome

- ○ State University of New York— Upstate Medical University
- ○ Texas A&M University—Texarkana
- ○ Thomas Jefferson University
- ○ Troy University Dothan
- ○ University of Baltimore
- ○ University of Central Texas
- ○ University of California—San Francisco
- ○ University of Colorado at Denver and Health Sciences Center— Health Sciences Program
- ○ University of Hawaii—West Oahu
- ○ University of Houston—Clear Lake
- ○ University of Houston—Victoria
- ○ University of Illinois at Springfield
- ○ The The University of Texas Health Science Center at Houston
- ○ The University of Texas Medical Branch
- ○ University of West Los Angeles
- ○ West Suburban College of Nursing
- ○ William Carey College

FUN FACT

Excelsior College prides itself on accommodating the needs of nontraditional students—to that end, the school has no residency requirement.

Moving to the Big Time

Two-year colleges from which students transfer at the highest rates to top-tier colleges

- ○ Blinn College
- ○ Deep Springs College
- ○ Kilgore College
- ○ Miami Dade Community College
- ○ Minneapolis Community and Tech College
- ○ New Mexico Military Institute
- ○ Orange Coast College
- ○ Pasadena City College
- ○ Santa Monica College
- ○ Simon's Rock College of Bard
- ○ Vista Community College

Test-Free Admissions

Schools that don't require the SAT/ACT for admission

- ○ Alberta College of Art & Design
- ○ Allentown Business School
- ○ American Academy for Dramatic Arts—East
- ○ American Academy for Dramatic Arts—West
- ○ Argosy University—Chicago

- ○ Arizona State University—Polytechnic Campus
- ○ Arkansas Baptist College
- ○ Arlington Baptist College
- ○ Art Institute of Atlanta
- ○ The Art Institute of Dallas
- ○ The Art Institute of Pittsburgh
- ○ The Art Institute of Washington
- ○ Barber Scotia College
- ○ Bard College
- ○ Bates College
- ○ Beacon College
- ○ Bellevue University
- ○ Berkeley College
- ○ Berkeley College—New York City
- ○ Berkeley College—Westchester
- ○ Bluefield State College
- ○ Boston Architectural Center
- ○ Boston Conservatory
- ○ Bowdoin College
- ○ Brandon University
- ○ Brooks Institute of Photography
- ○ Broome Community College
- ○ Brown College
- ○ California College for Health Sciences
- ○ California College of the Arts
- ○ Calumet College of Saint Joseph

- Cameron University
- Carlos Albizu University
- Cazenovia College
- Central Pennsylvania College
- Charter Oak State College
- Chatham College
- City University
- City University of New York—The College of Staten Island
- City University of New York—Hostos Community College

FUN FACT

The Rachel Carson Institute at **Chatham College**, named for the famed zoologist and biologist, offers curricula that focus on leadership roles for women in the field of environmental preservation and understanding.

- City University of New York—John Jay College of Criminal Justice
- City University of New York—Kingsborough Community College

- City University of New York—LaGuardia Community College
- City University of New York—Medgar Evers College
- City University of New York—Queensborough Community College
- Cogswell Polytechnical College
- The College of the Atlantic
- College of the Holy Cross
- Collins College
- Colorado Technical University
- Columbia College—Chicago
- Columbia College—Hollywood
- Columbia International University
- Cornish College of the Arts
- Davenport University—Kalamazoo
- DeVry Institute of Technology—Long Island City, NY
- DeVry University—Addison, IL
- DeVry University—Alpharetta, GA
- DeVry University—Bethesda
- DeVry University—Charlotte
- DeVry University—Chicago
- DeVry University—Colorado Springs, CO
- DeVry University—Columbus, OH
- DeVry University—Crystal City

- ○ DeVry University—Decatur, GA
- ○ DeVry University—Fremont, CA
- ○ DeVry University—Houston
- ○ DeVry University—Irving, TX
- ○ DeVry University—Kansas City, MO
- ○ DeVry University—Las Vegas
- ○ DeVry University—Long Beach, CA
- ○ DeVry University—Milwaukee
- ○ DeVry University—Miramar
- ○ DeVry University—North Brunswick, NJ
- ○ DeVry University—Orlando, FL
- ○ DeVry University—Philadelphia
- ○ DeVry University—Phoenix, AZ
- ○ DeVry University—Pomona, CA
- ○ DeVry University—Portland
- ○ DeVry University—Seattle
- ○ DeVry University—Tinley Park
- ○ DeVry University—West Hills, CA
- ○ DeVry University—Westminster
- ○ Dickinson College
- ○ Doane College
- ○ Dowling College
- ○ Drew University
- ○ Eastman School of Music— University of Rochester
- ○ Eugene Bible College
- ○ Florida Metropolitan University— Melbourne
- ○ Gibbs College
- ○ Gibbs College—Norwalk
- ○ Globe Institute of Technology
- ○ Goddard College
- ○ Golden Gate University
- ○ Goldey-Beacom College
- ○ Hamilton College
- ○ Hampshire College
- ○ Harrington College of Design
- ○ Hartwick College
- ○ Hebrew Union College—Jewish Institute of Religion
- ○ Herkimer County Community College
- ○ Herzing College
- ○ Hilbert College
- ○ Inter American University of Puerto Rico—Aguadilla
- ○ International Academy of Design & Technology—Tampa
- ○ International College
- ○ The Juilliard School
- ○ Juniata College
- ○ Katharine Gibbs School— Piscataway
- ○ Knox College
- ○ Lake Region State College

- Laura and Alvin Siegal College of Judaic Studies
- Lawrence University
- Lincoln University (CA)
- Lincoln University (MO)
- Lindsey Wilson College
- Loma Linda University
- Louisiana State University in Shreveport
- Lyme Academy of Fine Arts
- Manhattan School of Music
- Mannes College—The New School for Music
- Marygrove College
- Marymount College (CA)
- McGill University
- Memorial University of Newfoundland

FUN FACT

In 1974, Anne Waldman and Allen Ginsberg founded the Jack Kerouac School of Disembodied Poetics at **Naropa University**.

- Metropolitan College of New York
- Miles College

- Miles Community College
- Milwaukee Institute of Art and Design
- Mississippi University for Women
- Morrisville State College
- Mount Allison University
- Naropa University
- National American University
- National American Unversity (NM)
- National-Louis University
- New England College
- The New School for Jazz & Contemporary Music
- New World School of the Arts
- Northern State University
- Northwestern Michigan College
- Oakland University
- Ohio University—Chillecothe
- Onondaga Community College
- Oregon College of Art and Craft
- Pacific Northwest College of Art
- Pacific Oaks College
- Pitzer College
- Post University
- Purdue University—North Central
- Reformed Bible College
- Ringling School of Art & Design
- Rust College

- Sarah Lawrence College
- Seton Hill University
- Shawnee State University
- Sheldon Jackson College
- Shimer College
- Southeastern University
- Southern Maine Community College
- St. Lawrence University
- State University of New York—Empire State College
- State University of New York—Sullivan County Community College
- State University of New York—Upstate Medical University
- Stephens College
- Strayer University
- Susquehanna University
- Teikyo Loretto Heights University
- Thomas More College of Liberal Arts
- Tougaloo College
- Touro College
- Trinity (Washington) University
- Troy University Montgomery
- UM College of Technology
- Unity College
- University of Arizona

- University of Baltimore
- The University of British Columbia
- University of Central Texas
- University of the District of Columbia
- University of Great Falls
- University of Maine—Farmington
- University of Maine—Fort Kent
- University of Manitoba
- University of Mary
- University of Nevada—Las Vegas
- The University of Texas at Brownsville
- University of Victoria
- University of Waterloo
- Vanguard University of Southern California
- Villa Maria College of Buffalo
- Wadhams Hall Seminary College
- Wayne State College
- Weber State University
- Wesley College (DE)
- Westwood College of Technology
- Wheaton College (MA)
- Wilmington College (DE)

2400, Here They Come!

Schools whose incoming freshmen have the highest SAT scores

- ○ Amherst College
- ○ Brown University
- ○ California Institute of Technology
- ○ Carleton College
- ○ Columbia University
- ○ Dartmouth College
- ○ Deep Springs College
- ○ Duke University
- ○ Eastern Washington University
- ○ Franklin W. Olin College of Engineering
- ○ Harvard College
- ○ Harvey Mudd College
- ○ Howard University
- ○ Johns Hopkins University
- ○ Massachusetts Institute of Technology
- ○ Northwestern University
- ○ Pomona College
- ○ Princeton University
- ○ Rice University
- ○ Stanford University
- ○ Swarthmore College

- ○ University of Chicago
- ○ University of Pennsylvania
- ○ Washington University in St. Louis
- ○ Williams College
- ○ Yale University

36 Never Sounded So Good

Schools whose incoming freshmen have the highest ACT scores

- ○ Amherst College
- ○ Brandeis University
- ○ Brown University
- ○ Carleton College
- ○ Carnegie Mellon University
- ○ Case Western Reserve University
- ○ Claremont McKenna College
- ○ Colby College
- ○ Colgate University
- ○ College of William & Mary
- ○ Colorado College
- ○ Columbia University
- ○ Cornell University
- ○ Dartmouth College
- ○ Davidson College
- ○ Duke University

- Eastern University
- Eastern Washington University
- Emory University
- Franklin W. Olin College of Engineering
- Georgetown University
- Grinnell College
- Harvard College
- Howard University
- Illinois Wesleyan University
- Johns Hopkins University
- Kalamazoo College
- Kenyon College
- Louisiana State University
- Macalester College
- Marlboro College
- Massachusetts Institute of Technology
- Middlebury College
- New York University
- Northwestern University
- Oberlin College
- Pomona College
- Reed College
- Rice University
- Rose-Hulman Institute of Technology
- Scripps College
- Smith College
- St. John's College (NM)
- Stanford University
- Trinity University
- Tufts University
- Tulane University
- United States Merchant Marine Academy
- University of Chicago
- University of Illinois at Urbana-Champaign
- University of Michigan—Ann Arbor
- The University of North Carolina at Chapel Hill
- University of Notre Dame
- University of Pennsylvania
- University of Southern California
- Vanderbilt University
- Vassar College
- Washington and Lee University
- Washington University in St. Louis
- Wellesley College
- Wesleyan University
- Wheaton College (IL)
- Whitman College
- Williams College
- Yale University

Feel Like One in a Million

Schools with the highest admissions selectivity ratings (as determined by first-years' standardized test scores, class ranks, and high school GPAs; percentages of out-of-state first-years; and percentages of accepted applicants)

○ Amherst College
○ Bard College

FUN FACT

When choosing a major, all students at **Bard College** go through "Moderation," for which they submit a body of work for review to the department of their choice. The department faculty members then interview and evaluate the student.

○ Barnard College
○ Bates College
○ Boston College
○ Bowdoin College

○ Brandeis University
○ Brown University
○ Bryn Mawr College
○ Bucknell University
○ California Institute of Technology
○ Carleton College
○ Carnegie Mellon University
○ Claremont McKenna College
○ Colby College
○ Colgate University
○ College of William & Mary
○ Columbia University
○ Cornell University
○ Dartmouth College
○ Davidson College
○ Deep Springs College
○ Duke University
○ Emory University
○ Franklin W. Olin College of Engineering
○ Georgetown University
○ Grinnell College
○ Grove City College
○ Hamilton College
○ Harvard College
○ Harvey Mudd College
○ Haverford College

- ○ Johns Hopkins University
- ○ Kenyon College
- ○ Lafayette College
- ○ Lehigh University
- ○ Macalester College
- ○ Massachusetts Institute of Technology
- ○ Middlebury College
- ○ New York University
- ○ Northwestern University
- ○ Oberlin College
- ○ Pepperdine University
- ○ Pomona College
- ○ Princeton University
- ○ Reed College
- ○ Rice University
- ○ Scripps College
- ○ Stanford University
- ○ Swarthmore College
- ○ Tufts University
- ○ United States Air Force Academy
- ○ United States Coast Guard Academy
- ○ United States Military Academy
- ○ United States Naval Academy
- ○ University of California—Berkeley
- ○ University of California—Davis
- ○ University of California—Irvine
- ○ University of California—Los Angeles
- ○ University of California—San Diego
- ○ University of Chicago
- ○ University of Miami
- ○ University of Michigan—Ann Arbor
- ○ The University of North Carolina at Chapel Hill
- ○ University of Notre Dame
- ○ University of Pennsylvania
- ○ University of Richmond
- ○ University of Rochester
- ○ University of Southern California
- ○ University of Virginia
- ○ Vassar College
- ○ Wake Forest University
- ○ Washington and Lee University
- ○ Washington University in St. Louis
- ○ Webb Institute
- ○ Wellesley College
- ○ Wesleyan University
- ○ Whitman College
- ○ Williams College
- ○ Yale University

(Relatively) Breezy Admissions

Schools with the lowest admissions selectivity ratings (as determined by first-years' standardized test scores, class ranks, and high school GPAs; percentages of out-of-state first-years; and percentages of accepted applicants)

- Angelo State University
- Anna Maria College
- Arkansas Baptist College
- The Art Institute of California— San Francisco
- Barber Scotia College
- Berkeley College
- California State University— California Maritime Academy

FUN FACT

PAL, the Program for Advancement of Learning at **Curry College**, is designed to help students with language-based disabilities by offering weekly tutoring sessions and allowing untimed tests.

- Cameron University
- Cincinnati Bible College and Seminary
- City University of New York— Medgar Evers College
- Cleveland State University
- College of St. Joseph in Vermont
- Colorado State University—Pueblo
- Concordia College (NY)
- Curry College
- Dickinson State University
- Dowling College
- Eastern Illinois University
- Edinboro University of Pennsylvania
- Eugene Bible College
- Fairmont State College
- Gratz College
- Hilbert College
- Huston-Tillotson University
- Indiana Institute of Technology
- Indiana University East
- Indiana University—Northwest
- Indiana University—South Bend
- Indiana University—Southeast
- Indiana University—Kokomo
- Iowa Wesleyan College
- Jarvis Christian College
- Johnson State College

- Kendall College of Art and Design of Ferris State University
- Madonna University
- Massachusetts Maritime Academy
- Metropolitan College of New York
- Miles Community College
- Milwaukee Institute of Art and Design
- Minnesota State University—Moorhead
- Minnesota State University—Mankato
- Missouri Southern State University—Joplin
- Missouri Western State College
- Morris College
- Mount Senario College
- National-Louis University
- Neumann College
- Niagara County Community College
- North Carolina Central University
- North Carolina Wesleyan College
- Northwest Missouri State University
- The Ohio State University—Lima
- The Ohio State University—Mansfield
- The Ohio State University—Marion
- Ohio University—Zanesville
- Philander Smith College
- Prairie View A&M University
- Purdue University—Calumet
- Robert Morris College (IL)
- Saint Mary's College of Ave Maria University (MI)
- Saint Paul's College
- San Francisco State University
- Shawnee State University
- State University of New York—Broome Community College
- State University of New York—Cobleskill
- Sul Ross State University
- University of Maine—Fort Kent
- The University of Montana—Western
- University of New Hampshire at Manchester
- The University of Texas at San Antonio
- University of Wisconsin—Parkside
- Upper Iowa University
- Vaughn College of Aeronautics and Technology
- Villa Maria College of Buffalo
- Wadhams Hall Seminary College
- Winston-Salem State University
- Youngstown State University

Many Get In

Schools with the highest acceptance rates

- Academy of Art University (formerly The San Francisco Academy)
- Alaska Bible College
- American University of Puerto Rico
- Angelo State University
- Arkansas Baptist College
- Arlington Baptist College
- The Art Institute of California—

FUN FACT

Cameron University is the only college in Oklahoma to offer not only bachelor's and master's degrees, but also associate's degrees.

San Francisco
- The Art Institute of California— San Diego
- The Art Institute of Los Angeles— Orange County
- The Art Institutes International— Portland
- Auburn University—Montgomery

- Baker College of Muskegon
- Baker College of Owosso
- Baltimore Hebrew University
- Benedictine College
- Birmingham-Southern College
- Bluefield State College
- Boise Bible College
- Bryn Athyn College of the New Church
- Calvary Bible College and Theological Seminary
- Calvin College
- Cameron University
- Chaminade University of Honolulu
- Cincinnati Bible College and Seminary
- City University
- Clear Creek Baptist Bible College
- Colorado Mountain College— Alpine Campus
- Colorado Mountain College— Spring Valley
- Colorado Mountain College— Timberline Campus
- Conception Seminary College
- City University of New York—The College of Staten Island
- City University of New York— Medgar Evers College

- City University of New York—Queensborough Community College
- City University of New York—LaGuardia Community College
- Dakota State University
- Davenport University
- Dawson Community College
- Dickinson State University
- The Evergreen State College
- Fairmont State College
- Franklin University
- Freed-Hardeman University
- Gibbs College
- Glenville State College
- Herkimer County Community College
- Hope International University
- Huston-Tillotson University
- Indiana University—Purdue University Fort Wayne
- International College
- Jamestown College
- Jarvis Christian College
- Jones International University
- Lake Region State College
- Lincoln University (CA)
- Luther Rice Bible College and Seminary
- Lyme Academy of Fine Arts
- Lyndon State College
- Marycrest International University
- Marylhurst University
- McNeese State University
- Miles Community College
- Minot State University—Bottineau Campus
- Missouri Southern State University—Joplin
- Missouri Western State College
- Montana State University, College of Technology—Great Falls
- Montana State University—Billings
- Montana State University—Northern
- Montana Tech of the University of Montana
- Mountain State University
- National University
- National-Louis University
- Neumann College
- New School of Architecture and Design
- Niagara County Community College
- North Central University
- Northwestern Oklahoma State University

- ○ Notre Dame de Namur University
- ○ Oakland City University
- ○ The Ohio State University—Lima
- ○ The Ohio State University—Mansfield
- ○ The Ohio State University—Marion
- ○ The Ohio State University—Newark
- ○ Ohio University—Zanesville
- ○ Oklahoma Christian University
- ○ Our Lady of Holy Cross College
- ○ Ozark Christian College
- ○ Pacific States University
- ○ Piedmont Baptist College
- ○ Pikeville College
- ○ Purdue University—Calumet
- ○ Reedley College
- ○ Saint Joseph Seminary College
- ○ Salem International University
- ○ Shasta Bible College
- ○ Shawnee State University

- ○ Sheldon Jackson College
- ○ Southern University and Agricultural and Mechanical College
- ○ St. Charles Borromeno Seminary
- ○ State University of New York—Canton
- ○ Texas A&M University—Galveston
- ○ Texas A&M University—Kingsville
- ○ Texas College
- ○ Thomas University (GA)
- ○ Tougaloo College
- ○ Trinity Bible College
- ○ Troy University Montgomery
- ○ University of Houston—Downtown
- ○ University of Maryland—University College
- ○ University of Montana—Helena College of Technology
- ○ The University of Montana—Western
- ○ University of Phoenix
- ○ University of Regina
- ○ University of Sioux Falls
- ○ The University of Texas at Brownsville
- ○ The University of Texas at El Paso

FUN FACT

Have you ever wanted to run a town? Every mayor of Topeka, Kansas since 1989 was a graduate of **Washburn University**.

Let me guess . . . Poli Sci 101?

A Few Good Men and Women

Schools with the lowest acceptance rates

- Amherst College
- Bard College
- Barnard College
- Bates College
- Berea College
- Boston College
- Bowdoin College
- Brigham Young University—Hawaii
- Brown University
- California Institute of Technology
- California Institute of the Arts
- California State Polytechnic University—Pomona
- California State University—Dominguez Hills
- California State University—San Bernardino
- Carleton College
- City University of New York—Baruch College
- City University of New York—York College
- Claremont McKenna College
- Cleveland Institute of Music
- Colgate University
- The College of the Ozarks
- College of William & Mary
- Columbia University
- The Cooper Union for the Advancement of Science and Art
- Cornell University
- Dartmouth College
- Davidson College
- Deep Springs College
- Delta State University
- Duke University
- Eastman School of Music—University of Rochester
- Emily Carr Institute of Art and Design
- Flagler College
- Franklin W. Olin College of Engineering
- Georgetown University
- Harvard College
- Haverford College
- The Juilliard School
- Lane College
- Laura and Alvin Siegal College of Judaic Studies
- LeMoyne-Owen College
- Mannes College—The New School for Music

- Massachusetts Institute of Technology
- Middlebury College
- Mississippi Valley State University
- Northwestern University
- Pacific Union College
- Pomona College
- Princeton University
- Reinhardt College
- Rice University
- Ringling School of Art & Design
- Rutgers, The State University of New Jersey—College of Nursing
- Rutgers, The State University of New Jersey—Mason Gross School of the Arts
- Stanford University
- State University of New York—Purchase College
- Swarthmore College
- Tufts University
- United States Air Force Academy
- United States Coast Guard Academy
- United States Merchant Marine Academy
- United States Military Academy
- United States Naval Academy
- University of California—Berkeley
- University of California—Los Angeles
- University of Notre Dame
- University of Pennsylvania
- University of Southern California
- Vassar College
- Walla Walla College
- Washington and Lee University
- Washington Bible College
- Washington University in St. Louis
- Webb Institute
- Wesleyan University
- Wilberforce University
- Williams College
- Yale University

Get In . . . and Go!

Schools with the highest yields (i.e., percentages of accepted students who enroll)

- Alaska Bible College
- Alberta College of Art & Design
- American University in Dubai
- Arkansas Tech University
- Art Institute of Colorado
- The Art Institute of Pittsburgh
- Auburn University—Montgomery

○ Baker College of Owosso
○ Beulah Heights Bible College
○ Black Hills State University
○ Bryn Athyn College of the New Church
○ Columbia College—Hollywood
○ Conception Seminary College
○ The Culinary Institute of America
○ Davenport University
○ Deep Springs College
○ DeVry University—Addison, IL

FUN FACT

Arkansas Tech University is one of only two schools in the state to have the Accreditation Board for Engineering and Technology grant accreditation to their courses in electrical and mechanical engineering.

○ DeVry University—Westminster
○ East-West University
○ Emily Carr Institute of Art and Design
○ Florida College

○ Gratz College
○ Harding University
○ Heritage Bible College
○ Hillsdale Free Will Baptist College
○ Hope International University
○ Humphreys College
○ Huston-Tillotson University
○ Idaho State University
○ International College
○ Lancaster Bible College
○ Laura and Alvin Siegal College of Judaic Studies
○ Lourdes College
○ Luther Rice Bible College and Seminary
○ Marylhurst University
○ Metropolitan College of Court Reporting
○ Monroe College
○ Montana Tech of the University of Montana
○ Newman University
○ New School of Architecture and Design
○ Oak Hills Christian College
○ Ohio University—Zanesville
○ Oklahoma Panhandle State University

- Pacific States University
- Pontifical College Josephinum
- Saint Joseph Seminary College
- Salish-Kootenai College
- Shasta Bible College
- Southern University and Agricultural and Mechanical College
- St. Charles Borromeo Seminary
- University of Alberta
- University of Phoenix
- University of Tennessee—Knoxville
- Wadhams Hall Seminary College
- Warner Pacific College
- William Carey College
- Williston State College

Get In and Roam

Schools with the lowest yields (i.e., percentages of accepted students who enroll)

- Adelphi University
- Alabama State University
- Alaska Pacific University
- Albertson College of Idaho
- Albright College

- American University
- Arcadia University
- Arkansas Baptist College
- Assumption College
- Averett University
- Barry University
- Beloit College
- Bethel College (KS)
- Bishop's University
- Boston University
- Butler University
- California Institute of the Arts
- California State University—Chico
- California State University—Long Beach
- Capitol College
- Carnegie Mellon University
- Carthage College
- Case Western Reserve University
- Cedar Crest College
- Central State University
- Centre College
- Chicago State University
- City University of New York—Brooklyn College
- City University of New York—Hunter College

- City University of New York— Lehman College
- Clark University
- Coker College
- Colby-Sawyer College
- College of the Southwest
- Concordia College (NY)
- Culver-Stockton College
- Dominican University of California
- Dowling College
- Drew University
- Drexel University
- Emmanuel College
- Fairfield University
- Fordham University
- Franklin Pierce College

FUN FACT

Marietta College's campus is composed of three city blocks in downtown Marietta, Ohio.

- Goucher College
- Hanover College
- Harrington College of Design
- Hartwick College
- Heidelberg College

- Hobart and William Smith Colleges
- Hofstra University
- Hood College
- Humboldt State University
- Indiana Institute of Technology
- Iona College
- Ithaca College
- Johnson & Wales University
- Johnson & Wales University at North Miami
- Johnson & Wales University at Denver
- Kansas Wesleyan University
- Kentucky Wesleyan College
- Knox College
- Lake Forest College
- Lasell College
- Le Moyne College
- Lewis & Clark College
- Livingstone College
- Loyola College in Maryland
- Loyola University—Chicago
- Lynchburg College
- MacMurray College
- Marietta College
- Marquette University
- Marycrest International University
- McDaniel College

230

- Mercer University—Macon
- Merrimack College
- Mount St. Mary's University
- New England College
- Northeastern University
- Occidental College
- Our Lady of the Lake University (OLLU)
- Pace University
- Pennsylvania State University—Harrisburg
- Pitzer College
- Point Park University
- Post University
- Providence College
- Quincy University
- Quinnipiac University
- Randolph-Macon College
- Regis College
- Rhodes College
- Roanoke College
- Roger Williams University
- Rose-Hulman Institute of Technology
- Rust College
- Rutgers, The State University of New Jersey—Camden
- Rutgers, The State University of New Jersey—Newark
- Sacred Heart University
- Saint Anselm College
- Saint Joseph's College (IN)
- Saint Louis University
- Saint Mary's College of California
- Salem International University
- Salve Regina University
- San Diego State University
- San Francisco Art Institute
- San Francisco State University
- San Jose State University
- Santa Clara University
- School of the Museum of Fine Arts
- Seton Hill University
- Sonoma State University
- Southampton College of Long Island University
- St. John's University (NY)
- State University of New York at Binghamton
- State University of New York—The College at Old Westbury
- State University of New York—College at Oneonta
- State University of New York—Cortland
- State University of New York at Geneseo

- State University of New York—New Paltz
- State University of New York—Plattsburgh
- State University of New York University at Albany
- Stonehill College
- Suffolk University
- Talladega College
- Thiel College
- Tiffin University
- Trinity College (CT)

FUN FACT

The **University of San Francisco** is excellently situated in the city, thanks to its location Laurel Hill—beneath it, however, is what was once a cemetery.

- Tri-State University
- Tulane University
- Tusculum College
- United States International University
- University of Bridgeport
- University of California—Davis

- University of California—Irvine
- University of California—Riverside
- University of California—San Diego
- University of California—Santa Barbara
- University of California—Santa Cruz
- University of Charleston
- University of Hartford
- University of the Pacific
- University of Phoenix
- University of Puget Sound
- University of Rhode Island
- University of Rochester
- University of San Diego
- University of San Francisco
- The University of Scranton
- University of Vermont
- Utica College
- Valparaiso University
- Voorhees College
- Washington & Jefferson College
- Wells College
- Western New England College
- Whittier College
- Willamette University
- Wittenberg University
- Xavier University (OH)

Aid Me!

Schools with the highest percentages of students receiving any financial aid

- Alice Lloyd College
- Alma College
- Alvernia College
- Augustana College (IL)
- Baldwin-Wallace College
- Bethany College (KS)
- Briar Cliff University
- Bridgewater College
- Buena Vista University
- Carroll College (WI)
- Cascade College
- Central College
- Coker College
- College Misericordia
- The College of Saint Scholastica
- The College of Wooster
- Dakota Wesleyan University
- Davis & Elkins College
- Denison University
- DePauw University
- Dillard University
- Dordt College
- Fresno Pacific University
- Georgetown College
- Goshen College
- Grand View College
- Hampton University
- Hastings College
- Hood College
- Humphreys College
- Huntingdon College
- Jamestown College
- Jarvis Christian College
- Juniata College
- Lake Erie College
- Lebanon Valley College
- Lyon College
- Maharishi University of Management
- Manchester College
- Maryville College
- Milwaukee School of Engineering
- Monmouth College (IL)
- Morris College
- Muskingum College
- Northwest Nazarene University
- Northwestern College (IA)
- Oak Hills Christian College
- Rose-Hulman Institute of Technology
- Saint Vincent College

- Shorter College
- Spring Hill College
- St. Thomas University
- Tennessee Wesleyan College
- Transylvania University
- University of Mobile
- University of Saint Thomas (MN)
- Webber International University
- Westminster College (MO)
- Wisconsin Lutheran College
- Wittenberg University

Alone (With a Loan?)

Schools with the lowest percentages of students receiving any financial aid

- American Indian College of the Assemblies of God, Inc.
- Amherst College
- Arizona State University—West
- Bates College
- Bowdoin College
- Brandeis University
- Brigham Young University (UT)
- Brock University
- California State University—East Bay
- Cameron University

- Central Michigan University
- Christopher Newport University
- City University
- City University of New York— Queens College
- Cleary University
- Colby College
- Colgate University
- College of Charleston
- Columbia University
- Cornell University
- Eastern Illinois University
- Excelsior College
- Fitchburg State College
- Florida State University
- George Mason University
- Georgetown University
- Georgia College & State University
- Hampden-Sydney College
- Haverford College
- Johns Hopkins University
- Landmark College
- Michigan State University
- Middlebury College
- Missouri Southern State University—Joplin
- The Ohio State University— Columbus

- Otis College of Art & Design
- Pitzer College
- Purdue University—Calumet
- Sam Houston State University
- San Francisco State University
- Savannah College of Art and Design
- Skidmore College
- Sonoma State University
- St. John's College (NM)
- State University of New York—Empire State College
- Stephen F. Austin State University
- Texas State University—San Marcos
- Thomas Edison State College
- Trinity College (CT)
- Troy University
- Tufts University
- University of Chicago
- University of Connecticut
- University of Georgia
- University of Hawaii—Manoa
- University of Illinois at Urbana-Champaign
- University of Kansas
- University of Kentucky
- University of Maryland—Baltimore County
- University of Nebraska—Lincoln
- University of Tennessee—Chattanooga
- The University of Texas at Arlington
- University of Utah
- University of Virginia
- The University of Western Ontario
- University of Wisconsin—Whitewater
- Virginia Polytechnic and State University (Virginia Tech)
- Washington University in St. Louis
- Webb Institute
- Wesleyan University
- Western Carolina University

FUN FACT
Every summer, **Middlebury College** hosts the Breadloaf Writer's Conference, the oldest writer's conference in the United States.

Cha-Bling!

Schools that offer free tuition to all students

- ○ Berea College
- ○ The College of the Ozarks
- ○ The Cooper Union for the Advancement of Science and Art
- ○ Deep Springs College
- ○ Franklin W. Olin College of Engineering
- ○ United States Air Force Academy

FUN FACT

Getting into **Berea College** isn't just a question of grades. Since the school's goal is to cover full tuition for all students, an important criterion for acceptance is your family's income bracket. The less likely they are to be able to pay for your education, the more likely Berea will.

- ○ United States Coast Guard Academy
- ○ United States Merchant Marine Academy

- ○ United States Military Academy
- ○ United States Naval Academy
- ○ Webb Institute

Cha-Ching!

Schools with the highest price tags—private

- ○ Amherst College
- ○ Barnard College
- ○ Boston College
- ○ Boston University
- ○ Bowdoin College
- ○ Brown University
- ○ Bryn Mawr College
- ○ Bucknell University
- ○ Carleton College
- ○ Carnegie Mellon University
- ○ Chapman University
- ○ Claremont McKenna College
- ○ College of the Holy Cross
- ○ Columbia University
- ○ Cornell University
- ○ Dartmouth College
- ○ Dickinson College
- ○ Duke University
- ○ Emory University
- ○ Franklin & Marshall College

○ The George Washington University
○ Georgetown University
○ Hamilton College
○ Hampshire College
○ Haverford College
○ Hobart and William Smith Colleges
○ Lafayette College
○ Landmark College
○ Lehigh University
○ Manhattan School of Music
○ Massachusetts Institute of Technology
○ Mount Holyoke College
○ Northwestern University

Oh . . . she got in . . . that's . . . good news. Right?

- ○ Oberlin College
- ○ Reed College
- ○ Scripps College
- ○ Simon's Rock College of Bard
- ○ Skidmore College
- ○ Smith College
- ○ St. John's College (MD)
- ○ St. John's College (NM)
- ○ Swarthmore College
- ○ Trinity College (CT)
- ○ University of Chicago

FUN FACT

The **University of Pennsylvania** was founded by Benjamin Franklin and helped usher in the United States's first modern liberal arts course of study.

- ○ University of Notre Dame
- ○ University of Pennsylvania
- ○ University of Rochester
- ○ University of Southern California
- ○ Vanderbilt University
- ○ Vassar College
- ○ Wake Forest University

- ○ Washington University in St. Louis
- ○ Wellesley College
- ○ Wesleyan University
- ○ Wheaton College (MA)
- ○ Williams College
- ○ Worcester Polytechnic Institute

Cha-Ching, Part 2

Schools with the highest price tags—public, in-state

- ○ California State University— California Maritime Academy
- ○ The College of New Jersey
- ○ Fort Hays State University
- ○ Massachusetts Maritime Academy
- ○ Miami University
- ○ Montclair State University
- ○ New Jersey Institute of Technology
- ○ The Ohio State University— Columbus
- ○ Pennsylvania State University— Altoona
- ○ Pennsylvania State University— Beaver
- ○ Pennsylvania State University— Berks
- ○ Pennsylvania State University— Erie, The Behrend College

- Pennsylvania State University—Harrisburg
- Pennsylvania State University—Hazleton
- Pennsylvania State University—McKeesport
- Pennsylvania State University—Mont Alto
- Pennsylvania State University—University Park
- Ramapo College of New Jersey
- Richard Stockton College of New Jersey
- Rowan University
- Rutgers, The State University of New Jersey—New Brunswick/Piscataway
- St. Mary's College of Maryland
- State University of New York—College of Environmental Science and Forestry
- Temple University
- The University of Akron
- University of California—Davis
- University of California—Los Angeles
- University of California—Riverside
- University of California—San Diego
- University of California—Santa Cruz
- University of Cincinnati
- University of Connecticut
- University of Illinois at Urbana-Champaign
- University of Maryland—Baltimore County
- University of Maryland—College Park
- University of Massachusetts—Amherst
- University of Michigan—Ann Arbor
- University of Pittsburgh—Bradford
- University of Rhode Island
- University of Toledo
- University of Vermont

Cha-Ching, Part 3

Schools with the highest price tags—public, out-of-state

- Colorado School of Mines
- Indiana University—Bloomington
- Massachusetts Maritime Academy
- Miami University
- Michigan State University
- Michigan Technological University
- The Ohio State University—Columbus

- Oregon State University
- Pennsylvania State University—University Park
- Portland State University
- Rutgers, The State University of New Jersey—New Brunswick/Piscataway
- St. Mary's College of Maryland
- Temple University
- University of California—Davis
- University of California—Los Angeles
- University of California—Riverside
- University of California—San Diego
- University of California—Santa Barbara
- University of California—Santa Cruz
- University of Cincinnati
- University of Colorado—Boulder
- University of Connecticut
- University of Illinois at Urbana-Champaign
- University of Iowa
- University of Maryland—Baltimore County
- University of Michigan—Ann Arbor
- University of Minnesota—Duluth
- University of North Carolina at Greensboro
- University of Pittsburgh—Bradford
- University of Rhode Island
- University of South Carolina—Columbia
- University of Vermont
- University of Virginia
- University of Washington
- University of Wisconsin—Madison

part 2

Alumni

Hail to the Chiefs

Schools from which the greatest number of U.S. presidents received an undergraduate degree

- ○ College of William & Mary (3)
- ○ Harvard College (5)
- ○ Princeton University (2)
- ○ United States Military Academy (2)
- ○ Yale University (3)

Studying With the Stars

Schools famed for having many famous alumni

- ○ Columbia University
- ○ Harvard College
- ○ New York University
- ○ Princeton University
- ○ Stanford University

- ○ United States Military Academy
- ○ United States Naval Academy
- ○ University of California—Los Angeles
- ○ University of Southern California
- ○ Yale University

Giving Back

Schools with especially active alumni associations

- ○ Ball State University
- ○ Brigham Young University
- ○ Central Washington University
- ○ Clemson University
- ○ Colorado State University
- ○ Columbia University
- ○ Duke University
- ○ Florida State University
- ○ Georgia Institute of Technology

- ○ Harvard College
- ○ Massachusetts Institute of Technology
- ○ Northwestern University
- ○ The Ohio State University
- ○ Ohio University
- ○ Oregon State University
- ○ Princeton University
- ○ Stanford University
- ○ Texas A&M University

FUN FACT

On April 21st of every year, Aggies everywhere gather to take part in the "Muster," at which they honor **Texas A&M University** alumni who have died.

- ○ University of Arkansas
- ○ University of California—Berkeley
- ○ University of California—Los Angeles
- ○ University of California—Riverside
- ○ University of California—Santa Cruz
- ○ University of Connecticut
- ○ University of Houston
- ○ University of Illinois
- ○ University of Maryland
- ○ University of Michigan
- ○ University of Missouri
- ○ University of Notre Dame
- ○ University of Oregon
- ○ University of South Florida
- ○ University of Southern California
- ○ Yale University

chapter 7

Life On Campus— Dorms, Food, and Pets

Stephens College has a soft spot for furry friends in dorms, while Hampshire College offers up many a vegetarian-friendly dining option. Indeed, home is where the bunk is—and so we tell you which schools boast high rates of on-campus living, which have fair numbers of students who opt to live off-campus, and which are havens of Greek life. We also divulge where you may find sushi in the dining hall and where you can sip on free-trade coffee while you read the campus paper.

Another part of your campus experience—a large part, in fact—will derive from your peers. We covered their academic profiles in Chapter 6, but the level of diversity at the schools you're considering matters, as well. In this chapter, we tell you which schools have the highest proportions of women, for example (and which among those are classified as women's colleges).

Where you live, what you eat, and with whom you interact are three very important elements of your college experience. Find out what you can expect from the schools on your list.

part 1

Dorm Life

Dorm Me Up, Scotty!

Schools with the highest proportions of students living in university housing

- Agnes Scott College
- Albion College
- Amherst College
- Antioch College
- Asbury College
- Baptist Bible College and Seminary of Pennsylvania
- Bates College
- Beacon College
- Beloit College
- Bennington College
- Bethany College (WV)
- Bowdoin College
- Bryn Mawr College
- California Institute of Technology
- Carleton College
- Centre College
- The Citadel—The Military College of South Carolina
- Claremont McKenna College
- Colby College
- The College of Wooster
- Columbia University
- Conception Seminary College
- Connecticut College
- Cornell College
- Davidson College
- Deep Springs College
- Denison University
- DePauw University
- Dickinson College
- Divine Word College
- Dordt College
- Elmira College
- Emory University—Oxford College
- Erskine College

- ○ Franklin Pierce College
- ○ Franklin W. Olin College of Engineering
- ○ Furman University
- ○ Gettysburg College
- ○ Grove City College
- ○ Hamilton College
- ○ Hampden-Sydney College
- ○ Hampshire College
- ○ Hanover College
- ○ Harvard College
- ○ Harvey Mudd College

FUN FACT

Students at **Beloit College** note that they love theme parties (such as "Come as Another Beloit Student" and "Dress Like Your Celebrity Look-Alike"), and that ultimate Frisbee has an impressive number of participants.

- ○ Haverford College
- ○ Hobart and William Smith Colleges
- ○ Jewish Theological Seminary— Albert A. List College

- ○ Kenyon College
- ○ Knox College
- ○ Lafayette College
- ○ Landmark College
- ○ Lawrence University
- ○ Lincoln University (PA)
- ○ Marietta College
- ○ Martin Luther College
- ○ Massachusetts Institute of Technology
- ○ Massachusetts Maritime Academy
- ○ Middlebury College
- ○ Monmouth College (IL)
- ○ Mount Angel Seminary
- ○ Mount Holyoke College
- ○ Muhlenberg College
- ○ Northeastern University
- ○ Pomona College
- ○ Pontifical College Josephinum
- ○ Presbyterian College
- ○ Princeton University
- ○ Principia College
- ○ Saint John Vianney College Seminary
- ○ Saint John's Seminary College
- ○ Saint Michael's College
- ○ Saint Olaf College
- ○ Scripps College

- Sewanee—The University of the South
- Smith College
- Soka University of America
- South Carolina State University
- Southern Illinois University—Edwardsville
- St. Charles Borromeno Seminary
- St. Lawrence University
- Stanford University
- State University of New York—Maritime College
- Swarthmore College
- Sweet Briar College
- Tabor College
- Thomas Aquinas College
- Thomas More College of Liberal Arts
- Trinity College (CT)
- United States Air Force Academy
- United States Coast Guard Academy
- United States Merchant Marine Academy
- United States Military Academy
- United States Naval Academy
- University of Judaism
- University of Richmond

- Ursinus College
- Vassar College
- Virginia Military Institute
- Warren Wilson College
- Webb Institute
- Wellesley College
- Wesleyan University
- Wheaton College (IL)
- Wheaton College (MA)
- Williams College
- Wofford College

Security Deposit City

Schools with the lowest proportion of students living in university housing

- American Academy for Dramatic Arts—East
- American Conservatory of Music
- Antioch Southern California—Los Angeles
- Argosy University—Chicago
- Arizona State University—West
- Art Academy of Cincinnati
- Art Center College of Design
- Athens State University
- Augusta State University

- Berkeley College
- Bluefield State College
- California State University—Bakersfield
- California State University—Dominguez Hills
- California State University—East Bay
- California State University—Fullerton
- California State University—Los Angeles
- California State University—Sacramento
- Cardinal Stritch College
- Charter Oak State College
- Chicago State University
- City University of New York—Hostos Community College
- City University of New York—Baruch College
- City University of New York—Brooklyn College
- City University of New York—Hunter College
- City University of New York—Lehman College
- City University of New York—Medgar Evers College
- City University of New York—New York City College of Technology
- City University of New York—Queens College
- City University of New York—Queensborough Community College
- City University of New York—York College
- Clarkson College
- Clayton College & State University
- Cleary University
- Cleveland State University
- Colorado State University—Pueblo
- Columbia College—Hollywood
- Concordia University (QC)
- Davenport University
- Davenport University—Kalamazoo Campus
- Davenport University—Western Region
- DeVry University (Phoenix, AZ)
- East-West University
- Excelsior College
- Ferris State University—Kendall College of Art and Design
- Gibbs College
- Golden Gate University
- Governors State University

- Gratz College
- Hawaii Pacific University
- Heritage University
- Holy Family University
- Humphreys College
- Immaculata University College of Lifelong Learning
- Indiana University—Kokomo
- Indiana University-Purdue University Fort Wayne
- Indiana University-Purdue University Indianapolis
- International College
- Laura and Alvin Siegal College of Judaic Studies
- Long Island University—Brooklyn
- Lourdes College
- Madonna University
- Marylhurst University
- Medcenter One College of Nursing
- Medical University of South Carolina
- Mercy College
- Metropolitan College of New York
- Metropolitan State College of Denver
- Montana State University, College of Technology—Great Falls

- Mountain State University
- Naropa University
- National American Unversity (NM)
- National University
- National-Louis University
- New Jersey City University
- NewSchool of Architecture and Design
- Northeastern Illinois University
- The Ohio State University—Lima
- The Ohio State University—Marion
- Ohio University—Zanesville
- Oregon College of Art and Craft
- Our Lady of Holy Cross College
- Pacific Northwest College of Art
- Pacific Oaks College
- Park University
- Pennsylvania State University—Delaware County
- Pennsylvania State University—DuBois
- Pennsylvania State University—Fayette, The Eberly Campus
- Pennsylvania State University—Lehigh Valley
- Pennsylvania State University—Shenango

- Pennsylvania State University—Wilkes-Barre
- Pennsylvania State University—Worthington Scranton
- Pennsylvania State University—York
- Prescott College
- Purdue University—North Central
- Robert Morris College (IL)
- Saint Francis College (NY)
- Saint Joseph Seminary College
- San Francisco Art Institute
- San Francisco Conservatory of Music
- Silver Lake College
- Southeastern University
- Southern California College of Optometry
- Southern California Institute of Architecture
- Southern Maine Community College
- St. Joseph's College—New York (Brooklyn)
- St. Joseph's College—New York (Patchogue)
- State University of New York—Empire State College
- State University of New York—Erie Community College, City Campus
- State University of New York—Erie Community College, North Campus
- State University of New York—Erie Community College, South Campus
- State University of New York—Ulster Community College
- Strayer University
- Trent University
- Troy University Dothan
- Troy University Montgomery
- Union Institute & University
- University College of the Cariboo
- University of Arkansas—Little Rock
- University of Baltimore
- University of Central Texas
- University of Colorado at Denver and Health Sciences Center
- University of the District of Columbia
- University of Hawaii—West Oahu
- University of Houston—Clear Lake
- University of Houston—Downtown
- University of Maine—Augusta
- University of Michigan—Dearborn
- University of Michigan—Flint
- University of Montana—Helena College of Technology
- University of Phoenix
- University of Texas at Brownsville

- University of Texas Health Science Center at Houston
- Villa Maria College of Buffalo
- Wadhams Hall Seminary College
- Walsh College of Accountancy and Business Administration
- Weber State University
- Wilmington College (DE)

Want PSIS With That?

Schools with the greatest rates of participation in Greek life

- Adrian College
- Albion College
- Albright College
- Allegheny College
- Athens State University
- Auburn University
- Austin College
- Baker University—College of Arts & Sciences
- Bethany College (WV)
- Birmingham-Southern College
- Bradley University
- Bucknell University
- Butler University
- Case Western Reserve University
- Centenary College of Louisiana
- Centre College
- Clearwater Christian College
- Colgate University
- College of William & Mary
- Cornell College
- Cornell University
- Culver-Stockton College
- Dartmouth College
- Denison University
- DePauw University
- Doane College
- Drake University
- Drury University
- Duke University
- Elon University
- Emory University
- Eureka College
- Fairleigh Dickinson University—College at Florham
- Franklin College
- Furman University
- Georgetown College
- Gettysburg College
- Hanover College
- Harding University
- Hillsdale College
- Illinois Wesleyan University

- Kettering University
- Lafayette College
- Lambuth University
- Lehigh University
- LeMoyne-Owen College
- Lenoir-Rhyne College
- Linfield College
- Massachusetts Institute of Technology
- Millsaps College
- Missouri Valley College
- Newberry College
- Northwestern University
- Oglethorpe University
- Ohio Valley University
- Ohio Wesleyan University
- Oklahoma Christian University
- Otterbein College
- Ouachita Baptist University
- Parks College of Saint Louis University
- Phillips University
- Presbyterian College
- Randolph-Macon College
- Rensselaer Polytechnic Institute
- Rhodes College
- Rockhurst University
- Rollins College
- Rose-Hulman Institute of Technology
- Samford University
- Savannah State University
- Sewanee—The University of the South
- Simpson College (IA)
- Southern Methodist University
- Southwestern University
- Stetson University
- Stevens Institute of Technology
- Texas Christian University
- Transylvania University
- Trinity University
- Truman State University
- Tulane University
- Union College (NY)
- University of Richmond
- University of Rio Grande
- University of Virginia
- Upper Iowa University
- Vanderbilt University
- Voorhees College
- Wabash College
- Wake Forest University
- Washington & Jefferson College

- ○ Washington University in St. Louis
- ○ West Virginia Wesleyan College
- ○ Westminster College (MO)
- ○ Westminster College (PA)
- ○ Whitman College
- ○ Wiley College
- ○ Willamette University
- ○ William Jewell College
- ○ William Woods University
- ○ Wofford College
- ○ Worcester Polytechnic Institute

Student's Pet

Schools that allow pets—besides fish—in (some) dormitories

- ○ California Institute of Technology
- ○ Case Western Reserve University
- ○ Eckerd College
- ○ Massachusetts Institute of Technology
- ○ State University of New York—Canton
- ○ Stephens College
- ○ University of Pennsylvania (birds)

part 2

Eating In

How Have You Bean?

Schools that offer free-trade coffee in the dining hall/student center

- Albertson College
- American University
- Anderson University
- Antioch College
- Baylor University
- Biola University
- Boston College
- Boston University
- Brandeis University
- Case Western Reserve University
- Clark University
- Connecticut College
- Cornell University
- Drury University
- Eckerd College
- Emmanuel College
- Gallaudet University
- Georgetown University
- Goucher College
- Grove City College
- Hamilton College
- Harvard College
- Hobart and William Smith Colleges
- Idaho State University
- Ithaca College
- Lehigh University
- Lewis and Clark College
- Livingston College
- Loyola University—Chicago
- Massachusetts Institute of Technology
- Milligan College
- North Greenville College
- Northwestern University

- Otterbein College
- Point Loma Nazarene
- Saint Mary's College
- St. Joseph College (CT)
- St. Joseph's College of Maine
- University of California—Berkeley
- University of California—Davis
- University of California—Los Angeles
- University of California—San Diego
- University of California—Santa Cruz
- University of Connecticut
- University of Illinois at Chicago
- University of Iowa
- University of Minnesota—Twin Cities
- University of New Hampshire
- University of Notre Dame
- University of Puget Sound
- University of Rochester
- University of Washington
- Valparaiso University
- Wheaton College
- Yale University

Fresh Fish

Schools that serve sushi in the dining hall

- Brigham Young University (UT)
- College of William & Mary
- DePaul University
- Johns Hopkins University
- Massachusetts Institute of Technology
- Northeastern University
- Oberlin College
- The Ohio State University
- Princeton University
- Roger Williams University
- San Francisco State University
- Stanford University
- Union College
- University of Arizona
- University of California—Los Angeles
- University of California—Riverside
- University of Central Florida
- University of Hawaii—Manoa
- University of Kansas
- University of Louisiana at Monroe
- University of Maryland
- University of Michigan
- University of Pennsylvania

- University of Southern California
- University of Texas at Austin
- University of Vermont
- Wesleyan University
- Western Carolina University
- Yale University

Herbivore's Delight

Schools with many vegetarian/vegan-friendly options

- Bennington College
- Bowdoin College
- The College of Wooster
- Columbia University
- Connecticut College
- Cornell University
- Elmira College
- Hampshire College
- Indiana University
- New York University
- Oberlin College
- Smith College
- Stanford University
- Temple University
- University of California—Berkeley
- University of California—Santa Cruz
- University of Maryland—College Park
- University of Oregon
- University of Pennsylvania
- University of Texas at Austin
- Vassar College
- Virginia Polytechnic and State University (Virginia Tech)
- Wesleyan University

part 3

Student Body

To Have and To Hold

Students with the highest proportions of married students

- Abilene Christian University
- Brigham Young University (UT)
- Harding University
- University of Utah
- Ursinus College

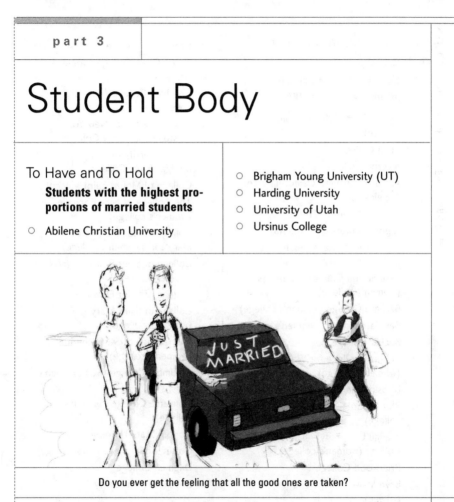

Do you ever get the feeling that all the good ones are taken?

Double X (Chromosomes, That Is!)

Schools with the greatest proportions of women

- Agnes Scott College (women's college)
- Allen College
- Alverno College
- Antioch Southern California—Los Angeles
- Aquinas College (TN)
- Argosy University—Atlanta
- The Art Institute of Boston at Lesley University
- Assumption College for Sisters (women's college)
- Barnard College (women's college)
- Bay Path College (women's college)
- Becker College
- Bennett College for Women (women's college)
- Blessing-Rieman College of Nursing
- Blue Mountain College (women's college)
- Brenau University—The Women's College (women's college)
- Briarwood College
- Bryn Mawr College (women's college)

- Cazenovia College
- Cedar Crest College (women's college)
- Chatham College (women's college)
- City University of New York—Hostos Community College
- City University of New York—Medgar Evers College
- College of Mount Saint Vincent
- The College of New Rochelle (women's college)
- College of Notre Dame of Maryland (women's college)
- College of Saint Benedict (MN) (women's college)
- College of Saint Elizabeth
- College of Saint Mary (NE) (women's college)
- The College of St. Catherine (women's college)
- Columbia College (SC) (women's college)
- Converse College (women's college)
- Coppin State University
- Cottey College (women's college)
- Daemen College
- Davenport University

- Davenport University—Kalamazoo
- Deaconess College of Nursing
- Dillard University
- Dominican University of California
- D'Youville College
- Elms College
- Emmanuel College
- Felician College
- Fontbonne University
- Georgia Baptist College of Nursing
- Georgian Court University (women's college)
- Goldey-Beacom College
- Gratz College
- Gwynedd-Mercy College
- Hollins University (women's college)
- Holy Family University
- Holy Names College
- Hood College (women's college)
- Humphreys College
- John F. Kennedy University
- Judson College (AL) (women's college)
- Laboratory Institute of Merchandising
- Lexington College (women's college)
- Lesley College
- Lourdes College
- Madonna University
- Mary Baldwin College (women's college)
- Marygrove College
- Marylhurst University
- Marymount Manhattan College
- Marymount University
- Maryville University of Saint Louis
- Medcenter One College of Nursing
- Medical College of Georgia
- Medical University of South Carolina
- Meredith College (women's college)
- Metropolitan College of Court Reporting
- Metropolitan College of New York
- Midway College (women's college)
- Mills College (women's college)
- Mississippi University for Women
- Molloy College
- Moore College of Art & Design (women's college)
- Mount Holyoke College (women's college)
- Mount Mary College

- Mount Saint Mary's College (CA) (women's college)
- Mount Saint Vincent University
- National American University—Denver
- Nazareth College of Rochester
- Nebraska Methodist College
- New York School of Interior Design
- Our Lady of Holy Cross College
- Our Lady of the Lake University (OLLU)
- Pacific Oaks College
- Parsons—The New School for Design
- Peace College (women's college)
- Pine Manor College (women's college)
- Presentation College
- Queens University of Charlotte
- Randolph College (women's college)
- Regis College (women's college)
- Rivier College
- Rosemont College (women's college)
- Rush University
- Russell Sage College (women's college)
- Saint Anthony College of Nursing
- Saint Joseph College (CT) (women's college)
- Saint Mary-of-the-Woods College (women's college)
- Saint Mary's College (IN) (women's college)
- Salem College (women's college)
- Samuel Merritt College
- Scripps College (women's college)
- Simmons College (women's college)
- Smith College (women's college)
- Sojourner Douglass College
- South College
- Southwestern Christian University
- Spelman College (women's college)
- St. John's College—Department of Nursing (IL)
- St. Joseph's College—New York (Brooklyn)
- St. Joseph's College—New York (Patchogue)
- State University of New York—Upstate Medical University
- Stephens College (women's college)
- Sweet Briar College (women's college)
- Texas Woman's University

- Thomas Jefferson University
- Trinity University (Washington, DC) (women's college)
- University of Colorado at Denver and Health Sciences Center— Health Sciences Program
- University of Houston—Victoria
- University of Maine—Augusta
- University of Nebraska Medical Center
- University of New England
- The University of Texas Health Science Center at Houston
- University of Texas Medical Branch at Galveston
- University of the Virgin Islands
- Ursuline College (women's college)
- Webster University
- Wellesley College (women's college)
- Wells College
- Wesleyan College (women's college)
- West Suburban College of Nursing
- Wheelock College
- William Woods University
- Wilson College (women's college)
- Xavier University of Louisiana

XY Havens

Schools with the greatest proportions of men

- California State University— California Maritime Academy
- Capitol College
- The Citadel—The Military College of South Carolina
- Clarkson University
- Clear Creek Baptist Bible College
- Cogswell Polytechnic College
- Colorado School of Mines
- Conception Seminary College (men's college)
- Daniel Webster College
- Deep Springs College (men's college)
- DeVry Institute of Technology— Long Island City, NY
- DeVry University—Columbus, OH
- DeVry University—North Brunswick, NJ
- DeVry University—Philadelphia
- DeVry University—Phoenix, AZ
- DeVry University—Pomona, CA
- DeVry University—Seattle
- DeVry University—Westminster

- Dominican School of Philosophy and Theology
- Embry Riddle Aeronautical University (AZ)
- Embry Riddle Aeronautical University (FL)
- Emmanuel Bible College
- Hampden-Sydney College (men's college)
- Henry Cogswell College
- Heritage Bible College
- Holy Apostles College and Seminary
- Illinois Institute of Technology
- Kettering University
- Landmark College
- Lawrence Technological University
- LeMoyne-Owen College
- Lock Haven University of Pennsylvania
- Luther Rice Bible College and Seminary
- Maine Maritime Academy
- Massachusetts Maritime Academy
- Michigan Technological University
- Milwaukee School of Engineering
- Morehouse College (men's college)
- Neumont University
- New Jersey Institute of Technology
- The New School for Jazz & Contemporary Music
- Pacific States University
- Polytechnic University—Brooklyn
- Pontifical College Josephinum (men's college)
- Rensselaer Polytechnic Institute
- Rose-Hulman Institute of Technology
- Saint John's University (MN) (men's college)
- South Dakota School of Mines & Technology
- Southern Christian University
- Southern Polytechnic State University
- St. Charles Borromeno Seminary (men's college)
- State University of New York—Maritime College
- Stevens Institute of Technology
- United States Air Force Academy
- United States Merchant Marine Academy
- United States Military Academy
- United States Naval Academy
- University of Missouri—Rolla
- Vaughn College of Aeronautics and Technology

- Virginia Military Institute
- Wabash College (men's college)
- Wadhams Hall Seminary College
- Webb Institute
- Wentworth Institute of Technology
- Westwood Aviation Institute—Houston
- Worcester Polytechnic Institute

Global Communities

Schools with the greatest proportions of international students

- Academy of Art University (formerly The San Francisco Academy)
- Alliant International University
- American InterContinental University
- Andrews University
- Art Center College of Design
- Babson College
- Berkeley College—New York City
- Berklee College of Music
- Beulah Heights Bible College
- Brigham Young University (HI)
- Brooks Institute of Photography
- Bryn Athyn College of the New Church

- Carnegie Mellon University
- City University of New York—Baruch College
- City University of New York—Borough of Manhattan Community College
- City University of New York—Kingsborough Community College
- City University of New York—LaGuardia Community College
- City University of New York—Queensborough Community College
- Cleveland Institute of Music
- The College of the Atlantic
- Concordia College (NY)
- The Cooper Union for the

FUN FACT

Andrews University has 885 international students hailing from 98 countries.

Advancement of Science and Art
- DeVry University—Charlotte
- DeVry University—Milwaukee
- Dominican School of Philosophy and Theology

- Eastman School of Music—University of Rochester
- East-West University
- Florida Institute of Technology
- Fort Hays State University
- Gallaudet University
- Grinnell College
- Hebrew College
- Hellenic College
- Illinois Institute of Technology
- The Juilliard School
- La Roche College
- Lake Superior State University
- Lincoln University (CA)
- Loma Linda University
- Macalester College
- Maharishi University of Management
- Manhattan School of Music
- Mannes College—The New School for Music
- Marymount College (CA)
- McGill University
- Monterey Institute of International Studies
- Mount Holyoke College
- National American University—Denver
- New England Conservatory of Music
- The New School for Jazz & Contemporary Music
- Northwood University (FL)
- Oklahoma City University
- Otis College of Art & Design
- Parsons—The New School for Design
- Principia College
- Rhode Island School of Design
- Saint Francis College (NY)
- Saint Mary's College of Ave Maria University (MI)
- Salem International University
- San Francisco Conservatory of Music
- St. John's University—School of Risk Management, Insurance and Actuarial Science
- School of the Art Institute of Chicago
- School of Visual Arts
- Soka University of America
- Southeastern University
- Union College (NE)
- United States International University
- University of Bridgeport

- University of Hawaii—Hilo
- University of New England
- University of the District of Columbia
- University of the Ozarks
- Wadhams Hall Seminary College
- Webber International University
- Wesleyan College

In a Different State

Schools with the highest out-of-state student populations

- American University
- Amherst College
- Armstrong University
- The Art Institute of Dallas
- Bates College
- Beloit College
- Bennington College
- Berklee College of Music
- Boston University
- Bowdoin College
- Brown University
- Bryant University
- Bryn Mawr College
- The Catholic University of America
- Colby College
- Colorado College
- Columbia University
- Connecticut College
- Dartmouth College
- Davidson College
- Deep Springs College
- Divine Word College
- Don Bosco College
- Duke University
- Eastman School of Music—University of Rochester
- Excelsior College
- Franklin Pierce College
- Franklin W. Olin College of Engineering
- Gallaudet University

FUN FACT

Deep Springs College is located on a self-sustaining cattle ranch and alfalfa farm in California's High Desert. The 27 male undergrads who comprise the student body appreciate the small student-to-faculty ratio (4:1) and full tuition scholarships that they all receive.

- The George Washington University
- Georgetown University
- Goddard College
- Green Mountain College
- Hampshire College
- Harvard College
- Haverford College
- Hellenic College
- Johns Hopkins University
- The Juilliard School
- Landmark College
- Loyola College in Maryland
- Marlboro College
- Martin Luther College
- Maryland Institute College of Art
- Massachusetts Institute of Technology
- Middlebury College
- Mount Angel Seminary
- New England Conservatory of Music
- Oberlin College
- Park University
- Princeton University
- Principia College
- Providence College
- Reed College
- Roger Williams University
- Salve Regina University
- Savannah College of Art and Design
- Simon's Rock College of Bard
- Spelman College
- St. John's College (MD)
- St. John's College (NM)
- Sterling College (VT)
- Swarthmore College
- Thomas More College of Liberal Arts
- Trinity College (CT)
- United States Air Force Academy
- United States Coast Guard Academy
- United States Merchant Marine Academy
- United States Military Academy
- United States Naval Academy
- University of Notre Dame
- University of Pennsylvania
- University of Richmond
- University of Washington
- Vanderbilt University
- Warren Wilson College
- Washington and Lee University
- Washington University in St. Louis
- Wellesley College

- ○ Wesleyan University
- ○ Williams College
- ○ Yale University

Keep It Local

Schools with the lowest out-of-state student populations

- ○ California State University—Chico
- ○ California State University—Dominguez Hills
- ○ California State University—East Bay
- ○ California State University—Fresno
- ○ California State University—Fullerton
- ○ California State University—Long Beach
- ○ California State University—Northridge
- ○ California State University—Sacramento
- ○ California State University—San Bernardino
- ○ California State University—San Marcos
- ○ California State University—Stanislaus
- ○ Cameron University

- ○ City University of New York—The College of Staten Island
- ○ City University of New York—Kingsborough Community College
- ○ City University of New York—LaGuardia Community College
- ○ City University of New York—Lehman College
- ○ City University of New York—New York City College of Technology
- ○ City University of New York—Queens College
- ○ City University of New York—Queensborough Community College
- ○ Georgian Court University
- ○ Harris-Stowe State College
- ○ Hebrew College
- ○ Illinois State University
- ○ Indiana University Northwest
- ○ Indiana University—Kokomo
- ○ Lamar University
- ○ Lawrence Technological University
- ○ Medaille College
- ○ Montana State University, College of Technology—Great Falls
- ○ National-Louis University
- ○ New Jersey City University
- ○ Northeastern Illinois University

- ○ Oakland University
- ○ Ohio University—Chillecothe
- ○ Ohio University—Lancaster
- ○ Pennsylvania State University—DuBois
- ○ Pennsylvania State University—Fayette, The Eberly Campus
- ○ Pennsylvania State University—Worthington-Scranton
- ○ Purdue University—North Central
- ○ Reedley College
- ○ Robert Morris College (IL)
- ○ Saginaw Valley State University
- ○ Saint Francis College (NY)
- ○ Saint Mary's College of Ave Maria University (MI)

FUN FACT

Students at **Lamar University** in Beaumont, Texas, take full advantage of the city's civic, business, and cultural opportunities.

- ○ Sam Houston State University
- ○ Samuel Merritt College
- ○ San Francisco State University

- ○ Sheridan College
- ○ Sonoma State University
- ○ State University of New York—Brockport
- ○ St. Joseph's College—New York (Brooklyn)
- ○ State University of New York—The College at Old Westbury
- ○ State University of New York at Geneseo
- ○ State University of New York—Institute of Technology at Utica/Rome
- ○ State University of New York—University at Buffalo
- ○ Texas State University—San Marcos
- ○ Texas Wesleyan University
- ○ University of Houston—Clear Lake
- ○ University of Houston—Downtown
- ○ University of Maine—Augusta
- ○ University of Mary Hardin—Baylor
- ○ University of Michigan—Flint
- ○ University of Montana—Helena College of Technology
- ○ University of New Hampshire at Manchester
- ○ University of Pittsburgh—Johnstown

- University of Texas at Brownsville
- University of Texas Medical Branch at Galveston
- The University of Texas—Pan American
- Ursuline College
- Vaughn College of Aeronautics and Technology
- Wayne State University

Diversity Universities

Schools with the greatest proportions of African American students

HBCU: Historically Black college/university

- Alabama A&M University (HBCU)
- Alabama State University (HBCU)
- Albany State University (GA) (HBCU)
- Alcorn State University (HBCU)
- Allen University (HBCU)
- Argosy University—Atlanta
- Barber-Scotia College (HBCU)
- Benedict College (HBCU)
- Bennett College (HBCU)
- Bethune-Cookman College (HBCU)
- Bloomfield College
- Bluefield State College (HBCU)
- Bowie State University (HBCU)
- Central State University (HBCU)
- Cheyney University of Pennsylvania (HBCU)
- Chicago State University
- City University of New York—Medgar Evers College
- Claflin University (HBCU)
- Clark Atlanta University (HBCU)
- Concordia College (AL) (HBCU)
- Coppin State University (HBCU)
- Delaware State University (HBCU)
- DeVry University—Chicago
- DeVry University—Crystal City
- DeVry University—Decatur, GA
- Dillard University (HBCU)
- East-West University
- Edward Waters College (HBCU)
- Elizabeth City State University (HBCU)

FUN FACT

Howard University's motto is Veritas et Utilitas, "Truth and Service."

- Fayetteville State University (HBCU)
- Fisk University (HBCU)
- Florida A&M University (HBCU)
- Florida Memorial University (HBCU)
- Fort Valley State University (HBCU)
- Grambling State University (HBCU)
- Guilford College
- Hampton University (HBCU)
- Harris-Stowe State College (HBCU)
- Howard University (HBCU)
- Huston-Tillotson University (HBCU)
- Interdenominational Theological Center (HBCU)
- Jackson State University (HBCU)
- Jarvis Christian College
- Johnson C. Smith University (HBCU)
- Kentucky State University (HBCU)
- Knoxville College (HBCU)
- Lane College (HBCU)
- Langston University (MO) (HBCU)
- LeMoyne-Owen College (HBCU)
- Lexington College
- Lincoln University (MO) (HBCU)
- Lincoln University (PA) (HBCU)

- Livingstone College (HBCU)
- Marygrove College
- Mercy College
- Miles College (HBCU)
- Mississippi Valley State University (HBCU)
- Morehouse College (HBCU)
- Morgan State University (HBCU)
- Morris Brown College (HBCU)
- Morris College
- Norfolk State University (HBCU)
- North Carolina A&T State University (HBCU)
- North Carolina Central University
- Oakwood College (HBCU)
- Paine College (HBCU)
- Paul Quinn College (HBCU)
- Philander Smith College (HBCU)
- Potomac College
- Prairie View A&M University (HBCU)
- Rust College (HBCU)
- Saint Augustine's College (HBCU)
- Saint Paul's College (HBCU)
- Savannah State University (HBCU)
- Shaw University (HBCU)
- Shorter College (HBCU)
- Sojourner Douglass College

- South Carolina State University (HBCU)
- Southeastern University
- Southern University and A&M College (HBCU)
- Southern University and Agricultural and Mechanical College (HBCU)
- Southwestern Christian College
- Spelman College (HBCU)
- Stillman College (HBCU)
- Talladega College
- Tennessee State University (HBCU)
- Texas College (HBCU)
- Texas Southern University (HBCU)
- Tougaloo College (HBCU)
- Trinity University (Washington, DC)
- Troy University Montgomery
- Tuskegee University (HBCU)
- University of Arkansas—Pine Bluff (HBCU)
- University of the District of Columbia (HBCU)
- University of Maryland—Eastern Shore (HBCU)
- University of the Virgin Islands (HBCU)
- Virginia State University (HBCU)
- Virginia Union University (HBCU)
- Virginia University of Lynchburg (HBCU)
- Voorhees College
- West Virginia State University (HBCU)
- Wilberforce University (HBCU)
- Wiley College (HBCU)
- Winston-Salem State University (HBCU)
- Xavier University of Louisiana (HBCU)

More Diversity Universities

Schools with the greatest proportions of Latino students

- American University of Puerto Rico
- Barry University
- Berkeley College
- California State University—Dominguez Hills
- California State University—Los Angeles
- California State University—San Bernardino
- City University of New York—Hostos Community College
- City University of New York—LaGuardia Community College

- ○ City University of New York—Lehman College
- ○ DeVry University—Long Beach, CA
- ○ DeVry University—Miramar
- ○ DeVry University—Pomona, CA
- ○ Dominican School of Philosophy and Theology
- ○ Florida International University
- ○ Heritage University
- ○ Inter American University of Puerto Rico—Aguadilla
- ○ Monroe College
- ○ Mount Saint Mary's College (CA)

- ○ Reedley College
- ○ Saint Peter's College
- ○ St. Mary's University
- ○ St. Thomas University
- ○ Sul Ross State University
- ○ Texas A&M University—Corpus Christi
- ○ Texas A&M University—Kingsville
- ○ University of Houston—Downtown
- ○ University of the Incarnate Word
- ○ University of La Verne
- ○ University of New Mexico
- ○ University of Texas at Brownsville
- ○ University of Texas at El Paso
- ○ The University of Texas—Pan American
- ○ The University of Texas at San Antonio
- ○ Vaughn College of Aeronautics and Technology
- ○ Woodbury University

FUN FACT

The student group STAND.com at **Monroe College** works to utilize the tools and knowledge gained in the classroom to improve the greater community.

- ○ National American Unversity (NM)
- ○ New Jersey City University
- ○ New Mexico State University
- ○ New World School of the Arts
- ○ Our Lady of the Lake University

Still More Diversity Universities

Schools with the greatest proportions of Asian students

- Art Center College of Design
- California Institute of Technology
- Chaminade University of Honolulu
- DeVry University—Pomona, CA
- Pacific States University
- San Jose State University
- Soka University of America
- University of California—Berkeley
- University of California—Davis
- University of California—Irvine
- University of California—Los Angeles
- University of California—Riverside
- University of California—San Diego
- University of Hawaii—Hilo
- University of Hawaii—Manoa
- University of Hawaii—West Oahu

Even More Diversity Universities

Schools with the greatest proportions of Native American students

- Alaska Pacific University
- American Indian College of the Assemblies of God, Inc.
- Central Wyoming College
- Fort Lewis College
- Heritage University
- Holy Apostles College and Seminary
- Montana State University—Northern
- Northeastern State University
- Presentation College
- Sheldon Jackson College
- Southeastern Oklahoma State University

FUN FACT

The most popular majors at **Heritage University** are business administration/management, elementary education and teaching, and social work.

- University of Alaska—Fairbanks
- University of North Carolina at Pembroke

- University of Science and Arts of Oklahoma

chapter 8

Extracurricular Life

Calling all rock climbers, gamelan players, and jugglers—this chapter is for you. Some of the best schools you'll find will embrace learning in all its various forms. While you may find yourself more loaded with schoolwork in college—and thus, more strapped for time—extracurricular activities should remain a vital part of your life. They will help you relieve stress, stay fit, meet new people, and even promote your career interests. You also might find that being able to schedule your own classes—on the times and days that work best for you—will make it easier to show up for volleyball practice, join a choral ensemble, or volunteer at the local children's hospital.

Your biggest challenge could actually be finding a school that will indulge your specific extracurricular desires—from learning lacrosse, even if you've never picked up a stick, to learning the steel pan. Not every university is going to offer competitive ballroom dancing, a juggling club, a well-respected literary magazine, or a wrestling program. If those things are important to you, pursue them—and use the lists here. Refer to this chapter throughout your college search, and stay connected with the schools that can meet your academic and extracurricular interests.

One last piece of advice: After you've found the school (or schools) that have the best combination of programs for you, don't forget to put all of your careful research to work. Get involved! At the beginning of the school year, most clubs host welcome meetings (free pizza is a common incentive). If you're a person with varied interests and talents, you are likely to find that your college experience rewards you in many wonderful and sometimes unexpected ways.

Something For Everyone

Schools with the greatest numbers of on-campus organizations

- Arizona State University—Tempe
- Auburn University
- Ball State University
- Boston University
- Brigham Young University (UT)
- California Polytechnic State University—San Luis Obispo
- California State University—Long Beach
- College of William & Mary
- Columbia University
- Cornell University
- Dartmouth College
- Florida State University
- Georgia Institute of Technology
- Indiana University—Bloomington
- Iowa State University
- Iowa State University of Science and Technology
- Kansas State University
- Louisiana State University
- Massachusetts Institute of Technology
- Miami University
- Michigan State University
- Mississippi State University
- New York University
- North Carolina State University
- Northwestern University
- The Ohio State University—Columbus
- Ohio University—Athens
- Oklahoma State University
- Oregon State University
- Pennsylvania State University—University Park
- Purdue University—West Lafayette
- Rutgers, The State University of New Jersey—New Brunswick/Piscataway
- Southern Illinois University—Carbondale
- Stanford University

FUN FACT

On the Friday before Homecoming, student and faculty teams at **Ball State University** compete in the Homecoming Bed Race, during which they wheel beds along a racecourse.

279

- State University of New York—College of Environmental Science and Forestry
- State University of New York—University at Buffalo
- Syracuse University
- Texas A&M University—College Station
- Texas Tech University
- University of Arizona
- University of California—Berkeley
- University of California—Davis
- University of California—Irvine
- University of California—Los Angeles
- University of California—Santa Barbara
- University of Central Florida
- University of Colorado—Boulder
- University of Connecticut
- University of Florida
- University of Georgia
- University of Houston
- University of Illinois at Urbana-Champaign
- University of Iowa
- University of Kansas
- University of Kentucky

- University of Maryland—College Park
- University of Michigan—Ann Arbor
- University of Minnesota—Twin Cities
- University of Missouri—Columbia
- University of Nebraska—Lincoln
- University of New Mexico
- The University of North Carolina at Chapel Hill
- University of Oklahoma
- University of Pennsylvania
- University of Pittsburgh—Pittsburgh Campus
- University of South Carolina—Columbia
- University of South Florida
- University of Southern California
- University of Tennessee—Knoxville
- The University of Texas at Arlington
- The University of Texas at Austin
- University of Utah
- University of Virginia
- University of Wisconsin—Madison
- Vanderbilt University
- Virginia Polytechnic and State University (Virginia Tech)
- Washington State University
- West Virginia University

Across the Pond
Schools in the Atlantic Coast Conference

- Boston College
- Clemson University
- Duke University
- Florida State University
- Georgia Institute of Technology
- University of Maryland—College Park
- University of Miami
- The University of North Carolina at Chapel Hill
- North Carolina State University
- University of Virginia
- Virginia Polytechnic and State University
- Wake Forest University

Top-Ten List
Schools in the Big Ten Conference

- Indiana University
- Michigan State University
- Northwestern University
- The Ohio State University
- Pennsylvania State University
- Purdue University
- University of Illinois
- University of Iowa
- The University of Michigan
- The University of Minnesota
- University of Wisconsin

Twelve Gates to the City
Schools in the Big 12 Conference

- Baylor University
- University of Colorado—Boulder
- Iowa State University
- University of Kansas
- Kansas State University
- University of Missouri—Columbia
- University of Nebraska—Lincoln
- University of Oklahoma
- Oklahoma State University
- The University of Texas at Austin
- Texas A&M University—College Station
- Texas Tech University

Eastern Education

Schools in the Big East Conference

- DePaul University
- Georgetown University
- Marquette University
- Providence College
- Rutgers, The State University of New Jersey—New Brunswick/Piscataway
- Seton Hall University
- St. John's University (NY)
- Syracuse University
- University of Cincinnati
- University of Connecticut
- University of Louisville
- University of Notre Dame
- University of Pittsburgh
- University of South Florida
- Villanova University
- West Virginia University

The Sun Sets Here

Schools in the Pacific Ten Conference

- Arizona State University—Tempe
- Oregon State University
- Stanford University
- University of Arizona
- University of California—Berkeley
- University of California—Los Angeles
- University of Oregon
- University of Southern California
- University of Washington
- Washington State University

Sunny Days

Schools in the Southeastern Conference

- Auburn University
- Louisiana State University
- Mississippi State University
- University of Alabama—Tuscaloosa
- University of Arkansas
- University of Florida
- University of Georgia
- University of Kentucky

- University of Mississippi
- University of South Carolina—Columbia
- University of Tennessee—Knoxville
- Vanderbilt University

Next Stop: The Big Leagues

Schools that have many professionally-drafted players

- Arizona State University—Tempe (football)
- Auburn University (football)
- Duke University (basketball)
- Florida State University (football)
- Oklahoma State University (basketball)
- The Ohio State University (football)
- Pennsylvania State University (football)
- Texas A&M University—College Station (baseball, football)
- University of Arizona (basketball)
- University of Cincinnati (basketball)
- University of Connecticut (basketball)
- University of Alabama (football)

- University of Kansas (basketball)
- University of Maryland—College Park (basketball)
- University of Miami (baseball, football)
- University of Michigan (football)
- University of California—Los Angeles (football)
- University of Georgia (football)
- The University of North Carolina at Chapel Hill (basketball)
- University of Notre Dame (football)
- University of Oklahoma (football)
- University of Pittsburgh (football)
- University of Southern California (football)
- The University of Texas at Austin (baseball, football)
- University of Virginia (football)
- University of Washington (football)
- University of Wisconsin—Madison (football)

Your Mascot Is What!?
Schools with unusual mascots

- Oglethorpe University (Stormy Petrels)
- Pittsburgh State University (Gorilla)
- Saint Louis University (Billiken)
- Southern Illinois University—Carbondale (Saluki)
- Syracuse University (Orangemen)
- University of California—Irvine (Anteater)

FUN FACT

UCLA's athletic teams have won 97 NCAA titles and 118 team titles in 19 different sports.

- University of California—Santa Cruz (Banana Slug)
- University of Richmond (Spider)
- University of South Carolina—Columbia (Gamecock)

Bullseye!
Schools with great archery programs

- Columbia University
- Diné College of Arizona
- James Madison University
- Long Beach State University
- Stanford University
- Texas A&M University—College Station
- University of California—Los Angeles
- University of Southern California
- The University of Texas

The World's Fastest Racquet
Schools with great badminton programs

- Bates College
- Boston University
- Bryn Mawr College
- Cornell University
- Swarthmore College
- University of California—Los Angeles

Diamond Days

Schools with great baseball programs

- Arizona State University
- California Polytechnic Institute
- California State University—Fullerton
- Clemson University
- Florida State University
- Long Beach State University
- Louisiana State University
- Mississippi State University
- Oregon State University
- Pepperdine University

Shouldn't I be a little bit lower? Guys...? Lower, right?

- ○ Rice University
- ○ Stanford University
- ○ Texas A&M University—College Station
- ○ Tulane University
- ○ University of Arkansas
- ○ University of Florida
- ○ University of Kansas
- ○ University of Mississippi
- ○ University of Missouri
- ○ University of Nebraska
- ○ University of North Carolina
- ○ University of South Carolina
- ○ University of Tennessee
- ○ The University of Texas at Austin

FUN FACT

The **University of Kentucky** has 13 former players in the NBA—that's the most of any school!

Slam Dunk

Schools with great basketball programs

- ○ Baylor University
- ○ Duke University
- ○ Michigan State University
- ○ North Carolina State University
- ○ Oklahoma State University
- ○ Purdue University
- ○ Stanford University
- ○ Syracuse University
- ○ University of Arizona
- ○ University of Arkansas
- ○ University of California—Los Angeles
- ○ University of Cincinnati
- ○ University of Connecticut
- ○ University of Kansas
- ○ University of Kentucky
- ○ University of Maryland—College Park
- ○ The University of North Carolina at Chapel Hill
- ○ University of Notre Dame
- ○ University of Southern California
- ○ University of Tennessee

Pugilists Unite!

Schools with great boxing programs

- The Citadel—The Military College of South Carolina
- Lock Haven University of Pennsylvania
- Pennsylvania State University—University Park
- United States Air Force Academy
- United States Military Academy
- United States Naval Academy
- University of Nevada—Las Vegas
- University of Nevada—Reno

Give Me a C-H-E-E-R

Schools with great cheerleading programs

- Arizona State University
- College of Charleston
- Duke University
- Michigan State University
- North Carolina State University
- Syracuse University
- Temple University
- University of Arizona
- University of Florida
- University of Kansas
- University of Kentucky
- University of Maryland—College Park
- University of Massachusetts—Dartmouth
- University of Oklahoma
- University of Tennessee at Martin
- University of Wisconsin—La Crosse

Row Your Boat

Schools with great crew/rowing programs

- Boston University
- Brown University
- Columbia University
- Cornell University

FUN FACT

Yale's mascot is Handsome Dan, the bulldog. When the first mascot died in 1897, his hide was stuffed and put on display, where it remains to this day in the Payne Whitney Gymnasium. The current incarnation is Handsome Dan XVI.

- Dartmouth College
- Georgetown University
- Harvard College
- Massachusetts Institute of Technology
- Mount Holyoke College
- Northeastern University
- Princeton University
- Rutgers, The State University of New Jersey
- Syracuse University
- United States Naval Academy
- University of California—Berkeley
- University of Pennsylvania
- University of Washington
- University of Wisconsin
- Yale University

Over the River and Through the Woods

Schools with great cross-country programs

- American University
- Arizona State University
- Brigham Young University (UT)
- College of William & Mary
- Dartmouth College

- Florida State University
- Georgetown University
- Iona College
- The Ohio State University
- Oklahoma State University
- Stanford University
- Texas State University
- University of Alabama
- University of Arizona
- University of Arkansas
- University of Colorado
- University of Florida
- University of Indiana
- University of Iowa
- University of Kansas
- University of Minnesota
- University of Notre Dame
- University of Portland
- University of Tennessee
- The University of Texas at El Paso
- University of Virginia

A Kinder, Gentler Game

Schools with great flag football teams

- Angelo State University
- Ball State University
- Baylor University
- California State University—Fullerton
- Campbell University
- Florida State University
- Georgia Southern University
- Louisiana State University
- Sam Houston State University
- Texas Institute of Technology
- Troy State University
- University of Central Florida
- University of Denver
- University of Florida
- University of the Pacific
- The University of Texas at San Antonio

Gridiron Glory

Schools with great football programs

- Auburn University
- Boston College

- Brigham Young University (UT)
- Clemson University
- Florida State University
- Georgia Institute of Technology
- Louisiana State University
- Northwestern University
- The Ohio State University
- The Pennsylvania State University
- Texas Christian University
- Texas A&M University—College Station
- Texas Institute of Technology
- University of Alabama
- University of California—Los Angeles
- University of Florida
- University of Georgia
- University of Louisville
- University of Miami

FUN FACT

The **University of Alabama**'s football team won national championships in 1925, 1926, 1930, 1934, 1941, 1961, 1964, 1965, 1973, 1978, 1979, and 1992.

- University of Michigan
- University of Nebraska
- University of Notre Dame
- University of Oklahoma
- University of Oregon
- University of Pittsburgh
- University of Southern California
- University of Tennessee—Knoxville
- The University of Texas at Austin
- University of Utah
- University of Virginia
- University of Washington
- University of Wisconsin—Madison
- Virginia Institute of Technology
- West Virginia University

FUN FACT

In September 2005, Men's Fitness named **Georgia Institute of Technology** the Fourteenth Fittest College in America.

Check Yourself

Schools with great hockey programs

- Boston College
- Boston University
- Colgate University
- Colorado College
- Cornell University
- Dartmouth College
- Ferris State University
- Harvard College
- Mercyhurst College
- Michigan State University
- Princeton University
- St. Cloud State University
- St. Lawrence University
- University of Denver
- University of Maine
- University of Miami
- University of Michigan
- University of Minnesota
- University of Nebraska—Omaha
- University of New Hampshire
- University of North Dakota
- University of Wisconsin—Madison

Par For the Course

Schools with great golf programs

- Arizona State University
- California State University—Berkeley
- The College of Wooster
- Cornell University
- Duke University
- Emory University
- Florida State University
- Furman University
- Georgetown University
- Georgia Institute of Technology
- Long Beach State University
- Middlebury College
- Northwestern University
- The Ohio State University
- Pennsylvania State University
- Pepperdine University
- Princeton University
- Stanford University
- Tulane University
- University of California—Davis
- University of California—Irvine
- University of California—Los Angeles
- University of California—Riverside
- University of California—San Diego
- University of Florida
- University of Georgia
- University of Miami
- University of Michigan
- The University of North Carolina at Chapel Hill
- University of South Florida
- University of Southern California
- The University of Texas
- University of Tulsa
- University of Virginia
- University of Washington
- Vanderbilt University
- Vassar College
- Wake Forest University
- Yale University

FUN FACT

Arizona State University's mascot, Sparky the Sun Devil, was created by the late Bert Anthony, an artist for Walt Disney.

Field of Greens

Schools with great on-campus golf courses

- Arizona State University
- The College of Wooster
- Cornell University
- Middlebury College
- The Ohio State University
- Pennsylvania State University
- Stanford University
- University of Florida
- University of South Florida
- Vassar College

Gymnast Utopia

Schools with great gymnastics programs

- College of William & Mary
- The Ohio State University
- Pennsylvania State University
- Southern Methodist University
- Stanford University
- Temple University
- United States Military Academy
- United States Naval Academy
- University of Alabama

- University of California—Los Angeles
- University of Georgia
- University of Illinois
- University of Iowa
- University of Michigan
- University of Minnesota
- University of Nebraska
- University of Oklahoma
- University of Utah

A Kinder, Gentler Baseball

Schools with great softball programs

- Arizona State University
- Auburn University
- Baylor University
- California State University—Los Angeles
- DePaul University
- Louisiana State University
- Northwestern University
- Oregon State University
- Stanford University
- Texas A&M University—College Station
- University of Alabama

- University of Arizona
- University of California—Los Angeles
- University of Georgia
- University of Louisiana—Lafayette
- University of Michigan
- University of Nebraska
- University of Oklahoma
- University of Tennessee
- The University of Texas
- University of Washington

Four Balls Up in the Air
Schools with great juggling clubs

- Bates College
- Boston University
- Brown University
- California Institute of Technology
- Colorado State University
- Harvard College
- Humboldt State University
- Indiana University
- Massachusetts Institute of Technology
- McMaster University
- Purdue University
- Renssalaer Polytechnic Institute
- Stanford University
- Syracuse University
- University of California—Berkeley
- University of Dayton
- University of Georgia
- University of Illinois at Urbana-Champaign
- University of Maryland—College Park
- University of Missouri—Rolla
- University of New Hampshire
- University of Notre Dame
- The University of Texas at Austin
- University of Vermont
- Whitman College
- Yale University

FUN FACT
The **University of Maryland** has produced its own ice cream since 1924; 25,000 gallons of it are produced there annually.

We Came Lacrosse These...

Schools with great lacrosse programs

- ○ Bucknell University
- ○ Cornell University
- ○ Duke University
- ○ Georgetown University
- ○ Johns Hopkins University
- ○ Northwestern University
- ○ Pennsylvania State University
- ○ Princeton University
- ○ Syracuse University
- ○ University of Maryland—College Park
- ○ University of Virginia

The Great Outdoors

Schools with great outdoor adventure clubs

- ○ Allegheny College
- ○ Amherst College
- ○ Bates College
- ○ Boston College
- ○ Brandeis University
- ○ Eastern Connecticut State University
- ○ Hampshire College

- ○ Harvard College
- ○ Massachusetts Institute of Technology
- ○ Pennsylvania State University
- ○ Providence College
- ○ Roanoke College
- ○ Skidmore College
- ○ Smith College
- ○ State University of New York at Binghamton
- ○ University of California—Riverside
- ○ University of California—Santa Cruz
- ○ University of Illinois
- ○ University of Maryland
- ○ Whitman College

Horse & Mallett

Schools with great polo programs

- ○ Colorado State University
- ○ Cornell University
- ○ Michigan State University
- ○ New Mexico State University
- ○ The Ohio State University
- ○ Oregon State University
- ○ Purdue University

- Skidmore College
- Stanford University
- Texas A&M University—College Station
- University of California—Davis
- University of Connecticut
- University of Georgia
- University of Louisville
- University of Massachusetts
- University of Southern California
- The University of Texas at Austin
- University of Virginia
- Vassar College
- Yale University

Cliffhanging
Schools with great rock-climbing clubs

- Colby College
- Harvard College
- Kansas State University
- Michigan Institute of Technology
- The Ohio State University
- University of California—Riverside
- University of Idaho
- University of Illinois
- University of Kentucky

- University of Minnesota
- University of Missouri—Columbia
- Virginia Institute of Technology

Artificial Mountain
Schools with great on-campus rock-climbing walls

- Eastern Mennonite University
- Harvard College
- Rutgers, The State University of New Jersey—New Brunswick/Piscataway
- Smith College
- Stanford University
- University of California—Riverside

FUN FACT

The **University of Idaho** has a "Found Money Fund." It started out with three cents in 1981 and, at last count, had $187,112.67.

- University of California—Santa Cruz
- University of Connecticut

295

- University of Northern Iowa
- University of Oregon
- University of Wisconsin—Stout

Call Me Ishmael
Schools with great sailing programs

- Bates College
- Boston College
- College of Charleston

FUN FACT

The **Texas A&M** mascot is Reveille, an American collie. Reveille holds the highest rank in the University's Corps of Cadets.

- Connecticut College
- Dartmouth College
- Harvard College
- Princeton University
- St. Mary's College of Maryland
- Stanford University
- State University of New York— Maritime College

- Tufts University
- United States Naval Academy
- University of California—Irvine
- University of Miami
- University of Rhode Island
- University of Southern California
- Yale University

Hit the Slopes
Schools with great skiing/snow-boarding opportunities

- Colby College
- Colorado College
- Middlebury College
- Montana State University
- University of Alaska—Fairbanks
- University of Colorado—Boulder
- University of Denver
- University of New Hampshire
- University of Utah
- University of Vermont
- Western State College of Colorado

Goal!!!

Schools with great soccer programs

- ○ Boston College
- ○ Brigham Young University (UT)
- ○ California State University—Fullerton
- ○ Duke University
- ○ Florida State University
- ○ Hartwick College
- ○ Indiana University
- ○ Marquette University
- ○ Old Dominion University
- ○ Pennsylvania State University
- ○ Santa Clara University
- ○ Texas A&M University—College Station
- ○ The University of Akron
- ○ University of California—Los Angeles
- ○ University of Connecticut
- ○ University of Maryland—College Park
- ○ University of New Mexico
- ○ University of North Carolina
- ○ University of Notre Dame
- ○ University of Portland
- ○ University of Virginia

From the High Dive You Can See For Miles

Schools with great swimming/diving programs

- ○ Auburn University
- ○ Dartmouth College
- ○ Emory University
- ○ Kenyon College
- ○ The Ohio State University
- ○ Stanford University
- ○ United States Naval Academy
- ○ University of California—Berkeley
- ○ University of Michigan
- ○ The University of Texas
- ○ Yale University

Surf's Up!

Schools with great surfing opportunities

- ○ Brigham Young University (HI)
- ○ Florida Atlantic University
- ○ Hawaii Pacific University
- ○ Humboldt State University
- ○ Pepperdine University
- ○ University of California—San Diego

- ○ University of California—Santa Barbara
- ○ University of California—Santa Cruz
- ○ University of Central Florida
- ○ University of Hawaii—Manoa

You Got Served

Schools with great tennis programs

- ○ Baylor University

FUN FACT

The bowling team at **Vanderbilt** is also a force to be reckoned with—it made its debut in the NCAA championship in 2006.

- ○ California State University—Berkeley
- ○ Duke University
- ○ Northwestern University
- ○ Pepperdine University
- ○ Rice University

- ○ Stanford University
- ○ University of California—Los Angeles
- ○ University of Florida
- ○ University of Georgia
- ○ University of Illinois at Urbana-Champaign
- ○ University of North Carolina
- ○ University of Notre Dame
- ○ University of Southern California
- ○ The University of Texas at Austin
- ○ Vanderbilt University

Indoor Decathalon

Schools with great track and field programs

- ○ Auburn University
- ○ Baylor University
- ○ Louisiana State University
- ○ Stanford University
- ○ University of Arizona
- ○ University of Arkansas
- ○ University of California—Los Angeles
- ○ University of Nebraska
- ○ University of Southern California

- University of Tennessee
- The University of Texas at Austin
- The University of Texas at El Paso

Some Folks Call It Flatball

Schools with great ultimate Frisbee clubs

- Brown University
- Bucknell University
- California State University—Humboldt
- Carleton College
- College of William & Mary
- Oregon State University
- Rutgers, The State University of New Jersey
- Smith College
- Stanford University
- University of California—Berkeley
- University of California—Davis
- University of California—San Diego
- University of California—Santa Barbara
- University of California—Santa Cruz
- University of Chicago

- University of Colorado
- University of Georgia
- The University of North Carolina at Chapel Hill
- University of Oregon
- University of Wisconsin
- Winona State University

Sideout

Schools with great volleyball programs

- Ball State University
- Brigham Young University (UT)
- George Mason University
- Harvard College
- Long Beach State University
- Loyola University—Chicago
- The Ohio State University
- Pennsylvania State University
- Pepperdine University
- Princeton University
- Stanford University
- University of California—Los Angeles
- University of California—Santa Barbara
- University of Hawaii—Manoa

- University of Miami
- University of Northern Iowa
- University of the Pacific
- University of Southern California
- University of Washington in St. Louis
- University of Wisconsin—Madison

Polo in Speedos
Schools with great water polo programs

- Arizona State University—Tempe
- California State University—Bakersfield
- California State University—Northridge
- Hartwick College
- Harvard College
- Indiana University—Bloomington
- Long Beach State University
- Loyola Marymont University
- Pepperdine University
- Princeton University
- San Diego State University
- San Jose State University
- Stanford University
- United States Naval Academy

- University of California—Berkeley
- University of California—Davis
- University of California—Irvine
- University of California—Los Angeles
- University of California—San Diego
- University of California—Santa Barbara
- University of Hawaii—Manoa
- University of Michigan
- University of Redlands
- University of Southern California

No Holds Barred
Schools with great wrestling programs

- Bowling Green State University
- Cornell University
- Grand Valley State University
- Iowa State University
- Lehigh University
- Maryville College
- Miami University
- Oklahoma State University
- Renssalaer Polytechnic Institute
- University of Central Florida

- ○ University of Florida
- ○ University of Iowa
- ○ University of Minnesota
- ○ University of New Hampshire
- ○ University of Northern Iowa

Lend a Hand

Schools that have active community service programs

- ○ Berea College
- ○ Brandeis University
- ○ Brigham Young University (UT)
- ○ Brown University
- ○ California State University—Monterey Bay
- ○ Clark University
- ○ College of William & Mary
- ○ Connecticut College
- ○ Darthmouth University
- ○ Elon University
- ○ Hampshire College
- ○ Harvard College
- ○ Hobart and William Smith Colleges
- ○ Macalester College
- ○ Northwestern University
- ○ Oberlin College
- ○ Pitzer College

- ○ Portland State University
- ○ Princeton University
- ○ Smith College
- ○ Spelman College
- ○ Stanford University
- ○ Swarthmore College
- ○ Texas A&M University—College Station
- ○ University of Alaska—Anchorage
- ○ University of California—Berkeley
- ○ University of California—Los Angeles
- ○ University of California—Santa Cruz
- ○ University of Maryland—College Park
- ○ University of Minnesota—Twin Cities
- ○ The University of North Carolina at Chapel Hill
- ○ University of Pennsylvania
- ○ University of Rhode Island
- ○ University of Southern California
- ○ University of Wisconsin—Madison
- ○ Vanderbilt University
- ○ Vassar College
- ○ Warren Wilson College
- ○ Wesleyan University
- ○ Williams College

Just Doo Wop It

Schools with great a cappella programs

- ○ Amherst College
- ○ Boston University
- ○ Brown University
- ○ College of William & Mary
- ○ Columbia University
- ○ Cornell University
- ○ Duke University
- ○ Eastman School of Music
- ○ Harvard College
- ○ Northwestern University
- ○ Pennsylvania State University
- ○ Princeton University
- ○ Smith College
- ○ Stanford University
- ○ State University of New York at Binghamton
- ○ Swarthmore College
- ○ Tufts University
- ○ University of Maryland—College Park
- ○ University of Michigan—Ann Arbor
- ○ The University of North Carolina at Chapel Hill
- ○ University of Oregon
- ○ University of Pennsylvania
- ○ University of Rochester
- ○ University of Southern California
- ○ University of Virginia
- ○ Vassar College
- ○ Washington University in St. Louis
- ○ Yale University

Strictly Mad Hot

Schools with great ballroom dancing programs

- ○ Bates College
- ○ Boston University
- ○ California Institute of Technology
- ○ Harvard College
- ○ Johnson & Wales University
- ○ Massachusetts Institute of Technology
- ○ New York University
- ○ North Carolina State University
- ○ Purdue University
- ○ Rice University
- ○ Rutgers, The State University of New Jersey—New Brunswick/Piscataway
- ○ Smith College
- ○ Tufts University
- ○ University of California—Berkeley

- ○ University of Delaware
- ○ University of Maryland—College Park
- ○ University of Massachusetts—Amherst
- ○ University of Michigan
- ○ University of Rhode Island
- ○ University of Toledo
- ○ Wesleyan University
- ○ Yale University

Bach 'Til You Drop
Schools with great choral ensembles

- ○ Brigham Young University (UT)
- ○ Columbia University
- ○ Cornell University
- ○ Dartmouth College
- ○ Eastman School of Music—University of Rochester
- ○ Gettysburg College
- ○ Harvard College
- ○ Iowa State University
- ○ The Juilliard School
- ○ Kent State University
- ○ Loyola Marymont University
- ○ Michigan State University

- ○ Princeton University
- ○ St. Olaf College
- ○ University of California—Berkeley
- ○ University of Michigan—Ann Arbor
- ○ The University of North Carolina at Chapel Hill
- ○ University of Pennsylvania
- ○ University of Rochester
- ○ University of Southern California
- ○ University of Utah
- ○ Westminster Choir College (NJ)
- ○ Yale University

Literary Landmarks
Schools with great literary magazines

- ○ Columbia University (*Columbia Journal*)
- ○ Emerson College (*Ploughshares*)

FUN FACT

Gettysburg College offers the BA, BS, and BM (in music performance).

- ○ Gettysburg College (*Gettysburg Review*)
- ○ Louisiana State University (*Southern Review*)
- ○ Massachusetts Institute of Technology (*Boston Review*)
- ○ The New School University (*LIT*)
- ○ Southern Methodist University (*Southwest Review*)
- ○ University of Alabama (*Black Warrior Review*)
- ○ University of Alaska—Anchorage (*Alaska Quarterly Review*)
- ○ University of California—Irvine (*Faultline*)

FUN FACT

The Eastman School of Music at the **University of Rochester** offers an innovative FORTE (four years plus teaching experience) program. The FORTE program is a ninth semester of tuition-free enrollment for selected music education majors that is devoted exclusively to completion of the student teaching experience.

- ○ University of California—Riverside (*Crate*)
- ○ University of Denver (*Denver Quarterly*)
- ○ University of Georgia (*Georgia Review*)
- ○ University of Houston (*Gulf Coast*)
- ○ University of Iowa (*Iowa Review*)
- ○ University of Massachusetts—Amherst (*Jubilat*)
- ○ University of Utah (*Western Humanities Review*)
- ○ University of Virginia (*Meridian*)

World Music

Schools with unusual musical groups

- ○ Bates College (Steelpan, Gamelan)
- ○ Blinn College (Steelpan)
- ○ California Institute of the Arts (Gamelan)
- ○ Cornell College (Steelpan)
- ○ Eastman School of Music (Gamelan)
- ○ Keene State University (Panpipes)
- ○ Massachusetts Institute of Technology (Gamelan)

- Pomona College (Gamelan)
- Swarthmore College (Gamelan)
- University of California—Los Angeles (Gamelan)
- University of California—Riverside (Gamelan)
- University of California—Santa Cruz (African Drums)
- University of Maryland—College Park (Gamelan)
- University of Southern Mississippi (Steelpan)
- Wesleyan University (Gamelan)

chapter 9

Religiously-Affiliated Schools

Everyone has heard of the Catholic University of Notre Dame and Mormon-affiliated Brigham Young University—two schools that offer outstanding academics, sports for one and all, and a hearty dose of faith. In addition to these prayer-friendly college giants, there are, of course, plenty of smaller schools that are religiously affiliated. Just how much faith you'll find on campus and how religion affects school policy and student preferences will vary from one college to the next. Some schools hold their students to strict codes of conduct, while others are as lax as some public institutions. Some require students to complete a certain number of hours of community service, and many integrate theology classes into the required curriculum. At the other end of the spectrum are schools that, if you didn't know otherwise, you'd never guess were tied to a particular religion. You'll need to do your homework to find out more about the schools on your prospective college-match lists.

A school's religious affiliation may give you some insight into the student body you're likely to find. Many of the schools on these lists tend to down-play or discourage wild parties in the interest of giving students a gentle push toward activities revolving around volunteer work and spiritual growth. Naturally, there are exceptions to this rule.

Most colleges—religiously affiliated or not—offer classes in religion even to non-majors, and many have various religiously-affiliated student groups. Beyond the curricular possibilities, most college towns are filled with a variety of houses of worship. Generally speaking, the bigger the school and/or college town, the more options you're likely to find.

This chapter introduces you to the names of colleges that are religously affiliated. Whether you're a devout follower of a specific faith or have always had an attraction or even a curiosity about one of these, the lists provide some schools you might want to look into further.

African Methodist Episcopal
- ○ Livingstone College
- ○ Morris Brown College

American Baptist
- ○ Alderson-Broaddus College
- ○ Eastern University
- ○ Franklin College
- ○ Keuka College
- ○ Linfield College
- ○ University of Sioux Falls

Assemblies of God
- ○ American Indian College of the Assemblies of God, Inc.
- ○ Northwest College
- ○ Southeastern College of the Assemblies of God
- ○ Vanguard University of Southern California

Baptist
- ○ Arkansas Baptist College
- ○ Arlington Baptist College
- ○ Baptist Bible College and Seminary of Pennsylvania
- ○ Baylor University
- ○ Belmont University

- ○ Benedict College
- ○ Bethel University (MN)
- ○ Blue Mountain College
- ○ Bluefield College
- ○ Brewton-Parker College
- ○ Campbellsville University
- ○ Carson-Newman College
- ○ Cedarville University
- ○ Central Baptist College
- ○ Chowan College
- ○ Corban College
- ○ Dallas Baptist University
- ○ East Texas Baptist University
- ○ Faith Baptist Bible College and Theological Seminary
- ○ Florida Memorial College
- ○ Gardner-Webb University
- ○ Georgetown College
- ○ Georgia Baptist College of Nursing
- ○ Grand Rapids Baptist Seminary

FUN FACT

Livingstone College is a Historically Black institution located in the Historic District of Salisbury, North Carolina.

309

- ○ Hardin-Simmons University
- ○ Howard Payne University
- ○ Judson College (AL)
- ○ Judson College (IL)
- ○ LeMoyne-Owen College
- ○ LeTorneau University
- ○ Liberty University
- ○ Louisiana College
- ○ Mars Hill College
- ○ The Master's College and Seminary
- ○ Mercer University—Macon

FUN FACT

Crown College instituted an online program, Crown Online, in 2000.

- ○ Morris College
- ○ Mount Olive College
- ○ Oakland City University
- ○ Samford University
- ○ Shasta Bible College
- ○ Shaw University
- ○ Southwestern College (AZ)
- ○ University of Mary Hardin—Baylor
- ○ University of Mobile
- ○ Virginia Intermont College

310

- ○ Virginia Union University
- ○ William Carey College
- ○ Wingate University

Buddhist
- ○ Institute of Buddhist Studies
- ○ Naropa University (Buddhist-inspired)
- ○ Soka University of America
- ○ University of the West

Christian & Missionary Alliance
- ○ Crown College
- ○ Nyack College
- ○ Simpson University

Christian (Nondenominational)
- ○ Alaska Bible College
- ○ Atlanta Christian College
- ○ Azusa Pacific University
- ○ Biola University
- ○ Boise Bible College
- ○ Central Christian College of the Bible
- ○ Colorado Christian University

- Cornerstone University
- Emmaus Bible College
- Gordon College
- Grace University
- Hope International University
- Huntington College
- Johnson Bible College
- Life Pacific College
- Limestone College
- Manhattan Christian College
- Multnomah Bible College and Biblical Seminary
- Northwestern College (MN)
- Ozark Christian College
- Palm Beach Atlantic University
- Philadelphia Biblical University
- Taylor University—Fort Wayne Campus
- Westmont College

Christian Reformed
- Calvin College
- Dordt College

Church of Brethren
- Ashland University
- Bridgewater College
- Elizabethtown College
- Juniata College
- Manchester College
- McPherson College

Church of Christ
- Abilene Christian University
- Cascade College
- Faulkner University
- Freed-Hardeman University
- Harding University
- Lipscomb University
- Lubbock Christian University
- Ohio Valley University
- Oklahoma Christian University
- Pepperdine University
- Rochester College

FUN FACT

Brigham Young University in Provo, Utah, ranked #1 on The Princeton Review's 2006 list of Best Value Private Colleges.

Church of God
- ○ Lee University
- ○ Mid-America Christian University
- ○ Warner Pacific College
- ○ Warner Southern College

Church of Jesus Christ of Latter-day Saints
- ○ Brigham Young University (ID)
- ○ Brigham Young University (UT)
- ○ Brigham Young University (HI)
- ○ Disciples of Christ
- ○ Barton College
- ○ Bethany College (WV)

FUN FACT

The core curriculum at **Hellenic College** traces the development of Greek culture from the ancient to the modern era.

- ○ Chapman University
- ○ Columbia College (MO)
- ○ Culver-Stockton College
- ○ Eureka College

- ○ Hiram College
- ○ Jarvis Christian College
- ○ Lynchburg College
- ○ Midway College
- ○ Texas Christian University
- ○ Transylvania University
- ○ William Woods University

Episcopal
- ○ Clarkson College
- ○ Kenyon College
- ○ Saint Augustine's College
- ○ Saint Paul's College
- ○ Sewanee—The University of the South
- ○ Voorhees College

Free Methodist
- ○ Greenville College
- ○ Spring Arbor University

Greek Orthodox
- ○ American Conservatory of Music
- ○ Hellenic College

Hindu
- ○ Banaras Hindu University
- ○ Hindu University of America

Jewish
- ○ Baltimore Hebrew University
- ○ Brandeis University
- ○ Gratz College
- ○ Hebrew College of Boston
- ○ Hebrew Union College—Jewish Institute of Religion
- ○ Jewish Theological Seminary—Albert A. List College
- ○ Laura and Alvin Siegal College of Judaic Studies
- ○ Spertus College
- ○ Touro College
- ○ University of Judaism
- ○ Yeshiva University

Lutheran
- ○ Augsburg College
- ○ Augustana College (IL)
- ○ Augustana College (SD)
- ○ Bethany College (KS)
- ○ California Lutheran University
- ○ Capital University
- ○ Carthage College
- ○ Concordia College (Moorhead, MN)
- ○ Concordia College (NY)
- ○ Concordia University—St. Paul
- ○ Concordia University (OR)
- ○ Concordia University—Austin
- ○ Concordia University—Irvine
- ○ Concordia University—Nebraska
- ○ Concordia University—Wisconsin
- ○ Concordia University—River Forest
- ○ Dana College
- ○ Gettysburg College
- ○ Grand View College
- ○ Gustavus Adolphus College
- ○ Lenoir-Rhyne College

FUN FACT

Tabor College was established in 1908 by those of the Mennonite Brethren and Krimmer Mennonite Brethren faiths. At the start of its first year, the school had just 39 students and three instructors. By the end of that year, enrollment had jumped to 104 students. Now, the school has 544 students.

- Luther College
- Martin Luther College
- Muhlenberg College
- Newberry College
- Pacific Lutheran University
- Roanoke College
- Saint Olaf College
- Susquehanna University
- Texas Lutheran University
- Thiel College
- Valparaiso University
- Wagner College
- Waldorf College
- Wartburg College
- Wisconsin Lutheran College
- Wittenberg University

Mennonite

- Bethel College (KS)
- Bluffton University
- Canadian Mennonite University
- Eastern Mennonite University
- Fresno Pacific University
- Goshen College
- Tabor College

Methodist

- Adrian College
- Albion College
- Albright College
- American University
- Baker University—College of Arts and Sciences
- Baldwin-Wallace College
- Bennett College
- Bethune-Cookman College
- Birmingham-Southern College
- Brevard College
- Centenary College
- Centenary College of Louisiana
- Central Methodist University
- Claflin University
- Clark Atlanta University
- Columbia College (SC)
- Cornell College
- Dakota Wesleyan University
- DePauw University
- Drew University
- Duke University
- Emory and Henry College
- Emory University
- Emory University—Oxford College
- Ferrum College

- ○ Florida Southern College
- ○ Green Mountain College
- ○ Greensboro College
- ○ Hamline University
- ○ Hendrix College
- ○ High Point University
- ○ Huntingdon College
- ○ Iowa Wesleyan College
- ○ Kansas Wesleyan University
- ○ Kendall College
- ○ Kentucky Wesleyan College
- ○ LaGrange College
- ○ Lambuth University
- ○ Lane College
- ○ Lebanon Valley College
- ○ Lindsey Wilson College
- ○ Lycoming College
- ○ MacMurray College
- ○ McKendree College
- ○ McMurry University
- ○ Methodist College
- ○ Millsaps College
- ○ Morningside College
- ○ Mount Union College
- ○ Nebraska Methodist College
- ○ Nebraska Wesleyan University

- ○ North Carolina Wesleyan College
- ○ North Central College
- ○ Ohio Northern University
- ○ Ohio Wesleyan University
- ○ Oklahoma City University
- ○ Otterbein College
- ○ Pfeiffer University
- ○ Randolph College
- ○ Randolph-Macon College
- ○ Reinhardt College
- ○ Roberts Wesleyan College
- ○ Rust College
- ○ Seattle Pacific University
- ○ Shenandoah University
- ○ Simpson College (IA)
- ○ Southern Methodist University
- ○ Southwestern College (KS)
- ○ Southwestern University
- ○ Texas College

FUN FACT

Moravian College is America's sixth-oldest college. It was founded in 1742 by followers of the Moravian bishop Jon Amos Comenius.

- ○ Texas Wesleyan University
- ○ Union College (KY)
- ○ University of Evansville
- ○ University of Indianapolis
- ○ Virginia Wesleyan College
- ○ Wesley College (DE)
- ○ Wesleyan College
- ○ West Virginia Wesleyan College
- ○ Willamette University
- ○ Wofford College

Moravian
- ○ Moravian College
- ○ Salem College

FUN FACT

College of the Ozarks manages to do the seemingly impossible: It charges $0.00 for tuition!

Muslim
- ○ Islamic American University

Nazarene
- ○ Eastern Nazarene College
- ○ MidAmerica Nazarene University
- ○ Mount Vernon Nazarene University
- ○ Northwest Nazarene University
- ○ Olivet Nazarene University
- ○ Point Loma Nazarene University
- ○ Trevecca Nazarene University

Pentecostal
- ○ Beulah Heights Bible College
- ○ Emmanuel College (GA)
- ○ Eugene Bible College
- ○ Heritage Bible College
- ○ North Central University

Presbyterian
- ○ Agnes Scott College
- ○ Alma College
- ○ Arcadia University
- ○ Austin College
- ○ Belhaven College
- ○ Bloomfield College
- ○ Buena Vista University
- ○ Carroll College (WI)
- ○ Centre College
- ○ Coe College

- ○ The College of the Ozarks
- ○ Davidson College
- ○ Davis & Elkins College
- ○ Eckerd College
- ○ Erskine College
- ○ Grove City College
- ○ Hampden-Sydney College
- ○ Hanover College
- ○ Hastings College
- ○ Illinois College
- ○ Jamestown College
- ○ King College (TN)
- ○ Knoxville College
- ○ Lafayette College
- ○ Lake Forest College
- ○ Lees-McRae College
- ○ Lindenwood University
- ○ Lyon College
- ○ Macalester College
- ○ Mary Baldwin College
- ○ Maryville College
- ○ Millikin University
- ○ Missouri Valley College
- ○ Monmouth College (IL)
- ○ Montreat College
- ○ Muskingum College
- ○ Pikeville College
- ○ Queens University of Charlotte

- ○ Rhodes College
- ○ Schreiner University
- ○ Sheldon Jackson College
- ○ St. Andrews Presbyterian College
- ○ Sterling College
- ○ The University of Tulsa
- ○ University of Dubuque
- ○ University of the Ozarks
- ○ Waynesburg College
- ○ Westminster College (MO)
- ○ Westminster College (PA)
- ○ Whitworth College
- ○ Wilson College

Quaker
- ○ Barclay College
- ○ Earlham College
- ○ Friends University
- ○ Guilford College

FUN FACT

Earlham College's Wilderness Program has a national reputation for outdoor leadership. The school is also home to a student-run, state-of-the-art equestrian center.

○ William Penn University
○ Wilmington College (OH)

Reformed Church
○ Central College
○ Northwestern College (IA)

Roman Catholic
○ Albertus Magnus College
○ Alvernia College
○ Alverno College
○ Anna Maria College
○ Aquinas College
○ Aquinas College (TN)
○ Assumption College
○ Avila University
○ Barat College of Depaul University
○ Barry University
○ Bellarmine University
○ Belmont Abbey College
○ Benedictine College
○ Benedictine University
○ Boston College
○ Brescia University
○ Briar Cliff University
○ Cabrini College
○ Caldwell College

○ Calumet College of Saint Joseph
○ Canisius College
○ Cardinal Stritch College
○ Carlow University
○ Carroll College (MT)
○ Chaminade University of Honolulu
○ Chestnut Hill College
○ Christendom College
○ Christian Brothers University
○ Clarke College
○ College Misericordia
○ College of Mount Saint Vincent
○ College of Mount St. Joseph
○ College of Notre Dame of Maryland
○ College of Saint Benedict/Saint John's University
○ College of Saint Elizabeth
○ College of Saint Mary
○ College of St. Joseph in Vermont
○ College of the Holy Cross
○ Conception Seminary College
○ Creighton University
○ DePaul University
○ DeSales University
○ Divine Word College
○ Dominican College

- Dominican School of Philosophy and Theology
- Dominican University
- Dominican University of California
- Duquesne University
- Edgewood College
- Elms College
- Emmanuel College
- Felician College
- Fontbonne University
- Fordham University
- Franciscan University of Steubenville
- Gannon University
- Georgetown University
- Georgian Court University
- Gonzaga University
- Gwynedd-Mercy College
- Hilbert College
- Holy Apostles College and Seminary
- Holy Family University
- Holy Names College
- Immaculata University College of Lifelong Learning
- Iona College
- John Carroll University
- King's College (PA)

- La Roche College
- LaSalle University
- Le Moyne College
- Lewis University
- Lexington College
- Loras College
- Lourdes College
- Loyola College in Maryland
- Loyola Marymount University
- Loyola University—New Orleans
- Madonna University
- Manhattan College
- Marian College
- Marian College of Fond Du Lac
- Marygrove College
- Marylhurst University
- Marymount College (CA)
- Marymount University
- Marywood University
- Merrimack College
- Molloy College
- Mount Marty College
- Mount Mary College
- Mount Mercy College
- Mount Saint Mary's College (CA)
- Mount St. Mary's University
- Neumann College

- Niagara University
- Notre Dame College
- Notre Dame de Namur University
- Ohio Dominican University
- Our Lady of Holy Cross College
- Pontifical College Josephinum
- Providence College
- Quincy University
- Regis College
- Regis University
- Rivier College
- Rockhurst University
- Rosemont College
- Sacred Heart University
- Saint Anselm College
- Saint Anthony College of Nursing
- Saint Francis College (NY)

FUN FACT
Seton Hall University was the first diocesan undergraduate institution in the United States.

- Saint Francis University (PA)
- Saint Joseph College (CT)

- Saint Joseph Seminary College
- Saint Joseph's College (IN)
- Saint Joseph's College of Maine
- Saint Leo University
- Saint Louis University
- Saint Martin's University
- Saint Mary-of-the-Woods College
- Saint Mary's College (IN)
- Saint Mary's College of California
- Saint Mary's University of Minnesota
- Saint Michael's College
- Saint Paul University
- Saint Vincent College
- Saint Xavier University
- Salve Regina University
- Santa Clara University
- Seton Hall University
- Seton Hill University
- Siena College
- Silver Lake College
- Spalding University
- Spring Hill College
- St. Ambrose University
- St. Bonaventure University
- St. Charles Borromeno Seminary
- St. Edward's University

- St. John's College—Department of Nursing (IL)
- St. John's University (NY)
- St. Mary's University
- St. Norbert College
- St. Thomas University
- Stonehill College
- The Catholic University of America
- The College of New Rochelle
- The College of Saint Rose
- The College of Saint Scholastica
- The College of Saint Thomas More
- The College of St. Catherine
- The University of Saint Francis (IN)
- Thomas Aquinas College
- Thomas More College
- Thomas More College of Liberal Arts
- University of Dallas
- University of Dayton
- University of Great Falls
- University of Mary
- University of Notre Dame
- University of Portland
- University of Saint Mary (KS)
- University of Saint Thomas (MN)
- University of San Diego
- University of San Francisco
- University of St. Francis
- University of St. Thomas (TX)
- University of the Incarnate Word
- Ursuline College
- Villa Maria College of Buffalo
- Villanova University
- Viterbo University
- Wadhams Hall Seminary College
- Walsh University
- Wheeling Jesuit University
- Xavier University of Louisiana

Roman Catholic-Jesuit
- Fairfield University
- Loyola University—Chicago
- Marquette University
- Saint Joseph's University (PA)
- Seattle University
- The University of Scranton
- University of Detroit Mercy
- Xavier University (OH)

FUN FACT

Griggs University has a student-to-faculty ratio of 3:1!

Seventh Day Adventist
○ Andrews University
○ Atlantic Union College
○ Bradford College
○ Columbia Union College
○ Griggs University
○ La Sierra University
○ Loma Linda University
○ Pacific Union College
○ Southern Adventist University
○ Union College (NE)
○ Walla Walla College

Southern Baptist
○ Baptist College of Florida
○ California Baptist University
○ Campbell University
○ Charleston Southern University

○ Hannibal-LaGrange College
○ Houston Baptist University
○ Luther Rice Bible College and Seminary
○ Mississippi College
○ Missouri Baptist College
○ North Greenville College
○ Oklahoma Baptist University
○ Ouachita Baptist University
○ Shorter College
○ Southwest Baptist University
○ Union University
○ Wayland Baptist University

United Church of Christ
○ Catawba College
○ Cedar Crest College
○ Defiance College
○ Dillard University
○ Doane College
○ Elmhurst College
○ Elon University
○ Heidelberg College
○ Lakeland College
○ Northland College
○ Olivet College
○ Pacific University
○ Talladega College

FUN FACT

Every student at **Olivet College** must complete a semester-long Service Learning course, which includes community service as well as guided reflection on that service.

United Methodist
Allegheny College
- ○ Houghton College
- ○ Indiana Wesleyan University
- ○ Southern Wesleyan University
- ○ Tennessee Wesleyan College
- ○ Wesleyan

chapter 10

Fun Stuff

So you've compared the schools that have attracted you inside and out, backwards and forwards, upside down and inside out. What's left? Have you thought about where you might run naked through campus (in the name of tradition), play (or be the victim of) an amazing prank, cheer on your school's team as they face their arch-rivals, or take a class on *Star Trek* and religion for credit?

Whether you're in the throes of the application process or a seasoned college sophomore, we highly recommend that you take a break from your required classes and peruse the course catalog of your college or prospective colleges. Check out some of the more unusual offerings. Sneaking in a whitewater rafting class can work wonders for the energy you have to put toward all of your schoolwork. The lists in this chapter are just a sample of the extraordinary classes available on many campuses. Many of the country's elite bastions of higher learning offer courses that diverge wildly from stuffier standards such as calculus, chemistry, and psychology. These classes are remarkable to say the least, and some border on the bizarre. Any one of them will add a jagged edge to your overall well-rounded education. Topics such as witchcraft, rap music, and The Beatles are the focus of real college classes.

While the search for the perfect college will end with your acceptance of a school's offer, the search for a perfect college experience will not. Throw yourself into a lively mix of the classes, extracurriculars, and services that your school offers, and you'll be a success with that search, too. If you can do something that broadens your perspective, brings joy to your life, and opens your eyes to new experiences—may you can get credit for it—you should go for it! In the real world, there will be far fewer opportunities to achieve while you explore.

Welcome to College

Schools with amazing freshman orientations

- Brigham Young University (UT)
- Bucknell University
- Catholic University of America
- Columbia University
- Harvard College
- Rice University
- Saint Vincent College
- Texas A&M University—College Station
- University of California—Riverside
- University of Chicago
- The University of Texas at Austin

You Took What!?

Schools offering unexpected courses for credit

- Brown University (See just how the times are a'changing with a course on Bob Dylan.)
- Bucknell University (We'll just say it: "Witchcraft and Politics.")
- Georgetown University (Join James Tiberius Kirk and Socrates for "Philosophy and *Star Trek*.")
- Indiana University—Bloomington (Set your phaser for stun with "*Star Trek* and Religion.")
- Maharishi University of Management (In business, focus is everything—perhaps that's why you can take classes in transcendental meditation.)
- New College of California (Help your imprisoned man with the "Prison Practicum Course.")
- Northern Illinois University ("Xtreme Lit"—read outdoor classics while engaging in the great outdoors.)
- Triton College (Embrace your inner clown with this course in "Circus Stunts.")
- University of Alabama (Take "The Beatles Era" to learn about twentieth-century history with the Fab Four as a soundtrack.)
- University of Alaska (Learn why "a horse is a horse, of course, of course" with "Basic Horse Behavior and Training.")

FUN FACT

West Virginia University also offers a three-credit horticulture course.

- University of California—Berkeley (Take the embattled and controversial "Male Sexuality" before its next legal snafu.)
- University of California—Davis (Go beyond simply tasting and get your degree in viticulture, AKA winemaking.)
- University of California—Los Angeles (Explore the development of bling with "Cultural History of Rap.")
- University of California—Santa Barbara (Argue for the betterment of nature with "Mock Environmental Summit.")
- University of Michigan (Break out the broomsticks with courses in the history and literature of witchcraft.)
- The University of Montana (Think of "Facial Reconstruction" as CSI 101.)
- University of Southern California ("The Beatles Albums: A Critical Appraisal." You'll love this, yeah, yeah, yeah...)
- West Virginia University (Brave the rapids with the "Whitewater Skills" course.)

For Those About to Rock (And Study), We Salute You

Schools offering performance-based rock classes for credit

- Belmont University
- Berklee School of Music
- California Institute of the Arts
- Columbia College (IL)
- Eugene Lang College—The New School for Liberal Arts
- Ithaca College
- University of Denver
- University of Miami
- University of North Texas
- University of Southern California
- University of Wisconsin—Oshkosh

8 Seconds to Glory

Schools with rodeo programs

- Black Hills State University
- California Polytechnic State University—Pomona
- California Polytechnic State University—San Luis Obispo
- California State University—Fresno
- Central Washington University
- Colorado State University
- Dickinson State University

- ○ Eastern Oregon University
- ○ Idaho State University
- ○ Iowa State University
- ○ Kansas State University
- ○ Michigan State University
- ○ Mississippi State University
- ○ Montana State University
- ○ New Mexico State University
- ○ North Dakota State University
- ○ Northwest Missouri State University
- ○ Northwestern Oklahoma State University
- ○ Oklahoma State University

Now this may be a generational thing, but as your teacher it's my job to let you know that I'm finding very little rockin' about what you're doing there.

- ○ Purdue University
- ○ Sam Houston State University
- ○ South Dakota State University
- ○ Southern Illinois University—Carbondale
- ○ Southwest Missouri State University
- ○ Southwestern Oklahoma State University
- ○ Texas A&M University—College Station
- ○ Troy State University
- ○ University of Arkansas—Monticello

- ○ University of Georgia
- ○ University of Idaho
- ○ University of Illinois
- ○ The University of Montana
- ○ University of Nebraska—Lincoln
- ○ University of Nevada—Las Vegas
- ○ University of Tennessee at Martin
- ○ University of West Alabama
- ○ University of Wisconsin—River Falls
- ○ University of Wyoming
- ○ Washington State University
- ○ Weber State University

It May Not Be School-Sponsored Per Se

Schools with their own Internet dating sites

- ○ Georgetown University
- ○ University of Florida
- ○ University of Washington
- ○ Wesleyan University

FUN FACT

In 1999, workers gutting **Harvard University**'s Holden Chapel in preparation for a renovation of the 1744 building found human bones buried beneath it. Due to the strategic cuts in the bones, it was apparent that they had had been used for medical instruction during 1782 and 1850. Holden Chapel was, as a result, declared an archaeological site.

Who You Gonna Call?

Schools thought to have haunted campuses

○ Boston University (The ghost of Eugene O'Neill is said to haunt a floor of Shelton Hall.)

○ Bucknell University (At Hunt Hall, a woman in a red raincoat is said to appear and play tricks on students.)

○ Fordham University (Built upon the old Rose Hill Manor and a hospital, this campus is said to be one of the nation's most haunted.)

No really, you two are nothing like my high school friends.

- Harvard College (Thayer Hall has been known to house Victorian spirits.)

- Huntingdon College (Everywhere you go on campus, chances are there's a ghost nearby—whether it's the temptress of Searcy Hall or the Houghton Library's phantom.)

- Illinois College (The campus is reputed to be one of the Midwest's most haunted locations.)

- Kent State University (A little girl in Allyn Hall searches for a playmate; there are mysterious marbles in Van Campen Hall; and a judgmental ghost hangs out in Koonce Hall.)

- Lake Erie College (A woman named Stephanie has reportedly been seen in the windows of the closed-off floor of College Hall.)

- Lindsey Wilson College (A lovelorn former student is known to frequent Phillips Hall.)

- Miami University (A violent past haunts Reid Hall.)

- Mount St. Mary's University (Beware of Room 252 in the residence hall, where even two priests couldn't quell the spirits.)

- Nyack College (A series of tunnels in the woods are said to be home to some ominous sightings.)

- Ohio University (Jefferson Hall features a room that locks and unlocks itself, and Wilson Hall is supposedly spook-free, having been built upon a pentagram.)

- San Jose State University (The gymnasium is said to have been a temporary internment location for Japanese-Americans during World War II, and it's rumored to have been haunted ever since.)

- Stetson University (The former school president, his wife, and dog are said to walk the grounds around Halloween.)

- University of Dayton (Come to the Theta Phi Alpha house for the parties, stay for the ghost.)

- University of Notre Dame (Washington Hall can count the "Gipper"—of the "Win one for the Gipper" fame—as one of its otherworldly tenants.)

- University of Vermont (There's nearly a ghost for every building—and block of cheese.)

- Weber State University (It's said to be haunted by a decidedly unruly ghost.)
- Western Kentucky University (There's a smiling picture in McClean Hall, not to mention a poltergeist in Schneider Hall—and don't even think about using a Ouija Board in Potter Hall.)

An Educated Joke
Schools with a history of amazing pranks

- California Institute of Technology (Altering the "Hollywood" sign to read "Caltech," exploiting a lucrative loophole in a McDonald's promotion, and asserting their dominance over MIT on the scoreboard at the Rose Bowl are just a few examples of these students' pranks.)
- Carleton College (The disappearing-reappearing bust of Schiller and the Goodhue Daylight Savings Time phenomenon are Carleton history-making events.)

- Cornell University (The university has seen a lion in the gym, a pumpkin and disco ball impaled upon the McGraw tower's spire, and—much to the GOP's embarrassment—the 1930 appearance of Hugo N. Frye.)
- DePauw University (Students here pulled a high-story stunt during class.)
- Harvard College (There was, to name just one prank, the kidnapping of a sacred codfish. *The Harvard Lampoon* and *The Harvard Crimson* have been exchanging pranks for years.)
- Harvey Mudd College (From relocating the dean's office to turning a student's room into an aquarium, students here know how to pull a good joke.)
- Haverford College (It's quite simple: Chevy Chase went here.)
- Johns Hopkins University (Every spoon in the cafeteria got "planted" on the lawn.)

- Massachusetts Institute of Technology (Besides introducing the word "hack" into the language, students here have turned the Great Dome into R2-D2's head, disguised the university president's door as a bulletin board, and inflated a massive balloon on the playing field during a Harvard-Yale game.)

- Princeton University (Students here created the "Veterans of Future Wars," a league of rather sarcastic gentlemen looking for their eventual wartime bonuses.)

- Rice University (An entire campus showed up at the student health care center with cups of urine after they received forged doctor's notes—what happened after wasn't pretty.)

- Stanford University (After losing a game to Berkeley, students here printed a fake newspaper to trick their rivals into believing the referees' ruling had been overturned.)

- University of California—Berkeley (Holding Stanford's mascot "The Tree" for ransom and duping USC's starting guard via instant messenger are but two drops in a sea of pranks.)

- University of Wisconsin—Madison (Students here successfully brought the Statue of Liberty to Madison—even if it was only plywood.)

- Wabash College (Students succeeded in stealing the Monon Bell from DePauw University.)

- Yale University (Students managed to have Harvard students raise signs that read WE SUCK—instead of signs that read GO HARVARD—at a game.)

Them Versus U.

Schools with famous/infamous rivalries

- Arizona State University vs. University of Arizona
- Auburn University vs. University of Alabama
- Brigham Young University vs. University of Utah
- California Institute of Technology vs. Massachusetts Institute of Technology
- Columbia University vs. Princeton University

- Cornell University vs. University of Pennsylvania
- Duke University vs. The University of North Carolina at Chapel Hill
- Florida State University vs. University of Miami
- Georgetown University vs. Syracuse University
- Harvard College vs. Yale University
- Louisiana State University vs. University of Arkansas
- The Ohio State University vs. University of Michigan
- Oklahoma State University vs. University of Oklahoma
- Stanford University vs. University of California—Berkeley
- Texas A&M University vs. The University of Texas
- Texas State University vs. University of Oklahoma
- United States Military Academy vs. United States Naval Academy
- University of California—Los Angeles vs. University of Southern California
- University of Cincinnati vs. Xavier University

- University of Connecticut vs. University of Pittsburgh
- University of Florida vs. University of Tennessee
- University of Indiana vs. Purdue University
- University of Kansas vs. University of Missouri—Columbia
- University of Kentucky vs. University of Louisville
- University of Notre Dame vs. University of Southern California
- University of Oregon vs. University of Washington

FUN FACT

The Commander-in-Chief's Trophy is the prize that that the **United States Military Academy**, United States Naval Academy, or United States Air Force Academy gets to take home after the triangular football series. The POTUS has, on a number of occasions, awarded the prize himself.

Shhh...It's a Secret

Schools with secret societies

- Baylor University (The NoZe Brotherhood)
- College of William & Mary (Bishop James Madison Society, Flat Hat Club)
- Cornell University (Quill and Dagger, Sphinx Head Society)
- Dartmouth College (Sphinx Senior Society)
- Georgetown University (Cloak and Dagger)

FUN FACT

President George W. Bush was a member of the Skull and Bones Society at **Yale University**.

- Georgia Institute of Technology (Anak Society)
- Northwestern University (DERU)
- Rutgers, The State University of New Jersey (Order of the Bull's Blood, Sword and Serpent)
- University of Alabama (The Machine)
- University of Georgia (Order of the Acropolis, Order of the Greek Horsemen)
- University of Hartford (The Vitruvian Society)
- University of Michigan—Ann Arbor (Michigamua)
- The University of North Carolina at Chapel Hill (Order of Gimghoul)
- University of Pennsylvania (Owl Society)
- The University of Texas at Austin (The Eyes of Texas)
- University of Virginia (IMP Society, Seven Society, Skull and Bones, Z Society)
- Wesleyan University (Mystical 7)
- Wittenberg University (Shifters)
- Yale University (Berzelius, Book and Snake, Elihu, Scroll and Key, Skull and Bones, Wolf's Head)

In The Name of Tradition

Schools with wacky traditions

- ○ Alfred University (Celebrate "Hot Dog Day"—just possibly the tastiest way to help charity...ever.)

- ○ Bates College (Each St. Patrick's Day, come for the "Puddle Jump," stay for the hypothermia.)

- ○ Brown University (There are too many to mention, but let's just say there's a gate you don't want to go through twice, a naked donut run, and sundry activities in the science library.)

- ○ Carleton College (Exorcise your pent-up frustration the night before finals with a campus-wide primal scream.)

- ○ Carnegie Mellon University (In a move that would make Tom Sawyer proud, students here are attempting to make "The Fence" the most heavily-painted object ever.)

- ○ Cornell University (Celebrate the first day of school by skipping class and relaxing with your fellow students on "Slope Day.")

- ○ Harvard College (Two of college's most time honored traditions— screaming and nudity—come together at the Primal Scream Run.)

- ○ Indiana University (Students...pedal your wheels...at the "Little 500.")

- ○ Mount Holyoke College (Each weeknight at 9:30 P.M., the cafeterias open to serve milk and cookies to students in need of some homey goodness.)

- ○ North Idaho College (Turkey bowling enthusiasts, mark your calendars for November!)

- ○ Pace University (The school prides itself on a pack of trained border collies that patrol the grounds to keep the campus goose-free.)

- ○ Pennsylvania State University (Fire up the 48-hour dance floor for this cancer fundraiser.)

- ○ Pomona College (Join the mysterious Muftis in their campus-papering exploits.)

- ○ Princeton University (Try as you might, you won't steer clear of the elements when you participate in the naked run through campus during the first snowfall of the year.)

- Sewanee—The University of the South (Know how to spot the smartest kids in class? They're the ones in the gowns. Earn high marks, and you too can join the "Order of the Gownsmen.")

- Tufts University (Whether in protest or in jest, paint the cannon to get your point across.)

- University of Hartford (Join fellow students in the pursuit of painting the massive anchor at the college entrance.)

- University of North Dakota (Each year, enjoy a football game along with more than two tons of French fries—now that's living.)

- Vassar College (Each year both students and faculty unite to witness freshmen serenade seniors, and seniors assault freshmen with water balloons, shaving cream, and flour. Ah, the perils of academia...)

- Wagner College (Fraternities give a whole new meaning to "chicken cutlet" thanks to eggs, sand, and a five-block run for pledges.)

Index

What's the right school for *you*?
Our experts can help.

THE BEST 366 COLLEGES, 2008 EDITION
978-0-375-76621-3
$21.95/$27.95 Can.

COMPLETE BOOK OF COLLEGES, 2008 EDITION
978-0-375-76620-6
$26.95/$34.95 Can.

THE ROAD TO COLLEGE
978-0-375-76617-6
$13.95/$17.95 Can.

BEST NORTHEASTERN COLLEGES, 2008 EDITION
978-0-375-76619-0
$16.95/$21.95 Can.

**Available everywhere books are sold
or at PrincetonReview.com**